Contributions to
South Asian Studies

Contributions to South Asian Studies 1

EDITED BY
GOPAL KRISHNA

DELHI
OXFORD UNIVERSITY PRESS
BOMBAY CALCUTTA MADRAS
1979

Oxford University Press
OXFORD LONDON GLASGOW
NEW YORK TORONTO MELBOURNE WELLINGTON
NAIROBI DAR ES SALAAM CAPE TOWN
KUALA LUMPUR SINGAPORE JAKARTA HONG KONG TOKYO
DELHI BOMBAY CALCUTTA MADRAS KARACHI

Filmset by All India Press, Pondicherry, printed by Pramodh P. Kapur at Rajbandhu Industrial Co., New Delhi 110027 and published by R. Dayal, Oxford University Press, 2/11 Ansari Road, Daryaganj, New Delhi 110002.

Preface

Contributions to South Asian Studies brings together scholarly work in the inter-related fields of history, religion, social and cultural anthropology, psychology, sociology and politics. It is conceived as a multidisciplinary publication which, in the aggregate, should enhance the understanding of man and society in South Asia.

South Asia is not merely a geographical region. The peoples of this area once shared a common civilization and a common historical experience. They also continue to share similar problems of social cohesion and the development of viable authority structures. *Contributions to South Asian Studies* will publish papers articulating these experiences of the peoples of South Asia, as also on their contemporary problems of authority, cohesion, and development.

In the first number we have contributions from two Indologists (Madhav Deshpande and Friedhelm Hardy) dealing with historical ideas of the Hindus (Deshpande) and religion in South India (Hardy); Michael Carrithers, an anthropologist, writes about the Buddhist *Sangha* in Sri Lanka; Rafiuddin Ahmed, a historian from Bangladesh, explores the process of Islamization in Bengal in the latter part of the nineteenth century; C. Shackle, a specialist in South Asian language problems, investigates aspects of language politics in Pakistan; and D.L. Sheth, a political sociologist, surveys the current state of research on the interaction between caste and politics.

Contributions to South Asian Studies will appear once a year and carry articles on these and other South Asian themes.

Contents

History, Change and Permanence: A Classical Indian Perspective

MADHAV DESHPANDE
Department of Linguistics
University of Michigan, Ann Arbor

I am neither a professional historian nor a professional anthropologist, and hence I must begin this study with a defence of myself. I started out as a professional Sanskrit grammarian, and at present I find myself involved in a study of the Indian grammatical tradition from a historical perspective. In conducting such a study, I recognized that one is essentially working with texts which do not share the same perspective of history as a modern historian does, and hence in writing a history of the theories of Sanskrit grammarians one is writing something which is not the intention of the Sanskrit grammarians themselves. This led me to a study of the concept of history of the Sanskrit grammarians themselves. In the same context I started studying the concepts of history, change and permanence as found in other branches of the classical Sanskrit literature. In this paper, I shall attempt to present some of my findings in this respect.

The modern Indian term for history is *itihāsa*. At present the term is almost redefined as a replacement for the English word 'history' and hence carries the same sense for a modern Indian historian. However, the term is quite old. The origin of the term is in the phrase: *iti ha āsa* 'Indeed thus it was'. We find that at the time of Yāska's *Nirukta* (about 500 B.C.), there existed a whole tradition called the tradition of the *aitihāsikas*. These were the scholars who tried to explain the contents of the Vedic hymns and the nature of the Vedic deities by referring to *itihāsa* or traditional accounts of events that were supposed to have happened sometime in the past.[1] Yāska quotes several such *itihāsa* passages to indicate possible explanations of certain Vedic hymns. In later times we find that the traditional Vedic scholars consciously use the *itihāsa* and *purāṇa* accounts to explain Vedic hymns, and stories narrated in the epics such as the Mahābhārata are often quoted as *itihāsas* 'histories'.[2] This tradition of 'history' is basically continued in later bardic poetry of Medieval Rajasthan and the *bakhar* literature of Maharashtra. Fairly professional expressions of traditional *itihāsa* may be seen in works like Kalhaṇa's *Rājataraṅgiṇī*. Though this literature is professional in its own way, it is not really what one may call 'critical history' in modern terms.

With respect to the concept of history in general, we may raise several important questions, and then see how the classical Indian tradition would have answered these questions. This is an important way of gaining insight into the workings of the classical Indian mind. History in some sense deals with the question of what there was at a particular time in a particular place. However, we face more difficult questions when we attempt to deal with epistemic and pragmatic aspects of history. How do we know what we think existed at a particular time in a particular place? As a matter of fact, the epistemology of a historian cannot be dissociated from his cultural and philosophical perspective. In this sense, we do find that there is a distinctly Indian perspective of historical epistemology.

The pragmatic aspect of history is equally important. Why do we want to know what there was at a particular time in a particular place? More specifically: How does our concept of what there was affect us? In what ways is history linked with the present and the future? These questions may be called pragmatic questions, and answers to these questions will greatly affect the outcome of a historian's craft. Like the epistemic aspects of history, the pragmatic aspects of history are also culture-specific. Thus the same 'hard fact' may be viewed differently by two historians with different cultural backgrounds. While the 1857 uprising against the British is called a mutiny by the British historians, the historians of independent India prefer to call it the beginning of the struggle for national independence, and hence the first war of independence. While the first description satisfies the British ego, it hurts the feelings of independent India. The second description may satisfy the Indian need; it may not fit the British conception. History is not just a presentation of 'what happened', but rather of what one thinks happened. There is absolutely no escape from this cage of 'what one thinks'. However undesirable the subjective element may be, any work on history is finally a 'conceptual construction' based on what one thinks the facts are. This game of conceptual construction is bound by the rules of cultural pragmatics. Colonial histories are different from independent histories, and the western histories of the east are different from the eastern histories of the east. The concept of truth in practice is closely related to the culture-specific facts of epistemic and pragmatic preconceptions.

Though we shall not go into the philosophical complexities of the Indian theories of epistemology, some aspects of these theories are closely linked with the classical Indian perspective of history, and hence must be studied. Every system of Indian philosophy deals with the question of means of valid cognition (*pramāṇa*) and the question of validity of cognition (*prāmāṇya*). Of several different theories of validity of cognition, I shall mainly refer to two prominent theories. The Vaiśeṣikas say that a cognition is neither valid nor invalid in itself, and that the validity or invalidity of a cognition must be proven separately by subsequent cognitions *(parataḥ prāmāṇyam* and *parataḥ aprāmāṇyam)*. The schools of monistic Vedānta and Bhāṭṭa Mīmāṁsā claim that a cognition is valid in itself, until and unless it is proven false by a subsequent cognition of a higher order (*svataḥ prāmāṇyam* and *parataḥ aprāmāṇyam*).[3] These two conceptions of epistemology are significantly different and have different implications for a historian.

If a historian wants to remain in his privileged ivory-tower of academic neutrality, he can indeed accept a doctrine such as that of the Vaiśeṣikas. He can perhaps afford to wait indefinitely to pronounce his final judgement on a certain event until he has evidence for all the pros and cons of the matter. The neutral academic historian is not personally involved in the subject matter of his investigation, and hence he is in no hurry to reach his final conclusions. However, in classical and medieval India, and elsewhere, there were very few such neutral academic historians. In those times we have 'applied' historians, men who were bards, kings, religious preachers, judges and lawyers. Recounting the past events as they saw them was only a part of their present concerns. The accounts of past events were relevant for the present in various ways and to various degrees. Thus their perception of these past events was coloured not just by an accident, but they had to be professionals in perceiving events in their own ways. By the urgent needs of their professions, certain aspects of past events were prone to be magnified, and others pushed into the background. Thus a Kauṭilya and a Buddha could not perceive the same event in the same way. Had they done so, they would cease to be what they were. The concerns of these classical personalities, be they kings or bards, priests or ascetics, were certainly not academic, and hence not neutral. These personalities were involved in their own present situations for which the past events and their interpretation had an immediate importance. They could not have waited indefinitely to make up their minds about a certain event. Under such non-academic circumstances of total present involvement, the non-dualist theory of epistemology becomes more valuable. A cognition is true or rather accepted to be true, until and unless it is proven false. This is what I would call a pragmatic theory of epistemology. Only such a view of cognition can be the basis for a working world.

Along with this pragmatic attitude towards cognition, Śaṅkara also exhibits a pragmatic attitude towards the process of inference. With the doctrine that inference is not an absolutely reliable means of knowledge of the ultimate reality, Śaṅkara recognizes that this non-absoluteness of inference is indeed a beneficial aspect of the process of inference in this world. This leaves room for constant improvement. One can always accept a better reasoning and abandon the previous false view. There is no reason to remain ignorant, because one's ancestors were ignorant, even after one realizes that they were ignorant.[4] This applies to all inferences, and particularly in the context of history, to inferences of past events based on present information, and to inferences of future events based on the past information. Since most of the texts on Vedic interpretation and rules of socio-religious life presuppose this pragmatic epistemology of Vedānta and Mīmāṁsā, it is important to know the theory in order to be able to understand the world-view of the religious literature of classical India.

The pragmatic background of history is bound not only with the particular professional requirements of its users, but is also bound with a more pervading and persuasive factor, namely the culture-specific concept of the direction of change of the world on the scale of time in terms of good and bad. If the direction of change on the scale of time is perceived to be rather neutral in terms of good and bad, then the past does not have to be particularly good or bad in relation to the present. However, if time is perceived as a necessary change from good to bad or bad to good, then the culture-specific concept of history is valuably altered. In this respect, India, particularly classical India, presents a stark contrast to the western concept of evolution. From Aristotle to Darwin, the concept of evolution, of whatever kind, seems to point out that man is moving from an imperfect state to a perfect state. It may be viewed as a movement from bad to good. This may be strengthened by the Judeo-Christian conception of original sin and its final redemption. With this given direction of change in time from bad to good to better, a western anthropologist finds his distinctions such as 'primitive *versus* developed' fitting in with his own cultural preconceptions.

In classical India, we find a stark contrast in this respect. The commonly accepted theory of cycles of four ages goes against the western conception. The first age (*yuga*) is the age of absolute truth (*satya*) and highest moral standards with no need for the enforcement of moral laws nor any need for the punishment for violation. This is what we might call goodness-utopia. Then things start deteriorating gradually and in the *tretā* and *dvāpara* ages the bad element starts becoming dominant. In the final age of *kali* 'quarrel', the bad becomes overpowering, and finally the good element completely disappears. When that happens, God is compelled to destroy the world, and create a new world with its beginning cycle of the age of truth. According to traditional calculations, we are somewhere in the last age of darkness.[5]

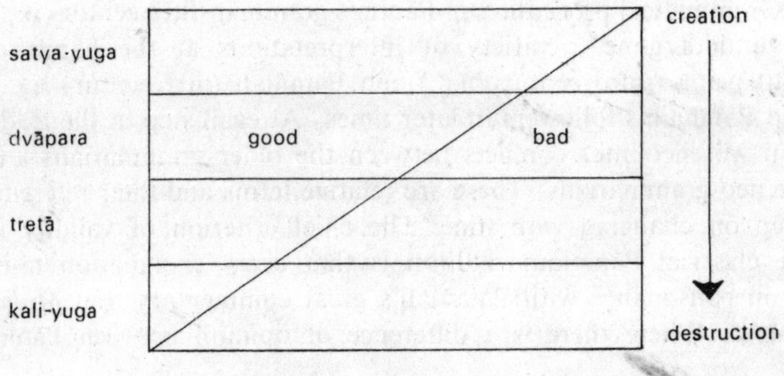

What are the implications of these contrasting views of the direction of change for the conception of history? In the conception of the four ages as presented above, whatever good there is in the world today is the inheritance from the past ages, and whatever is evil today is there because civilization has been continuously losing the good elements. Thus the story of civilization from the viewpoint of the theory of four ages is the story of gradually losing the golden past for an inferior present and future. Thus to keep up the spirits, it is necessary to constantly look back and take pride in the past. In several different traditions, there is a concerted attempt to depict the history of man as a history of the loss of intellectual and physical abilities. Many traditions claim that shorter versions of longer older texts were prepared by the sages because the people of later ages just did not have the intellectual and physical ability to understand the original longer texts.[6] It is not very clear why such a doctrine of decline developed in ancient India. It is conceivable that the invasion of the Greeks and the emergence and dominant political and social position of the non-Vedic religions like Buddhism and Jainism were viewed to be 'darker times' in comparison with the previous ages, and this might have led to the theory of four ages.[7] We find that the Bengali people viewed the beginning of the Muslim rule in Bengal to be like the beginning of the *kali* age.[8]

While the theory of four ages is generally accepted by the Hindu peoples, different philosophical systems and sciences such as grammar have developed different conceptions of history, change, permanence and authority. First we shall study this conception of history as it has been developed by the tradition of Sanskrit grammarians.

Grammatical procedures in Pāṇini's grammar (fifth century B.C.) have undergone a variety of interpretations at the hands of Kātyāyana (third century B.C.) and Patañjali (first century B.C.), and Patañjali's followers in later times. At each step in the tradition we encounter conflicts between the older grammarians and the neo-grammarians. These are relative terms and their referents keep on changing with time. The chief criterion of validity in the classical Pāṇinian tradition is that every explanation must be in consonance with Patañjali's great commentary, the *Mahābhāṣya*. Where there is a difference of opinion between Pāṇini and Kātyāyana, or between Kātyāyana and Patañjali, or between all the three, the classical Sanskrit grammarians attach a higher value to the views of Kātyāyana than to those of Pāṇini, and a higher value again to those of Patañjali than to those either of Kātyāyana or Pāṇini. Kielhorn remarks 'that such should be the case is not unnatural'.[9] The well-known maxim of the classical Pāṇinian tradition says: 'The later the sage, the greater his authority'. Grammarians belonging to a later period in history are bound to have more information. Ideally they possess knowledge of earlier grammars and also knowledge of linguistic changes which took place later on. However, this procedure is no doubt unhistorical from another point of view. The original meaning of the rules of an ancient grammar is gradually lost under the weight and supposed authority of later grammarians.

Patañjali himself has often tried to keep the historical and the synchronic perspectives separate from each other. On so many interpretations of Pāṇini's rules, he says: 'The correct result is established thus, but the method becomes un-Pāṇinian'.[10] In this statement, Patañjali draws a line of demarcation between the notions of theoretical or applicational effectiveness of an interpretation and its historical validity or its conformity with Pāṇini's intentions. Most of the later grammarians, with a few occasional exceptions,[11] have not carried this open historical approach into their own work. They are rarely concerned with Pāṇini's own intentions. They are more concerned with what Patañjali says. Their final authority on Pāṇini is not Pāṇini himself, as the case should be, but Patañjali. They refuse to look at Pāṇini except through the vision provided by Patañjali. Several classical grammarians were so obsessed with Patañjali's authority that they claimed that the earlier grammarians had already recognized the authority of Patañjali who was to come later.[12] This traditional approach to the study of Sanskrit grammatical literature is in clear contrast with the approach of a modern historian of this literature. The aim of a modern historian of the Pāṇinian tradition is not to prove Pāṇini's grammar to be absolutely perfect, complete and free of errors. His function is to see how Pāṇini stands in his own right.

The conception of history of the Sanskrit grammarians was directly affected by the socio-political and religious developments in ancient India. I have demonstrated this change in the attitudes of Sanskrit grammarians towards dialects in a recent paper.[13] I shall only briefly refer here to the views concerning history, change and permanence as reflected in their treatment of Sanskrit dialects. Along with forms which are purely optional, Pāṇini deals with regional dialectal variations as well as other dialectal variations which were recorded by previous grammarians. Pāṇini refers to these teachers and regions. The forms marked by the regions and teachers are thus 'restricted' forms and were used only in the limited dialectal domains. Certain forms were optional only within the restricted dialectal domain, and hence Pāṇini's rules provide us with dialectal options. These distinctions are real distinctions for him.

Surprisingly enough, all these distinctions are openly ignored and rejected by Kātyāyana, Patañjali and the rest of the grammatical tradition. They consider references to teachers and regions as simply a way of indicating a general option. To some extent, this has been the result of the doctrine of eternality of language which was accepted by these post-Pāṇinian grammarians. If grammar were to 'produce' linguistic usages and control their production, then it could easily restrict the 'production' of particular dialectal forms to particular dialectal domains. But the linguistic usage is by now thought to be eternal and without beginning. Thus there is no restriction on the 'production' of linguistic usages. Hence, the dialectal options are no different from other options. What has happened to 'history' in this case? Siddheshwar Varma looks at this 'height of formalism' and says: 'So a historical fact was victimized at the altar of formal consistency'.[14]

Patañjali's own work shows that dialects did in fact exist in his days.[15] However, at the same time, he declares all dialectal forms in Pāṇini to be pure options. We can perhaps explain the situation by referring to the changing history of ancient India during this period. Due to changes in political influences and the religious domination of non-Vedic movements like Buddhism, Sanskrit became more and more restricted to the academic and ritual domains of the orthodox brahmins. It no longer remained the common parlance of a major segment of Indian society. The only way Kātyāyana could justify the study of Sanskrit was by making an appeal to religious merit.[16] By the time of Patañjali, even the learned sages used Prakrit languages at home, and used

Sanskrit only in teaching and in rituals.[17] The Northwestern part of India was conquered by the Greeks who were trying to settle there and make further inroads into the northern plains. This must have led to conservatism and strong preservationist tendencies. The Sanskrit language as recorded by Pāṇini had to be preserved in its entirety, irrespective of the dialectal limitations which had become irrelevant in this age of conservative preservationism. The rise of the philosophy of linguistic eternalism itself may be viewed in the context of the historical situation of the Mauryan era, when the Brahmanic culture — threatened by the rise of non-Vedic and anti-Vedic movements such as Buddhism — was trying to reassert itself. Most probably Pāṇini did not particularly adhere to this doctrine which gained prominence in later times. The doctrine of the eternality of language helped project the present into the past, and thus support the claim that the Sanskrit language as it was known by then, and the entire Brahmanic culture, had existed in this form since the first day of creation. Thus there was no history in a real sense. All forms always existed, and it is a matter of pure accident that certain forms are or are not found in a particular text, a particular time or a particular region. Thus the problem of 'existence' was separated from the problem of 'attestation'. Non-attestation did not imply non-existence. While eternal existence was the fact, the attestation and non-attestation of forms was a matter of historical accident.

A similar conservative attitude is seen in the system of Mīmāṁsā and in the Dharmaśāstra literature. Most of the available literature on Mīmāṁsā and Dharmaśāstra is clearly post-Buddhistic, and it is quite conceivable that the degree of conservatism and preservationism exhibited by this literature is a direct result of Brahmanic society facing the trauma of the Greek invasion and the success of Buddhism and Jainism. The assertion of the eternalism of the existing Brahmanic socio-religious order grew stronger and stronger as the confrontation with the Buddhists increased. The resulting conceptions about history, change and permanence are reflected in classical Dharmaśāstra literature.

The Vedic statements carry the highest degree of authority. Ideally no two Vedic statements should conflict with each other. If there is a conflict, it must be only a surface conflict, and a Vedic scholar should remove that conflict by interpretation. If a conflict is finally unavoidable, then the two statements should be viewed as reflecting a valid option. The next in authority is the *Smṛti* literature, or the literature of the Law-Books, such as the Law-Book of Manu. These are ideally based on Vedic authority, and derive their authority from the Vedic texts. If a law-book statement is in consonance with a Vedic statement, then there is no problem. If a law-book statement is contrary to Vedic statements, then Vedic authority prevails and the law-book statement is rejected. If a statement in a law-book is not contrary to Vedic statements, but is not explicitly supported by the existing Vedic statements either, then it is assumed that there existed a Vedic statement upon which this law-book statement was based. However, the original Vedic statement is now lost. This way the authority of the law-book statement was always derived from a Vedic statement, attested or assumed (*anumita*). The behaviour of contemporary élites was the next authority. This behaviour was ideally based on statements in the classical law-books, which in turn were ideally based on the Vedic texts. If a certain kind of élite behaviour went against the law-books and the Vedic texts, it was to be rejected. However, if a certain kind of behaviour was neither supported explicitly, nor was contrary to the law-books and the Vedic texts, then supporting statements were assumed to have existed in the law-books and in the Vedic texts. In this manner the past was directly linked with the present, and the past was the authority for the present and future.

The most important part of this hierarchy of authority is the assumption of lost Vedic texts and law-texts to support the practices of later times which are not contrary to the older authority. This presents to us a very different conception of history. A modern researcher looks at the Vedic texts and says that certain things existed in Vedic times since they are mentioned in the Vedic texts. However, as far as the things which exist now and are not mentioned in the Vedic texts are concerned, a modern historian cannot say that those things also existed in Vedic times. However, the classical Indian tradition used a device like 'the benefit of doubt' to project the present into the past. The Vedic Aryans were supposed to have behaved exactly like their medieval and modern Indian successors. Justification for the present was sought in the past, but in this process, often an imaginary past was built to justify a concrete present. While the early western scholars of Vedic literature concluded that the Vedas were produced by 'primitive' peoples and that later the Indian religion developed into a 'non-primitive' form, the traditional Hindus cannot accept such conceptions. For them, the Vedic Aryans are the ultimate authority in every matter, and hence they must be at least as much 'developed' as the modern Hindus, if not more. The Hindu theory of declining ages combined with the notion of the authority of the past for the present leads to an inevitable construction of a more developed and a more glorious past. A primitive past cannot be considered to be an authority for the developed present. This is the western conception of history. In the Hindu conception, the past must have been more developed than the present, since the past is the authority for the present. This conceptual conflict played an important role in the history of modern India. The concept of 'progress' was defined by different groups in different ways. For some 'progress' meant getting away from the old Indian ideas and moving toward westernization. However, a significant number of Indian élites defined 'progress' as a movement towards achieving the heights of the glorious past. Thus a conception of a welfare state expressed in the term *Rāmarājya* 'the kingdom of Rāma' is a modern attempt at recreating a golden age in the past.

The concepts of eternality and history are always in conflict with each other, and the gap can be bridged in different ways. The opponents of the idea of the eternality of the Vedic texts argued that the texts often describe a particular action of a particular sage at a particular time. If the Vedic text is a true description, then the description of that particular action must come after the fact of that action has been accomplished. If so, the Vedas cannot be eternal. This is a very good argument and makes sense from the viewpoint of modern history. An inscription describing a grant of a village by a king could not have been carved out before the king was born. The inscription must come after the grant was made, and thus must have particular spatio-temporal coordinates. Faced with such a difficult situation, what can the Mīmāmsakas say? They were indeed ingenious pundits, and had an answer of their own.[18] According to them, the Vedas are beyond time and have nothing to do with the cycles of the creation and destruction of the universe. However, the successive cycles of the creation and destruction of the universe are exact carbon copies of each other. What this means is that if a particular sage performed a particular action at a particular time in the present cycle then he has been performing the same action at the same time in every cycle. Thus a description of such an action does not by any means make the Vedas non-eternal. While the Vedas are beyond time and history, history is a matter of ever repeating identical cycles of existence. It is important to recognize the conceptual gap between the eternal truth of the Vedas and the non-eternal cycles of history.

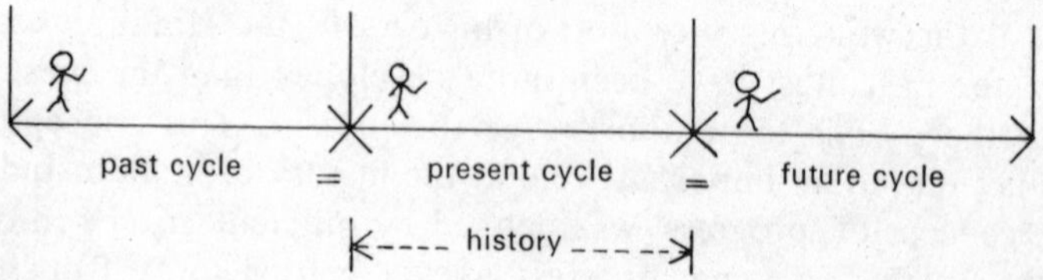

There is a conception of existence which is to some extent shared by the traditions of grammar and Dharmaśāstra in which all the different historical states and stages of a civilization are imposed on a flat atemporal ground. Thus the entire contents of the history of a civilization are in fact taken care of, but in a most unhistorical manner. This is a synchronic approach to diachronic problems.

Pāṇini's grammar takes care of Vedic Sanskrit as well as classical Sanskrit. Within Vedic Sanskrit, Pāṇini does refer to all kinds of sub-distinctions. Within the domain of the Classical language (*bhāṣā*), he refers to regional variation, though not quite exhaustively. In modern linguistics, one clearly makes a distinction between historical linguistics and descriptive linguistics. In a strict sense, descriptive grammars deal with the synchronic states of languages at particular points in time. Each state is studied and described independently. When we have descriptive grammars of many successive states of a language, then by comparing and contrasting these successive states one can write a historical grammar of that language indicating losses, developments and retentions. Thus a clear sense of the temporal sequence of changes is constantly maintained in modern historical linguistics.[19] This can be seen from the figure below:

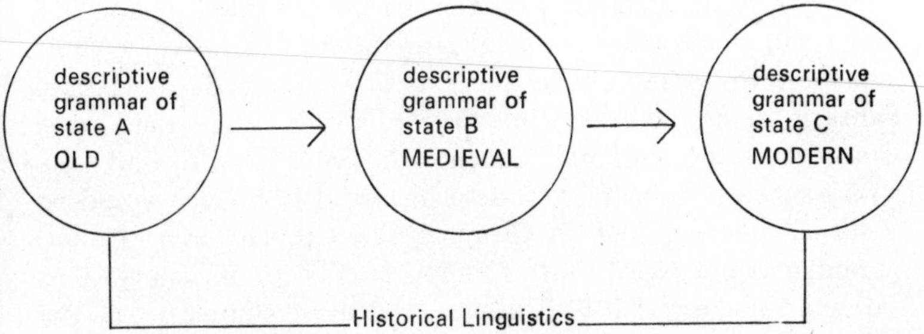

In Pāṇini's grammar of the Sanskrit language, the concept to history has been taken care of in a non-historical manner. He is not interested in history, but he is interested in describing every kind of Sanskrit known to have existed. Thus he deals with different historical periods in the development of Sanskrit in terms of different domains of Sanskrit usage. Within the total field of Sanskrit usage, there are different domains. Some of these domains are historical states of Sanskrit, while some are synchronic domains such as the domains of regional and scholastic dialects. Pāṇini is aware of all these domains and is interested in giving a single description of all of them. He, as if conceptually, brings all these different domains on a single flat plain which is atemporal. Once all the domains are placed on this flat plain, he abstracts their linguistic common factor. This linguistic common factor is the starting point of Pāṇini's linguistic description. Pāṇini's general rules are thus applicable to this common factor of all the domains. Wherever the smaller domains differ from this common factor, Pāṇini gives domain-specific rules to take care of these 'deviations'. Thus he deals with Vedic peculiarities as 'deviations' from the linguistic norm, the common factor. This atemporal synchronic concept of the field of linguistic usage is beautifully described by Patañjali:[20]

The domain of the usage of words is very extensive. The earth has seven continents. There are the three worlds. There are the four Vedas along with their ancillary texts and commentaries, and these Vedas are variously split. There are one hundred schools of Yajurveda, one thousand ways of Sāmaveda, twenty-one-fold Ṛgveda, ninefold Atharvaveda, debate texts, historical narratives, mythologies and medicine. All this is the domain of the usage of words. Without having 'heard' this entire domain of the usage of words, it would indeed be a venture to say that there are words which are not used.

With such an atemporal concept of the flat plain of linguistic usage, Pāṇinian grammarians give a rule such as this: 'In Vedic, *h* of the verbs *hṛ* and *grah* changes to *bh*'.[21] The verbs in Classical Sanskrit are *hṛ* and *grah*, while the Vedic verbs are *bhṛ* and *grabh*. Considering the temporal sequence of Vedic Sanskrit and Classical Sanskrit, the rule in modern historical linguistics would be: Vedic *bh* changes to *h* in Classical Sanskrit. However, Pāṇini's grammar is not based on this temporal concept of history. Considering the entire Sanskrit usage, *hṛ* is more common than *bhṛ*. Therefore, for the Sanskrit grammarians, the verb *hṛ* is to some extent more basic, while *bhṛ* is an occasional deviation for *hṛ* in the domain of Vedic Sanskrit.

This concept of atemporal synchronic linguistic usage does imply the concept of eternality of language which is explicitly developed and defended by later grammarians. In the classical Indian mind, the Vedas have never ceased to exist, and hence there is no reason to deal with them as a matter of the past. Similarly, the classical language is not just a matter of new creation, but it has been there all the time. Thus the past and the present are not distinct from each other, but the past is alive in the present, and the prensent was there in the past. The classical term for the Hindu religion is *sanātana-dharma*, and this term carries this very same meaning of having been there in this very form all the time. Thus the past forms of religion and medieval and modern developments in religion are all equally *current* and valid. Similarly they are all viewed to be equally ancient. These classical concepts have continued into the modern times, and there is always an attempt in modern India to interpret the present in terms of past and the past in terms of present.

In the *Purāṇas* and in the *Dharmaśāstra* literature, one finds a kind of historical syncretism, an absence of a critical historical perspective. It may be partly unintentional, but it could to a certain extent have been caused by certain pragmatic considerations.

Modern historical scholarship holds that the Indian population is not a single racial stock, but is a result of several successive historic and prehistoric migrations of different peoples. The oldest people believed to have settled in India were Negritos, whose traces can be seen in certain aborigines of India and Ceylon.

Then followed waves of Austro-Asiatic peoples from the east, and these survive today in the form of the Munda-Santal peoples of central India. Modern linguistic research also indicates that the Dravidians were the next to come to India from the west and settle in large tracts of northern and southern India.[22] Perhaps these were the peoples who developed the Indus Valley Civilization, though not much can be said with high certainty in this respect.[23] Dravidians were followed by the Aryans, who migrated to India in several waves. These waves of Aryans were probably somewhat different from each other in language and culture.[24] The relations between Aryans and non-Aryans as seen in the Ṛgveda are rarely friendly. In most cases the Ṛgvedic Aryans hated the non-Aryans, i.e. Dāsas, Dasyus and Paṇis, though occasionally there were some military alliances and patronage given to Aryan poets by the non-Aryan kings like *Bṛbu.* The Ṛgvedic Aryans were more like their linguistic and religious kinsmen, the Iranians, than like their eastern Indian contemporaries. The non-Aryans are accused by the Aryans of having dummy gods, of being phallus-worshippers and of not believing the Vedic gods.

The difference between the Vedic heroes and sages and the later Brahmins and Kṣatriyas is quite considerable. Hermann Oldenberg points out that 'in ancient times for instance, the Aryans of the Northwestern part of further India had not yet entered deep into the borderland by the use of force and were still the brothers and almost neighbours of the Zarathustrian Aryas of Iran, or rather of the Aryans who were opponents of Zarathustra. The situation changed in later times. Hinduism spread all along the peninsula with the Aryan character ever weakening, with the blood of the natives mingling in their bloodstream in a never ceasing continuity and with an infinite series of shades of complexion, ranging from the fair to the dark, observable in the populace. It will not do to mix up the old times with the modern times.'[25] He further differentiates the Ṛgvedic Aryans from the later bearers of the Hindu culture: 'The linguistic affinities between the Veda and the Avesta have been compared with the dialectal refinements of the incriptions of Aśoka; or, if we, on the other hand, compare the Vedic gods with the Avestic gods, or if we compare the Vedic sacrifice, the priests and the special designations of priests with their counterparts in the Avesta, and then, on the other side, if we observe what revolutionary changes have been introduced in the gods and in the sacrifices by the cult of Viṣṇu or Siva . . . , and how the externals as well as the inner meanings of religion have been profoundly changed . . . , we can say that there has been here a development corresponding to that between the script of the Aśokan rock-edicts and the present Devanagari script.'[26]

The Ṛgvedic Aryans were very much conscious of the Aryan–non-Aryan distinction, but the scene changed in later times. The original Vedic Aryans settled in northwestern India and gradually expanded to the east and to the south. The original non-Aryan population underwent Aryanization and the non-Aryan religion and culture were gradually Sanskritized. Eventually the earlier distinctions lost their value. Already in the *Brāhmaṇa* texts, we hear of dark-complexioned Brahmins proving themselves academically superior to the fair-complexioned Brahmins.[27] The author of the *Mahābhārata* is the dark-complexioned (*kṛṣṇa*) Vyāsa, who is also the progenitor of the Kauravas and Pāṇḍavas, and has himself a non-Aryan mother (the fishergirl Matsyagandhā). It is to him that the Indian tradition attributes the beginning of the process of editing and redacting the Vedas. With the prominence of Kṛṣṇa, the dark Lord, the *Mahābhārata* shows emergence of the dark Aryanized personalities in religious and political life.

By the end of the *Brāhmaṇa* period, the speakers of the Sanskrit language were not the pure Vedic Aryans, but were already a mixed people. The development of the caste-system shows to what extent the non-Aryan elements were Aryanized in the historical development of Hinduism.[28] Non-Aryans and non-Vedic Aryans were raised to the status of Brahmins and warriors and the Ṛgvedic enemies like Paṇis seem to have been absorbed into the Vaiśya caste.[29] This makes one wonder if the descendents of the original Vedic Aryans were numerically not a minority in this mixed Aryanized society. In the words of R.N. Dandekar:[30] 'In the long and continual history of Hinduism, the age of the Veda must be said to have occurred more or less as an interlude.' In classical Hinduism, the pre-Aryan proto-Hinduism regained its strength in an Aryanized form, so much so that the Vedic gods like Indra and Varuṇa and their elaborate fire-sacrifices almost became extinct, while Kṛṣṇa, Śiva and a host of other gods and goddesses came to dominate the field, with the claim that they still represented the essence of the Vedas. For instance, the *Bhagavad-Gitā* (15.15) speaks of Kṛṣṇa's claim that he alone is to be known from all the Vedas. Such statements for every different god in Hindu mythology can be found in the Purāṇas and in later literature. Such a syncretism has been the chief mark of classical Hinduism. This syncretism can perhaps be totally justified on a deeper philosophical and spiritual level; philosophically Viṣṇu and Śiva do not have to be different from each other, and yet in terms of the real history of the development of ideas, mythology, sects etc., the classical literature is certainly unhistorical in its syncretism.

In the classical *Dharmaśāstras* and *Purāṇas*, we do not find any acknowledgement of the history of the Hindu religion and culture which modern scholarship claims to have discovered and believes to have taken place. For the orthodox Indian tradition, the Aryans and the Dravidians were not racially different, nor did they ever come from outside into India. The orthodox socio-religious world-order as envisaged by the classical *Dharmaśāstra* and *Purāṇa* literature was believed to have been created directly by God in the centre of his creation, in India itself. The account of the creation of the world in the first chapter of Manu's Law-Book and similar other accounts of creation in the *Purāṇas* were trusted by the classical Indian mind, and were believed to be factual descriptions. According to these accounts, God himself created the Sanskrit language, the Vedas, the eternal code of conduct, and the caste-system, along with everything else in the world. In the *Puruṣa-sūkta* in the *Ṛgveda*, different castes were said to have originated from different limbs of the Cosmic Man, the first principle of reality. In the *Bhagavad-Gitā* (4.13), Kṛṣṇa says that he created the fourfold caste-system in accordance with the qualities and functions of the people. Manu (1.87ff) presents a similar account. Since India and particularly the north Indian plain was supposed to have been the centre of the world-creation, man was created by God right here and did not have to migrate into this region from any other place. Manu was directly familiar with the existing system of castes, caste-duties and rights etc., which the historians of India regard to be a result of a long historical process of racial and cultural conflict and fusion. The starting point and the end point of this historical process cannot obviously be considered to be identical by a modern historian.

However, Manu was not an academic historian. He was a store-house of the traditionally accumulated wisdom and a person with a great concern about the preservation of that traditional wisdom. For him the known socio-religious order was so ancient and so well established that it had to be considered to be a given fact. It also had to be enforced and preserved in an undiluted form for posterity. He had no reason to doubt that all the ancestors of the contemporary Brāhmaṇas he knew might not have been pure Vedic Aryans a hundred generations ago. Taking for granted the absoluteness of the then existing socio-religious order, Manu and others projected it back into the past to the first acts of creation. It was necessary to do this in order to claim divine sanction for the existing order. But Manu also knew that there were outcastes, tribals, regional peoples not fully under the Vedic order, and foreigners such as the Greeks, Persians and Chinese. Given the firm faith that God created man in India, and that the first orders of men were indeed only the orders of the four castes, Manu had to explain the entire world-population known to him in terms of his concept of the creation of the world. Chapter ten in Manu's Law Book deals with his explanation of the origin of these peoples external to the caste system. Many different historical peoples are explained here as an outcome of intercaste marriages. For example, the child of a Brahmin father and a Śūdra mother belongs to the Niṣāda caste. Many regional peoples such as Māgadhas, Vaidehas, Mallas, Licchavis, Khasa and even the Drāviḍas are said to have been born out of these 'illegal' intercaste relations (Manu 10.8ff). Manu (10.43ff) says: 'But in consequence of the omission of the sacred rites, and of their not consulting Brāhmaṇas, the following tribes of Kṣatriyas have gradually sunk in this world to the condition of Śūdras.' He includes the following peoples in this category:

1) Pauṇḍrakas; 2) Coḍas; 3) Draviḍas; 4) Kāmbojas; 5) Yavanas; 6) Pāradas; 7) Pahlavas; 8) Cīnas; 9) Kirātas; 10) Dāradas.

The entire history of the world's population known to Manu has been explained as an outgrowth of the divinely created caste-system.

The classical Indian tradition looked upon the Sanskrit language and the Sanskritic culture as eternal entities. They were viewed as God's creations at the beginning of time, but often they were viewed as self-existing realities independent of even God and his creation. Different philosophical traditions hold different views in this regard. However, these entities were placed by the classical tradition at the head of history, rather than viewing them as outcomes of a long historical development. These were the unquestionable first principles from which everything else had to be logically deduced. While western science and civilization seem to be based on a continuously self-improving process of experimentation and induction of new general principles, classical Indian tradition 'claims' to be authoritative by being a purely deductive tradition whose first principles have been unalterably established by the creator himself and which have been realized and stated by the Vedic sages in the scriptures. History as viewed from this deductive perspective is not a matter of new creation of events or new inventions, but simply an unfolding of implicit aspects and values of the eternally self-existing reality. Deduction does not give us any new information, but the conclusion of a deductive argument is an extraction of information already implicit in the first premise. The validity of deduction rests on the validity of the first principle and the method of deduction. The only self-improvement in the eyes of classical Indian tradition is to come up not with new truths, as there can be none to be newly discovered, but to come up with better methods of deduction, or, to use a more common expression, to come up with a better interpretation. A so-called new theory can be in fact nothing but a new interpretation of the old theory. The present can be nothing but a new interpretation of the past.

This presents to us a complicated situation. Is there nothing new in the works of classical Indian thinkers? Is everything they say only an interpretation of the old thoughts? If that is the case, then the Indian civilization may appear to the western mind as a decaying civilization, or at best a civilization which barely maintains itself but does not grow. This has been the criticism of several modern western scholars. I perceive the Indian situation in a somewhat different light. The Indian mind particularly in classical times functioned simultaneously in two ways. Obviously the Indian philosophical systems make constant references to *anubhava* 'experience' as the ultimate means of vaild cognition. Indian philosophers, technocrats and grammarians were thinking constantly and coming up with startling new conclusions shattering the old conceptions. That is clearly reflected in the rise and fall of several different schools of thought. However, after a conclusion was independently reached, and after a thinker was absolutely convinced of the truth of that conclusion, the cultural setting would take over. Whatever a thinker found to be true must be in total agreement with what the Vedas say. Thus starting from an independent personal investigation and self-conviction about a doctrine, the thinker had to turn himself into an interpreter of old scriptures and try to show that the scriptures indeed sanctioned what he believed in firmly. Thus the roles of independent thinker and interpreter were necessarily combined into a single personality, and the results of textual interpretation were in fact results of prior independent thinking. This fusion of the two roles in one personality creates immense problems for modern historical studies. What we call the philosophy of Śaṅkarācārya is claimed by him to be the philosophy of the Upaniṣads, and not his own creation or invention. But the same philosophy of the Upaniṣads or of the Bhagavadgītā changes from non-dualism to dualism when seen from the point of view of Madhvācārya. He does not claim dualism to be his own invention, but ascribes it to the same texts in which Śaṅkara finds non-dualism. Thus one has to evaluate every interpretation of the Hindu scriptures from two distinct points of view. An interpretation may be a good interpretation of an original text, but not consistent as a philosophical doctrine. On the other hand, an interpretation may be a bad textual interpretation, but may represent a very consistent philosophical doctrine. For instance, M. G. Mainkar finds that Śaṅkara 'is the greatest philosopher of India and an ingenious commentator, but perhaps for this very reason, not a very reliable faithful interpreter.'[31] Whatever the value of Mainkar's judgement of Śaṅkara, his statement significantly points out these two distinct aspects of Indian thinkers. Thus as a matter of the claim of the classical Indian tradition, there was no independent thinking and that all thinking was directed towards a faithful interpretation of the older scriptures where the first principles of Hindu religion and philosophy were stated. However, every interpreter was at the same time an original independent thinker, and the more independent he was as a thinker, the harder was the task of interpreting an old text to fit his philosophy. Thus despite the classical Indian claim of no new development, in fact there was a great deal of development of thought in classical India.

What has this 'unhistorical history' done to India? The historians of modern times look at Manu and others with a contempt which is similar to the contempt expressed against the rewriting of history done by the communist thinkers. A Russian version of Russian history appears to be too coloured to an American historian and he vows to write a matter-of-fact history of Russia. A nation's history has often been subjected to the 'designs' of the historian and his socio-political background. If Manu was not writing a critical history of the Indian peoples, did he have any 'designs' of his own which might have forced him to adjust the historical facts to fit his purpose? S.K. Chatterji talks about the 'Hindu Reconstruction of Ancient Hindu History'. He points out that 'a significant point in this reconstruction is that the great fact of different races of people having brought in diverse elements of Hindu culture . . . has not been taken note of, either unwillingly, or deliberately and with a purpose.'[32] We certainly do not know the real cause of Manu's failure to take note of the facts of Indian history as our modern historians perceive it. However, the historical impact of this 'unhistoric history' has been quite significant. By failing to recognize the foreign and racially different origins of the different peoples in India, and by focusing on their synchronic socio-religious positions, rights and duties, the classical Indian tradition brought about a wonderful racial and cultural synthesis of Indian peoples. 'Ignorance is bliss', a modern historian may comment in despair. However, for one who aims at such a synthesis, wilful ignoring, and not ignorance, may indeed serve a grand practical purpose. As Chatterji puts it: 'Here was a deliberate sacrifice of history for a larger issue. And this larger issue was the reconstruction of a new historical standpoint, in which peoples of various races and colours and languages were looked upon as limbs of a single body, a body which came to be felt as an organic whole.'[33] The synchronic feeling of socio-religious unity was more important than the historical fact of diverse origins, and therefore, to serve a synchronic purpose, the synchronic unity had to be projected back into history to the first acts of creation.

Manu's 'designs', unconscious or deliberate, succeeded in unifying the Indian peoples from the Himalayas to Kanya Kumari. Banaras and Rameshwara were parts of the same pan-Indian scheme of holy pilgrimages. Very few people were ever aware that the great Śaṅkarācārya hailed from Kerala in the south. That fact was irrelevant for his all-India prestige and function. A fair Kashmiri Brahmin and a dark Tamil Brahmin were no different at the gates of Sanskrit learning. They were absolute equals. Their complexions and languages were accidentally different, but these differences did not affect their valuable core-reality of Brahmanism. Sanskrit was equally studied all over India and was never felt to be a northern imposition on the south. The Dravidian grammarians of older eras not only wrote grammars of Dravidian languages in the Sanskrit languages, but they were convinced that their languages were as much derived from Sanskrit as the languages of the north. The dark Tamilians were as much Aryan in their own minds as the rulers of Taxila in classical times. The worship of Rāma, a northern destroyer of the southern Rāvaṇa, is as strong in the south as in the north. This cultural unity was so strong in classical times that all the foreign invaders were sucked into this whirlpool of united culture. The Greeks, the Śakas, the Kuṣāṇas were all absorbed by the Hindu culture, and these originally foreign peoples became devout defenders of the Indian culture in later times. The same drive for national unification and playing down the differences is clearly manifest in modern India.

In comparison with the historical impact on Indian society of the 'unhistorical histories' reconstructed by Manu and other classical writers, the impact of modern academic scholarship and history on Indian society is quite divisive. Modern historical scholarship has destroyed the grand designs of Manu. If historians have done a great service to their own fields, their conclusions have had an enormous socio-political impact in India. While classical India never saw the Aryan-Dravidian racial and cultural tensions, the Aryan-Dravidian linguistic identities and political conflicts became stronger after the publication of Robert Caldwell's *Comparative Grammar of Dravidian Languages* in the middle of the nineteenth century. The forgotten historic and prehistoric divisions were resurrected to divide a culturally unified subcontinent. The destruction of the ignorance of the historical diversity lead to the destruction of the unity based on that purposeful ignorance.

The northerners started viewing themselves as pure Aryans and the Dravidian-speaking population was reminded that they were not Aryans. Who were the real barbarians? Who was culturally superior, the invading Aryans or the invaded Dravidians? In the early nineteenth century works of Indo-Europeanists and Sanskritists, we find that the racial and cultural superiority of the invading Aryans was always emphasized. This concept not only appealed to the colonial rulers of India, who felt that they were doing the task which the Aryans had done centuries ago, but also to the intellectuals of northern India. The Maharashtrians who were traditionally counted among the five Dravidian Brahmin groups, wanted to realign themselves with the superior northerners, the Aryans. This obviously created tensions in India. In southern India itself, the Brahmins were looked upon as representatives of the northerners and hence the Brahmin–non-Brahmin tensions took a slightly different form in the southern regions. Rāma's destruction of Rāvaṇa began to be looked upon as the defeat of the lowly southerners by the superior northern Aryans. In contrast to this result of the early research, the recent researches indicate that the pre-Aryan civilizations of India were probably more developed and civilized than the invading Aryans. A significant fact has been brought forward by modern linguistic researches, i.e. that the form in which we know the north Indian Aryan languages now is a result of the adoption of the foreign Aryan language by the Dravidian-speaking populations in the northern regions.[34] Thus there is no reason for northerners in India to feel that they represent pure Aryan blood. The fact of racial integration is a pan-Indian phenomenon, and it may be impossible to find even one person who really has the so-called pure Aryan blood. However, these recent researches are too recent to have any impact on political feelings in India today. Thus history cannot remain neutral in its impact, even if the historian intends to remain neutral. No Indo-Europeanists intended to produce the deadly dragon of the 'pure Aryan' Nazism, and yet the academic neutrality of scholars was of no avail to stop its fury.

The most important fact of sociological importance is the continuity of this classical Indian perception in modern India in some form or the other. In modern times there have been two different avenues of individual upliftment in India. The first has been described by sociologists like M.N. Srinivas by the term 'Sanskritization', while the other drive is 'Westernization'. These are not necessarily exclusive of each other. Modern Indian intellectuals are affected by both these drives, though in varying degrees. These two drives in their extreme form represent totally different attitudes toward Indian history. While the proponents of Sanskritization as a way to Indian progress keep on feeling that their ideal lies somewhere in the past ideals, the exclusively westernized Indians feel that they must get rid of the vestiges of the binding past in order that the country might go ahead on the path of technological development.

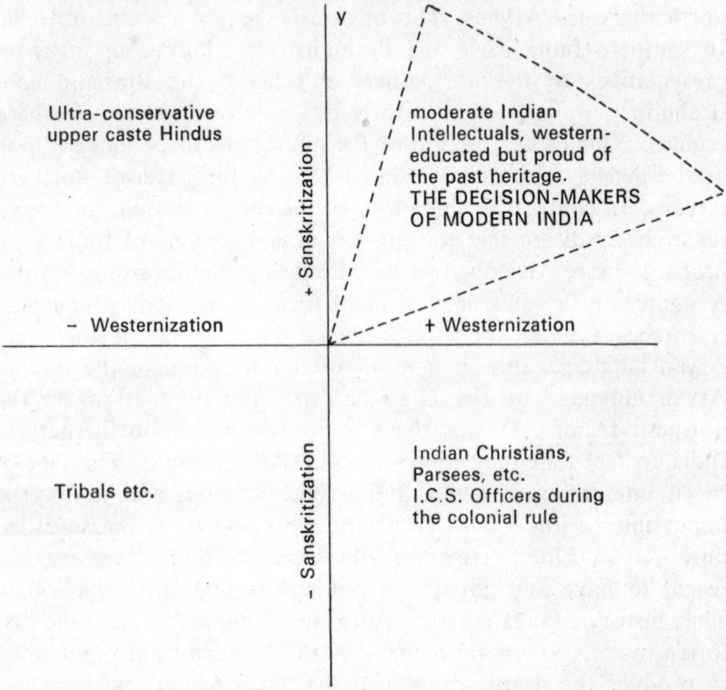

The above diagram in a most general manner sums up the attitudes of the modern Indian population in terms of Sanskritization or traditional orthodoxy and Westernization. The decision-making class of modern India is mostly made up of western-educated Indians who are professionals in their own technological fields, but who are at the same time proud of the past heritage of India. While the ultra-conservative traditionalists would ideally like to drive India back in the direction of the past golden ages in the name of progress, and while the ultra-westernized Indians would like to see their country transformed overnight into a European land, these extreme views do not influence the large intellectual population of India. They like to adopt as much as they can from the western civilization and retain enough good things of the past heritage, so that in their own mind they can still interpret their present as a continuation of the past ideals, without giving up the amenities provided by western technology. Hindu intellectuals like P.B. Gajendragadkar would like to assert that the secularism of the Indian Constitution is in essence a continuation of the universalism of the classical Hindu tradition. Rejecting Max Müller's conception that the Indian mind is permeated with otherworldliness and that the Hindus are indifferent to the events and incidents in human life, Gajendragadkar asserts: 'Hindu culture has always been dynamic and progressive and it is because of this aspect that it has continued to be youthful throughout its course of more than three-thousand years.'[35] He further claims: 'The Hindu society in its very early days was not a sacred society or a theocratic society; it was a secular society.'[36] Gajendragadkar, in my opinion, is trying to project the present into the past in order to justify that the present is not a deviation from the past. I have heard the previous ambassador of India to the United States, Mr. T.N. Kaul, say that the tradition of representative democracy in India is as old as the city-states of the age of the Buddha. Obviously, to strengthen the present conception of democracy in India, Mr. Kaul had to emphasize a minor occurrence in Indian history to the exclusion of the great authoritarian empires and centuries of feudal conflicts. Several modern Swamis are found justifying that modern science including nuclear physics is already implicit in the statements of the Upaniṣads. All these are modern attempts to project the present into the past, and essentially they are not different from the attempts in classical times. The classical attempts are different not in kind, but only in detail.

I hope I have demonstrated that it is extremely important to understand the attitudes of the classical Indian thinkers towards history, change, permanence and authority. This is necessary not only for its own sake, but we cannot understand classical Indian history and philosophy by blindly applying the methods of western critical history to a literature which does not share the same views of time and change. An understanding of the classical attitudes is also necessary to understand modern Indian developments. Despite the changes of governments and fusions of western ideas and technology, there is, I believe, a strong residue of classical ideas in the minds of modern Indian intellectuals, and this residue may explain several aspects of modern Indian decision-making. The past is still alive in present-day India.

NOTES

1 *Nirukta*, 2.16; 12.1 and 10.

2 Cf. Sāyaṇa's commentary on the *Ṛgveda*, published by the Vaidika Saṁśodhana Mandala, Poona, vol. I, p.30.

3 For a general discussion of these different theories in Indian epistemology, see: *Gaṅgeśa's Theory of Truth*, J.N. Mohanty, Shantiniketan, 1966, pp. 5ff.

4 Śaṅkara on the *Brahma-sūtra* 2.1.11.

5 For a brief account, see: *A Classical Dictionary of Hindu Mythology*, John Dowson, Indian Reprint Edition, Delhi, 1973, on the word *Yuga*.

6 See: Kullūkabhaṭṭa's commentary on Manu 1.58. *Nirukta* (1.20) contains a similar idea. A commentary on the *Sārasvata* system of Sanskrit grammar says that the Sanskrit grammar written by Maheśvara was as extensive as an ocean. The grammar composed by Bṛhaspati was like a half potful of water from the earlier grammar. Indra's grammar was but a part of a chapter of Bṛhaspati's work. Pāṇini's grammar is no more than a drop of water picked up by a blade of grass.

7 For a more detailed exploration into the origins of the concept of the *Kali* age, see my monograph: *Socio-Linguistic Attitudes in India, An Historical Reconstruction*, Karoma Publishers, Ann Arbor, Michigan, 1978, (Chapter II).

8 *Marriage and Rank in Bengali Culture*, Ronald B. Inden, University of California Press, Berkeley, 1976, p. 50.

9 *Kātyāyana and Patañjali, their Relation to each other and to Pāṇini*, Franz Kielhorn, Bombay, 1876, p. 52.

10 *Mahābhāṣya* by Patañjali, ed. Kielhorn, Poona, 1880, vol.I, p. 14. For a discussion of this concept, see: *Critical Studies in Indian Grammarians, 1, the Theory of Homogeneity*, Madhav Deshpande, *The Michigan Series in South and Southeast Asian Languages and Linguistics*, 2, 1975, Ann Arbor, 4-5.

11 Bhaṭṭojī Dīkṣita says: 'Pāṇini did not write his rules after having seen the comments of Kātyāyana'. *Śabdakaustubha*, *Chowkhamba Sanskrit Series 2*, Banaras, 1933, p. 39.

12 This is the view advocated by Maitreyarakṣita in his *Tantra-Pradīpa*. See: Introduction to *Dhātupradīpa* by Maitreyarakṣita, ed. S.C. Chakravarti, Rajshahi, Bengal, 1919, pp. 2-3.

13 'Pāṇinian Grammarians on Dialectal Variation', by Madhav Deshpande, in the *Adyar Library Bulletin*, 1978.

14 'Scientific and Technical Presentation as Reflected in the Mahābhāṣya of Patañjali', Siddheshwar Varma, *Vishveshvarananda Indological Journal*, vol. I, 1, 1966.

15 *Mahābhāṣya*, vol. I, pp. 7-8.

16 The very first statement by Kātyāyana on Pāṇini's grammar deals with this problem which has been discussed in detail by Patañjali.

17 *Mahābhāṣya*, vol. I, p. 11.

18 The problem is introduced and answered in the *Mīmāṁsā-sūtras* 1.1.27-32, and the answer mentioned above is found in the commentary *Siddhāntacandrikā* on Pārthasārathi Miśra's *Śāstradīpikā*, Nirnaya Sagara Press, Bombay, 1915, p. 162.

19 For a general discussion, see the first two chapters of A.M. Ghatage's *Historical Linguistics and Indo-Aryan Linguistics*, University of Bombay, 1962.

20 *Mahābhāṣya*, vol. I, p. 9.

21 This is not a rule by Pāṇini himself, but a statement by Kātyāyana. *Mahābhāṣya*, vol. III, p. 404. However, this is quite in line with Pāṇini's own approach.

22 see: 'Linguistic Prehistory of India', by M.B. Emeneau, *Proceedings of the American Philosophical Society*, vol. 98, 1954; 'India as a Linguistic Area', by M.B. Emeneau, *Language*, vol. 32, 1956; 'The Descent of the Dravidians', by Kamil Zvelebil, *International Journal of Dravidian Linguistics*, vol. I, No. 2, 1972; 'Linguistic Stratigraphy of North India', by Franklin C. Southworth, *International Journal of Dravidian Linguistics*, vol. III, No. 2, 1974.

23 Asko Parpola ('Tasks, Methods and Results in the Study of the Indus Script', *JRAS*, 1975) intuitively assumes that the Indus Valley language is a form of ancient Dravidian. On the other hand, S.R. Rao's recent work ('The Indus People Begin to Speak', *Journal of the Andhra Historical Research Society*, vol. XXXIII, 1972-3) tries to depict the Indus language as an ancient Aryan language. However, the issue is far from being settled.

24 See my paper: 'Some Aspects of Prehistoric Indo-Aryan', in the *Diamond Jubilee Volume of the Annals of the Bhandarkar Oriental Research Institute*, Poona, 1978.

25 Hermann Oldenberg, *Vedic Research*, originally published in *ZDMG*, vol. 50, recently translated into English by V.G. Paranjpe, Poona, 1973, 39.

26 Ibid, 39-40.

27 *Indianism and the Indian Synthesis*, by S.K. Chatterji, University of Calcutta, 1962, pp. 69-70.

28 M.B. Emeneau, 'Indian Linguistic Area Revisited', *International Journal of Dravidian Linguistics*, vol. III, No. 1, 1974; K.A. Nilakanta Sastri, *Cultural Contacts Between Aryans And Dravidians*, P.C. Manaktala and Sons, Bombay, 1967, pp. 48ff.

29 K.M. Panikkar, *The Hindu Society at Cross Roads*, Bombay, 1961, p. 31.

The Sanskrit word *vaṇij* 'merchant' is directly related with the Vedic word *paṇi*, a name of a non-Aryan trading tribe.

30 R.N. Dandekar, *Some Aspects of the History of Hinduism*, University of Poona, 1967, pp. 28-29.

31 M.G. Mainkar, *The Gītā-Bhāṣya-Prakāśa*, Sangli, 1951, p. 110.

32 S.K. Chatterji, op. cit, p. 83.

33 Ibid, p. 85. On p. 86, Chatterji comments: 'Thus in this way there was created in India a sort of a restatement of the great facts of the national history and the national social order. This was not strictly historical, and would not bear scrutiny of present-day historical criticism. But it did its work in an uncritical age, when the good and peaceful life were more thought of than the preservation of historical memories.' Though I agree with Chatterji's main conclusions, he is himself projecting the present into the past by using the loaded terms 'national' history and 'national' social order. India was not a 'nation' in the past in the modern sense of the term 'nation'.

34 See note 22. Also see my paper: 'Genesis of Rgvedic Retroflexion, An Historical and Socio-Linguistic Investigation', in *Aryan and Non-Aryan in India*, edited by Madhav Deshpande and Peter Hook, published by the Centre for South and Southeast Asian Studies, The University of Michigan, Ann Arbor, Michigan, 1978.

35 P.B. Gajendragadkar, 'Secularism: Its Implications for Law and Life in India', in a collection by the same title, the Indian Law Institute, Bombay, 1966, p. 1.

36 Ibid., p. 1. One may also compare in this respect the political philosophies of Mahatma Gandhi and Lokamanya Tilak. The first preached a non-violent movement while the other taught a very strong active resistance to the British. However, both felt the need to prove that their paths were essentially the same as the path of the *Bhagavad-Gītā*. Several modern Indian élites try to project the present political unity of India into the past centuries, when in fact it did not exist, and then they argue why India ('as a single unit') did or did not do certain things in the past. After independence, several medieval rulers like Śivājī, who were certainly regional rulers in their own days, have been viewed as national ideals. Epics like the Mahābhārata and the Rāmāyaṇa are often interpreted in modern India in the light of modern political conceptions. Even the Indian communists have occasionally felt the need to find support for their doctrines in the classical literature of India. In the state of Maharashtra today, democrats and communists alike have to vow to bring about the kingdom of Śivājī if they will win a given election. During the days of the struggle for national independence, the concept of Mother India in the image of the fierce goddess Durgā became a very effective psychological appeal. The trend still continues in modern times.

The Tamil Veda of a *Śūdra* Saint

(The Śrīvaiṣṇava Interpretation of Nammāḻvār)

FRIEDHELM HARDY
King's College, University of London

1.00 *Introduction*

My *bhakta* will not be lost; for whoever takes refuge with me — even women, *vaiśyas*, and *śūdras* — will reach the highest goal . . .

This assurance of the *Gītā*,[1] when taken out of its textual and historical contexts,[2] could potentially antagonize the premises of orthodox Hinduism. The latter, as formulated for example by Śaṅkara, defends itself against such a possibility in quite definite terms:

> It remains, however, a settled point that they [viz. *śūdras*] do not possess any such qualification with regard to the Veda.[3]

One would expect another exponent of the Vedânta, viz. Rāmânuja, to take a different view; after all, not only does hagiography mention a number of instances in which he is presented as displaying a much more positive personal attitude towards *śūdras*,[4] but he is also venerated as the leading *ācārya* of South Indian Vaiṣṇavism which claims to be heir to the Āḻvār movement. His remarks, however, on the same *sūtras*[5] of Bādarāyaṇa are, if anything, less compromising. Firstly, he specifies unmistakably that the *śūdras* are not qualified for the knowledge of *brahman*, just in case one might claim that such knowledge were possible outside the Vedas.[6] Secondly, he attacks the *advaitins* for being unable to prove the premise: only his system is capable of maintaining the position that *śūdras* do *not* qualify for the realization of *brahman*, because it avoids the internal contradictions which result from the *advaita* position.[7] Even if one ascribed such a staunch Vedic position to that period in Rāmânuja's life which, according to hagiography, preceded his joining the Vaiṣṇava *bhaktas* around Yāmuna, his brief commentary on the *Gītā* which may well belong to that later period,[8] is so vague *ad* IX,32 that we can certainly not regard it as proof of a change in his attitude.[9]

1.2. This doctrinal attitude of Rāmânuja, however, does not correspond to the whole of the actual social and religious situation in South India, although it illustrates very clearly the ideological obstacles which had to be overcome in order to materialize alternatives. The present study will investigate the significance of a particularly powerful symbol which occurs in the same Śrīvaiṣṇava tradition, figuring as a catalyst of socio-religious tension and as motivation for its solution in terms of the initial quotation from the *Gītā*. This symbol evolved out of the interpretation which the Śrīvaiṣṇavas imposed upon a specific historical person, Caṭakōpaṉ (usually called Nammāḻvār), and his poetry. This important fountainhead of the Vaiṣṇava movement in the South composed four collections of songs and poems in Tamil, claiming that these are the 'revelation' of Viṣṇu himself and expressing in them a novel form of bhakti. Moreover, later hagiographers regarded him unanimously as a *śūdra* while at the same time he was included in the *guru-paramparā* of Rāmânuja. The major problems which all this presented in terms of Hindu 'orthodoxy' and also in terms of other strands within the Śrīvaiṣṇava movement are apparent. Nevertheless, the motivational power of the symbol which resulted from the solution of these problems has remained operative over a millennium. The emphasis of the present paper will be on the evolution of the symbol itself, which means, on the history of the interpretation of Nammāḻvār; thus reference to the concrete social reality, the application of the symbol, will be made only to the extent necessary to illustrate the interaction of the religious symbol with social practice. The source-material is extensive, but the selective picture which is presented in the following will, I hope, provide a representative impression.[10] The Śrīvaiṣṇava interpretation of the Āḻvār can fairly naturally be differentiated into three separate strands. I have called the first one 'sāmpradāyika'; it represents the official or normative line of interpretation. I have subdivided it further into three sections. Firstly, I trace in outline the hagiographic developments which produced a 'life of Nammāḻvār' (along with an iconographic type); secondly, I turn to various mythological conceptions which place this 'life' in a larger context; finally, the systematic discussion of various Ācāryas will be considered. The second strand contains material of popular and local inspiration; both in idiom and content it differs considerably from the 'official' version. Thirdly, an approach exploiting the technique of Sanskrit *kāvya* poetic style will be illustrated. By spreading the analysis out over such a variegated range of source-material, insight will be gained not only into the multi-level mechanism of resolving socio-religious conflicts in the South Indian Hindu tradition, but also into the process of 'myth-making' around a historical person and a temple-complex. Incidentally, this study will reveal poetic imagination and association of symbols to be an undercurrent also of theological thought.

1.3. Nammāḻvār referred to himself as *nāṭaṉ* and *vaḷa-nāṭaṉ*. These titles may well contain the key for our understanding of the sociological environment within which the Āḻvār figured originally; the present paper will, nevertheless, restrict itself to some suggestions. Both *nāṭu* and *vaḷa-nāṭu* are terms which have been studied for the medieval Cōḻa kingdom; our knowledge of these institutions may, however, prove useful when applied to an earlier period (seventh century. A.D.) and to an area far removed from the Cōḻa homeland (the southern part of the ancient Pāṇḍya kingdom).[11] Various inscriptions,[12] dating from the eleventh to thirteenth century. A.D.,[13] document the activities of the *periya-*, or *vaḷa-*[14] *nāṭu*, provincial agricultural assemblies. One such organization mentions in an inscription at the Trivikrama-pPerumāḷ temple in TirukKōvalūr (one of the 108 *divyadeśams* of the Śrīvaiṣṇavas) that they had a Bhūmi *vigraha* consecrated and were making a special endowment for it.[15] Clearly concerned not only with secular but also with religious matters, this assembly introduces itself as:

> We, the members of the *citramēḻi periya-nāṭu*, who are the children of the glorious earth-goddess and have been born into all four *varṇas*, have studied and understood the fine Tamil and Sanskrit . . .[16]

Thus affairs like those of a temple are dealt with by an institution which consists of twice-born and *śūdras* and which prides itself on the fact that its members are conversant with both the cultures of the North and the South. By including *śūdras* it transcends the division of *sabhā* and *ūr*[17] on the village level. The smaller organization called 'nāṭu' has been described as 'comprising various ethnic groupings whose social and cultural interactions constituted a microregion'.[18] It is precisely this social and cultural interaction of all four *varṇas* in religious matters which is denoted by the symbol whose evolution will be traced now.

2.00 *Aspects of Nammāḻvār's Hagiography*

2.1. The life-story of Caṭakōpan̲[19] which evolved in Śrīvaiṣṇava circles derives its essential themes from his works,[20] particularly from the *śruti-phala* stanzas which conclude the individual songs. To this may be added a few old *tan̲iyan̲* and *muktaka* verses, and perhaps some locally evolved traditions. But it appears to me that the legends are not derived from any oral traditions of strictly historical value. What we are dealing with is almost from the beginning of the hagiographic developments a *vaibhavam*, a legendary account of the marvels and miracles in the life of a supernatural being.

2.11. The locality of Nammāḻvār is evident from the *śruti-phalas*: the temple town Kurukūr (once Kurukai)[21] on the bank of the Porunal[22] (Skt.: Tāmraparṇī) — today Alvartirunagari in the Tirunellvely District. The town has 'dense' *māṭams* (viz. *gopurams)* 'comparable to mountains' and 'walls of fortification,'[23] and the river the *caṅkaṇi tur̲ai*[24] (viz. ghat). The poet refers to himself as Caṭakōpan̲[25] (this appears later sanskritized as Śaṭhakopa, Śaṭhâri, Śaṭhârati, Śaṭhavairī, etc.), Caṭakōpan̲ Mār̲an̲,[26] Mār̲an̲ Caṭakōpan̲,[27] Mār̲an̲,[28] and finally as Kāri Mār̲an̲ Caṭakōpan̲.[29] He describes himself as *Val̲uti nāṭan̲* and *Val̲uti vaḷa nāṭan̲,*[30] *nakarān̲,*[31] *kōn̲,*[32] and also as *tur̲aivan̲.*[33] The interpretation of these names and titles is difficult and complex,[34] but certain points seem clear. 'Mār̲an̲' and 'Caṭakōpan̲' are personal names of the author (note that one is Tamil and the other Sanskrit), while 'Kāri' ought to be his father's name.[35] The titles suggest that he was a 'chieftain' (tur̲aivan̲) or 'leader' (kōn̲), an 'official' (nakarān̲), and a dignitary in organizations in and around Kurukūr (*nāṭan̲* and *vaḷa-nāṭan̲*).[36] Once he mentions that 'his chest is adorned by a garland of *makiḻ* flowers',[37] which gave rise to the Sanskrit name 'Bakulâbharaṇa'.[38]

2.12. Of the songs themselves, three are of particular interest here: TVM IV, 10; III, 7; and VII, 9. The first of these songs is dedicated to the temple in TirukKurukūr; apart from mentioning the two names by which Viṣṇu in that temple is referred to in later works, viz. 'Ādippiraṉ' (primordial lord) and 'polintu niṉṟa piraṉ' (the lord who abounds in splendour, or similar),[39] it concerns itself with proclaiming Viṣṇu's superiority over other gods. The tone of the song is pronouncedly polemic; he calls Śiva the Nude Lord[40] and discards his worshippers:

> What can they achieve, the *liṅga*-worshippers, by speaking evil against the master of Kurukūr. . .![41]

We may interpret the song as the expression of the Āḻvār's missionary, sectarian zeal against Śaivites in his home town. TVM III, 7 sings the praise of the true devotees of Viṣṇu. The poet sets up a new scale of values which supersedes the (Sanskritic) *varṇa* system. In v.9 he says:

> Our masters are those who serve the servants of the enlightened ones who [have realised with clarity] that they are the slaves of Viṣṇu, although they may be [like] Caṇḍālas [even in the eyes] of Caṇḍālas, not possessing any respectability (nalam) whatsoever and being below any of the four *jātis* which are the basis for a noble lineage (kulam).[42]

Of particular interest in this verse is the metaphorical master—servant/slave symbolism of bhakti which replaces the *varṇa* system. TVM VII, 9 shows how the Āḻvār understood his own activity as poet:

> What can I say about Him. . . who speaks inside me, Himself singing His own praise with His own words, while arranging for the sweet stanzas to be spoken by me in my words. . .?[43]

> The Most High makes me sing sweet verses about Himself, having taken me over [as His instrument] because of my lack of talent to compose by myself fine poems, after seeing His beauty. . .[44]

Thus the Āḻvār feels 'inspired' and impelled to compose his poems by the experience of Viṣṇu's beauty, and in fact regards himself merely as an instrument for Viṣṇu's own activity of revealing himself to men.

2.13. Still included in the *Prabandham*, the corpus of the poetry of the twelve Āḻvārs, is a small song by 'Madhurakavi'[45] called *Kaṇṇi nuṇ ciṟu ttāmpu* (Knct). Its author expresses his complete loyalty and devotion for Caṭakōpaṉ, and structurally it imitates many features of Nammāḻvār's own poetry.[46] Madhurakavi tells us that his vocation is 'to wander about, singing the sweet songs of Nampi[47] of Kurukūr' (v.2); that he will 'recite the poems written by Caṭakōpan̲ in fine Tamil, so that all the quarters come to know them' (v.7). This would indicate that Madhurakavi was perhaps a bard who, a century or two after Nammāl̲vār, travelled through the country and recited the Āl̲vār's works. V.4 indicates that in his time these works (and their reciter) had not yet achieved the recognition of some orthodox circles:

> Since those masters of the four Vedas. . .consider me low-and-impure, Caṭakōpan̲ whose very nature it is to rule over me as father and mother, is my master.[48]

But he expresses more than an external transfer of 'lordship' from the orthodox *Caturvedins* to the Āl̲vār; vs. 8f display a most daring internal reorientation:

> He expounded the meaning of those[49] Vedas difficult to understand. . . and out of compassion sang thousand splendid Tamil [stanzas, the TVM].[50]
>
> He has fixed in my mind the inner meaning of the Vedas which are recited by the brahmins.[51]

Thus the works which the *bhakta* bard recites are understood by him to be a Tamil rendering of the Vedas, expounded so that even those despised by the brahmins can come to know their meaning and 'praise His grace' (v.8). Their author is regarded already as a (semi) divine being, and Madhurakavi's phraseology is so ambiguous that we can well understand how later Śrīvaiṣṇava exegesis interpreted Nammāl̲vār as Madhurakavi's *iṣṭadevatā*.[52]

2.21. The next stage in the development is represented by three early brahmin Ācāryas, or better, three individual stanzas ascribed to them. Nāthamuni is credited in Śrīvaiṣṇava hagiography with the collecting and editing of the *Prabandham*. Born in the Cōl̲a-country, he is said to have gone to Kurukūr and obtained there the works of Nammāl̲vār with the help of a local resident, a disciple of Madhurakavi, called Parâṅkuśadāsa.[53] Another person born in Kurukūr, Kurukai kkāval appan̲, is said to have become his disciple and to have accompanied him during his later years.[54] Nāthamuni speaks in the stanza attributed to him of Caṭakōpan̲'s work TVM as 'the ocean of the Tamil Veda in which the Upaniṣads of the thousand branches[55] flow together'.[56] His son Īśvaramuni mentions that the Āl̲vār 'rendered the difficult Vedas in the [Tamil] *antâti* form'.[57] His son Yāmunâcārya, Nāthamuni's grandson, alluding to Madhurakavi's v.4, says

> I bow down with my head to the holy feet of the first lord of our lineage (kula-pati), which are attractive through the *bakula* flowers and which were mother, father . . . of my ancestors.[58]

2.22. Thus it is clear that by now a particular brahmin family from the Cōḻa-country, through personal contacts with Kurukūr, had acquired the knowledge of Nammāḻvār's works and had in fact accepted them as Tamil renderings of the Vedas, looking upon their author as the fountain-head of their lineage. According to the hagiographic accounts, Yāmuna himself failed to draw Rāmânuja into the fold of his community, but various disciples of his succeeded in doing so. Rāmânuja does not seen to have dealt with Nammāḻvār, except, perhaps, in one instance.[59] But it is clear that by the end of the twelfth century A.D. his disciples were engaged in an intensive study of the Āḻvār and his works; this is difficult to explain without assuming some encouragement from Rāmânuja himself. One of his disciples, Tiruvaraṅkatt' Amutaṉār, goes so far as to say that

> Rāmânuja found the true life by taking refuge at the feet of Māṟaṉ who lives on in his poetry[60]

and that Rāmânuja made

> the people on this broad earth realise that the Tamil songs which display the qualities He manifested to Māṟaṉ are indeed the Vedas.[61]

2.31. The first full-length account of Nammāḻvār's 'life' was written in the late twelfth or early thirteenth century[62] by Garuḍa-vāhana. His *mahākāvya Divyasūricaritam* (DSC), of which the fourth canto (89 stanzas) deals with Nammāḻvār, is the basis for most later hagiographic writing.

> There is . . . in the realm of the Pāṇḍya king a town called Kurukā[63] on the bank of the Tāmraparṇī river (1). Where the Primordial Lord who can be known by those who know the Upaniṣads,[64] whose chest is made radiant by Śrī, and who cures the afflictions of those who take their refuge with him (prapanna), had gone in former times (4); where the *prapannas* born into all four *varṇas* always wait upon him,[65] their minds made radiant through bhakti towards him (8); and where in particular *śūdras* who were dedicated in bhakti to Viṣṇu, strove after righteousness which is *dharma*'s fortune (9);[66]— there was born among

the foremost of *śūdras* a certain excellent *bhāgavata* [called] Śrīmad-Va_luti-rājêndra[67] who possessed an abundance of extraordinary virtues (10).

Va_luti-rāja's lineage continues through Dharmadhara etc. down to Kāri in the seventh generation.[69] This Kāri marries a girl called Nāthanāyikā (17) who becomes eager for a son (18).

When she was returning on a certain occasion from her father's village[69] to her husband's house, she prostrated herself before Kuraṅgêśa[70] on the way and requested him for a son (19). He granted her the desired boon: 'Daughter, I shall become your son; go!' thus he spoke (20). Nāthanāyikā in great joy returned to her husband's home. Kuraṅgêśa assigned Viṣvaksena to be her son,[71] and in a short time she conceived (21/22a).

At the end of her pregnancy, 'Nāthanāyikā gave birth to a son in the month Vaiśākha. . . .'[72] The birth of this son is accompanied by various miraculous events.

Bhagavān in the form of Varāha went to the lying-in chamber and gave *jñāna* to the newly born child. In the *muhūrta* in which Nāthanāyikā gave birth to a son, Śeṣa was born in that town in the form of a 'never-sleeping'[73] tamarind tree. When by the grace of Śrīpati the baby had received *jñāna*, he did not accept the milk of his mother's breast, nor did he wet his bed, nor cry. Then the parents gave their son the Tamil name Māra_n, because he rejected (saṃnyāsāt) impure (heya) objects like mother-milk etc. The son of Kāri, his *ātman* filled with the knowledge of Bhagavān, then remained in silence at the foot of the tamarind tree which had grown and aged instantaneously. . . . Riding on Garuḍa, Viṣṇu manifested himself there in the sky. When Viṣṇu who transcends even Revelation became visible to him [viz. Māra_n], his eyes filled with tears of joy, his body bristled with excitement, and he began to radiate. The Highest Man, wanting to render the four Vedas through his mouth into Tamil, on account of His protecting the world,[74] looked at the son of Kāri. (34-42)

By Viṣṇu's grace he learns all the vedas and *śāstras*, and remains seated under the tree in silence for sixteen years.

When sixteen years had come to an end, his overwhelming happiness burst forth from within him, like water from a full lake, [appearing] in the form of his poems. When he had composed various songs which were lovely by virtue of Bhagavān's qualities [they described], he immersed himself in the ocean of His bliss, swooned, and then recovered. (45f)

Garuḍavāhana now turns to Madhurakavi. He tells us that this Āḻvār was born in Kōḷūr (a Vaiṣṇava temple town a few miles SE of Kurukūr) as the son of an excellent brahmin belonging to a *śākhā* of the Sāma-Veda. When grown up, Madhurakavi practised the *aṣṭâṅga-yoga* and meditated on Viṣṇu in the temple of his home-town. Then he visited many temples of Viṣṇu all over India. By chance he saw a bright light in the South, and realized that a great *yogī* must live there (59/60). Proceeding in the direction of the light, he arrived in Kurukūr where he found Nammāḻvār who for his sake abandoned his yogic trance and became his teacher.

> That Parâṅkuśa began to relate to Madhurakavi who was eager to hear, the greatness of the Tamil Veda (66). 'In order to protect all beings, He who is born of Himself (svabhūḥ) made through my mouth these Tamil stanzas [filled] with the meaning of the Vedas'(70)

V.65 explains the names Śaṭhakopa and Parâṅkuśa: 'because of his achievements in uprooting the doctrines which are false and lie outside'; v.87 mentions that Hari gave the Āḻvār a garland made of *bakula* flowers and that he is therefore also called 'Bakulâbharaṇa'.

2.4. The Teṉkaḷai *Guruparamparāprabhāvam*[75] (GPPT), apart from embellishing this story with further details, presents Madhurakavi on the one hand as Nammāḻvār's disciple, but on the other hand also says

> he had a *vigraha* of the Āḻvār in the form of an *arcā* consecrated, and arranged for the permanent and seasonal rituals to be performed as great festivals.[76]

We also find here a story about disciples of 'Caṅkattār' who objected to Nammāḻvār being called 'Perumāḷ who rendered the Vedas in Tamil'. Madhurakavi wrote a song of the Āḻvār on a leaf and told them to take it to Maturai and place it there on the *caṅka-ppalakai*. When they did so, that *palakai* (plank) threw off three hundred Tamil poets, keeping the leaf. The leader of the *caṅkam* got frightened and composed a poem in honour of the Āḻvār.[77] This amusing anachronistic episode is intended to show that Nammāḻvār's poetry is the culmination also of the ancient *caṅkam* literature.

2.5. The Vaṭakaḷai *Guruparamparāprabhāvam*[78] (GPPV) contains a very short version of the legend. It repeats that the Āḻvār was the child of 'honest *śūdras* and devotees of Bhagavān.'[79] In greater detail it treats the theme of Caṭakōpaṉ's *dīkṣā*. Lakṣmī and Viṣṇu send Viṣvaksena, of whom Nammāḻvār is an *aṃśa*, down to earth to teach him all the *rahasyas*. The heavenly general does so and performs the Śrıvaiṣṇava initiation.[80]

2.6. When we compare these legends with the meagre information which Nammāḻvār provided about himself, the question arises how to account for a number of the themes which appear here for the first time. Since this will throw some light on the mechanism by which hagiography evolves, some details may be looked at here. It is in fact possible to trace many of these themes back to a fanciful exegesis of certain statements and phrases in the Āḻvār's poems.

2.61. The theme of the Āḻvār's seven *bhāgavata* ancestors is derived from phrases like: 'the master of Tiruvēṅkaṭam is the ancestor of the father of the father. . . of my father';[81] 'seven' in Tamil often means 'all, entire'.

2.62. The connection of the Āḻvār with Vaṇparicāram through his mother appears to be based on a mixture of curious exegesis and local tradition. He refers to that temple (two miles north of Nagarkoil) in TVM VIII,3, v.7, calling Viṣṇu 'Tiru vāḻ mārpaṉ of mine,'[82] and also mentioning 'those who come and go'. In the temple itself, Viṣṇu faces a couple said to be Kāri and Uṭaiyanaṅkai.[83]

2.63. That the couple had to wait for a long time before a son was born to them is derived from TVir 37: 'born after worshipping the feet of Kaṇṇaṉ for a long time. . .'[84]

2.64. The idea that Nampi of Kuṟuṅkuṭi (a temple between Kurukūr and Vaṇparicāram) was implicated in the Āḻvār's birth was derived from metaphorical descriptions of rapture given in his song dedicated to the temple. For example in v.7 we hear: 'he has filled my soul and stays hidden in it' or in v.9; 'he does not leave my heart'.[85]

2.65. That the baby did not eat or drink is based on a literal interpretation of the following metaphorical statement: 'the riçe I eat, the water I drink, and all vegetables I consume are Kaṇṇan'.[86]

2.66. Other themes are more difficult to trace. All versions discussed so far agree that the Āḻvār was a *śūdra*, but I cannot tell from which indications in his works they derive this. A comparison of the titles and attributes found in the *śrutiphala* stanzas of other Āḻvārs makes it however fairly clear that he could not have been a brahmin or *kṣatriya*.[87] The date of his birth, given with such precision, is clearly of practical importance in order to celebrate annually the *janmôtsava*. But I cannot tell how it was calculated or what kind of horoscope can be derived from it.

2.67. The different versions of the legend show an unresolved tension between two contradictory traditions. On the one hand, Nampi of Kuruṅkuṭi promises to become Uṭaiyanaṅkai's son, but on the other hand, the Āḻvār is said to be Viṣvaksena's *aṃśâvatāra*. The latter idea is typical of the speculation of the Acāryas about the *paramparā* and the history of Viṣṇu's grace (see 3.00 below); the choice of Viṣvaksena[88] appears to be inspired by the Pāñcarātra. The former idea represents a type of thought typical of local mythology in connection with a temple (see 5.2/3 below).

2.68. Finally there is the theme of the tamarind tree. Of impressive size and quite ancient, its branches intermingling with the architectural components of the Āḻvār's temple, its leaves not closing during the night — thus it appears today to the visitor of Kurukūr. I do not know of any reference to the tree in the Āḻvār's own works, but considering the pan-Indian importance of *sthalavṛkṣas* in connection with temples, it need not surprise us that the *sthalavṛkṣa* of the Āḻvār's temple figures prominently in the hagiography about him.

2.7. The legends about the Āḻvār are visually summarized in an iconographic type (see Figure I); it appears in the minds of the poets as a mental image, and underlies the *vigrahas* of the Āḻvār. The GPPT describes the content of the picture as follows. Quoting an anonymous *dhyānaśloka*, it says:

> As has been stated in this [Sanskrit stanza]:
>
> 'I honour the highest teacher Parâṅkuśa who is seated in the lotus-position, his mind fixed on the feet of Para and [holding his hand] in the *mudrā* of teaching the highest truth,'[89]
>
> Śrī Parâṅkuśa was full of all knowledge as the highest teacher; in the shade of the 'sleepless' tamarind tree he had his eyes closed;[90] sixteen years of age, like the full-moon consisting of sixteen *kalās*, seated in the lotus-position and holding his hand in the *mudrā* of teaching the highest truth.[91]

I Nammālvār

2.81. It is remarkable how clearly hagiography spells out that the Āḻvār Caṭakōpaṉ was a *śūdra.* It could be argued that certain themes in the legend are intended to weaken the impact of that fact; by stating that the newly born baby did not drink his mother's milk, that he then never married and never took on a profession, is implied that he avoided the three crucial areas of caste identity (and caste pollution): sharing food, marriage, and profession. But this can only be a partial explanation, the emphasis being clearly on pointing out that the Āḻvār became a *saṃnyāsī*[92] right from his birth onward. Thereby he did not only leave all caste ties behind, but he also became the ideal sage, uniquely qualified to receive Viṣṇu's revelation and to communicate it to the world.

2.82. When Nammāḻvār is presented as a *saṃnyāsī*, as a *yogī* and Vedic *ṛṣi* 'seeing Viṣṇu' and as an *ācārya*, the kind of religion he himself expresses in his songs and poems becomes thereby implicitly accepted.[93] The legends themselves draw our attention to it in a few places. His works are said to be the emotional outpourings of an intense mysticism and particular mention is made of his 'swooning three times for six months on account of the stories of Kṛṣṇa's stealing the butter etc.'[94] What we are dealing with is in fact a new form of religion, ecstatic, erotic, and aesthetic, unknown in earlier Hinduism and stimulated by the beauty of the temple images of Viṣṇu and his mythical exploits.[95] The Vedic *ṛṣi* has become a mystic (using the word in its common western sense).

2.83. The following may be regarded as a tentative reconstruction of the developments which we have discussed so far.[96] Sometime during the seventh century A.D. or so, in a provincial part of the old Pāṇḍya kingdom, in the town Kurukūr which had, we may assume, only recently acquired a Viṣṇu temple, a local chieftain or dignitary who was still familiar with the old literary tradition of the Tamil 'caṅkam', joined the Vaiṣṇava movement and composed numerous poems and songs in Tamil which praise Viṣṇu and promulgate his cult. It is impossible to say anything about his relationship with the local orthodox brahmins or the temple *pūjārins*, but we may suspect that this popular Vaiṣṇava cult, with some of its roots in older strata of Māyōṉ worship[97] and with its own hierarchy of classes (where a true *bhakta* of Caṇḍāla origin can become 'master'), did not find the approval of the whole brahmin community.[98] Madhurakavi shows that after Caṭakōpaṉ's death a particular tradition of reciting his works continued and also that he himself had become a cult figure. He is clear about the fact that certain brahmins were opposed to this popular religious movement. Taking into consideration the tamarind tree *outside* the temple of Kurukūr, the reference to an actual *pratiṣṭhā* of an *arcā* of the Āḻvār under that tree and to the institutionalized worship of that *vigraha*, we can infer that certainly in the twelfth century or so, but probably much earlier, a separate popular cult outside the actual temple, around what probably was the *sthalavṛkṣa*, was flourishing, which included the recitation of the Āḻvār's works as similar to, and in place of, the chanting of the Vedas. Other questions concerning the earlier period in the history of that cult, for example to what extent Nammāḻvār himself had been involved in that cult, to what extent Madhurakavi contributed to it, whether or not right from the beginning brahmins were also participating in it (and whether the legend is in fact correct in regarding Madhurakavi as brahmin), and how far the cult radiated into neighbouring areas, cannot be answered here. It is however fairly certain that during the late ninth or early tenth century a particular brahmin, Nāthamuni, came to know of the cult and prepared the way for its integration into 'orthodox', brahmin and Sanskritic, Vaiṣṇavism. He acknowledged the Tamil sage as teacher within the Vedic tradition; this is also precisely what the hagiographic accounts and the iconographic type aim at, to present the Āḻvār as recipient and teacher of Vedic knowledge.

We may now turn to the manner in which this conception of Nammālvār was related to the remaining Āḻvārs and in which it was placed in the larger context of the history of Viṣṇu's grace.

3.00 *The Twelve Āḻvārs and the History of Viṣṇu's Grace*

3.1. Nāthamuni is said to have compiled the *Prabandham* which contains the works of twelve Āḻvārs; thus the remaining eleven Āḻvārs and their works had to be drawn into the interpretation of Nammāḻvār. Moreover, the particular claim, expressed by Madhurakavi and repeated in the stanza ascribed to Nāthamuni, viz. that Nammāḻvār had rendered the Vedas into Tamil, had to be related to the existence of a Sanskrit Veda and to an interpretation of Vedic lore and Viṣṇu's revelations. The present section will explore various solutions which were put forward mainly by the hagiographic works.

3.21. The theme that Viṣṇu sends a companion of his from Vaikuṇṭha to be born on earth, illustrated so far by Viṣvaksena becoming Nammāḻvār, is applied to all Āḻvārs. Possibly the earliest expression of this is found in a stanza attributed to Vaṅkipuratt' Ācci:[99]

> Ordered by Viṣṇu the store-house of compassion, the eternally liberated companions of His (nityās) descended and were born 100 on earth in many places, like Śrīraṅgam etc., as the sages of splendid qualities.[101]

The DSC elaborates on this:

> [Viṣṇu in Vaikuṇṭha speaks] 'Sages of great wisdom will be born in different *varṇas* and live in different places. By composing various works which are *vivartas*[102] of the Upaniṣads and performing various acts of ritual service which proceed along lines appropriate for all *varṇas*, they will lead, through *stotras* in Tamil set to music and displaying my qualities, the people who are attached to the objects of the senses like sound etc.,

who have studied evil doctrines, who are completely deluded by the wicked darkness of alien systems, and who are comparable to elephants lost in the jungle of *saṃsāra*, step by step, into my vicinity, like elephants [are led] to the big column to which they are tied, after letting them meet with *bhaktas* and bringing them to the path of *prapatti*. From the sages I shall then accept them here (. . .) and shall always enjoy their worship and service.'

He sent the *nitya-sūris*, the *muktas*,[103] his weapons, Śrī, and Bhūmi to be born on earth, each one in the appropriate place. Bhagavān himself, out of compassion for all beings, made his abodes in the form of the *arcās* in Śrīraṅgam etc.[104]

From the time of the GPPT[105] onwards, this stratagem of Viṣṇu is connected with the famous stanzas in the *Bhāgavata-Purāṇa* 'In the *kali-yuga* there will be in the Tamil country. . .'[106]

3.22. The DSC distribute the following *nityas* as *aṃśas* of the Ālvārs:

five weapons of Viṣṇu: the four Early Ālvārs and Parakālan;
the *kaustubha*, garland, and *śrīvatsa*: Kulaśekhara, Toṇṭaraṭippoṭi, and TirupPāṇ-Ālvār;
Bhūmi, Garuḍa, Kumuda:[107] Aṇṭāḷ, Periyâlvār, Madhurakavi;
Viṣvaksena: Nammālvāṛ.
Ananta: the tamarind tree under which Nammālvār meditated; then Rāmânuja; then Maṇavāḷa mā muni.

3.23. Later works interpret Nammālvār's relationship with the other *avatāras* of Viṣṇu's companions in terms of body and limbs:

Nammālvār who has all the Ālvārs as his limbs (avayava);[108]
Viṣṇu serves him as head, the Ālvārs as hands, arms, and body, the early Ācāryas as hips, thighs, and lower legs. . .[109]

The latter quotation clearly alludes to, and in fact reverses, the famous *Puruṣa-sūkta* about the cosmic Man out of whose sacrificed limbs the four *varṇas* arose, the *śūdras* from his feet. This theme is, however, not developed further in Śrīvaiṣṇava literature.

3.31. These incarnations of Viṣṇu's companions are related to his own manifestations in the world of space, time, and matter. The general tenor of the various accounts that deal with this topic is that a progressively efficient and intensive struggle of Viṣṇu to save humanity underlies and motivates the history of his manifestations. Thus we hear in the DSC,

> [Lakṣmī asks Viṣṇu] 'The functions of creation, maintenance, and destruction [of the universe] depend on you eternally. While formerly you delegated the tasks of creating and destroying to Brahmā and Śiva, you in the specific form of Viṣṇu perform the remaining [task, viz.], the protection of the world. In your mercy you created the Vedas which have no end and which teach about *karma* and *brahman*,[110] and also the *śāstras* which elaborate upon them (upabṛṃhaka). But the people whose perception of their true nature has been spoiled by the faults [caused by] karmic seeds (vāsanā) despise those [sacred works] and wilfully continue on the wrong path. Therefore, like a king sets out in person to defeat those who disobey his orders, you descended down to earth many times in the form of the *avatāras* Rāma, Kṛṣṇa, etc. You went in the hope of catching them, but you returned here without having caught them. How can this be?' (Viṣṇu replies 'with a smile') 'The people on earth despised me who had taken on many *avatāras*, because of their demon-like nature[111] and as the effect of their former sins; as the result of their karmic seeds they are deluded and would not be guided. Like the vessels on a water-wheel, they pass through births in hell.[112] With the senses that I have given them they enjoy the objects of the senses, which is similar to the cutting off the tail of a cow with a knife (given) to cut fire-wood. I have now decided to save them. I require an infallible means which comprises [the efficiency of] all other [stratagems used previously]. The *antaryāmī* did this only incompletely for the *paratva*, *vyūha*, and *vibhava* [forms of my previous manifestations]. Therefore I shall now resort to manifesting myself in the form of the *arcā*.'[113]

This passage is based on Pāñcarātra theology which teaches that the transcendental Viṣṇu (paratva) is present in, or manifests himself to, the world in four different forms: as *vyūha*, *vibhava* or *avatāra* in the strict sense, as the immanent world soul (antaryāmī), and as icon (arcā). This structure which originally must have been static, is in Śrīvaiṣṇava literature interpreted as a dynamic history of grace.

3.32. The passage discussed above only alludes to, but does not spell out, another point, which must be discussed in conjunction with the conception of the history of Viṣṇu's grace. In another place of the same *kāvya*, Nammāḻvār is depicted as telling Madhurakavi about the 'greatness of the Tamil Veda'. There we hear:

> Corresponding to the sequence of Hari's manifestations as *paratva*, *vyūha*, *vibhava*, and *antaryāmī*, the scriptures in praise of Him were: the Vedas, Pāñcarātra-Scriptures, *Itihāsas*, and *Smṛtis*.
>
> After that, when He had taken on the form of the *arcās* which are made

> of wood, metal, or stone, His words became the hymns in Tamil composed as containing the meaning of the Vedas.
>
> The rewards which in the *kṛta*, *treta*, and *dvāpara yugas* could be gained by meditation, yoga, and worship, in the *kali yuga* a man obtains by singing the praise (kīrtanāt) of Viṣṇu.
>
> To protect all beings, Viṣṇu composed through my mouth the Tamil works with the meaning of the Vedas. (. . .)[114]

Thus the five different modes of Viṣṇu's being, seen as stages of a dynamic history of grace, are each related to a particular corpus of sacred scriptures. This could be done without violating the character of these scriptures themselves. The *vyūha* concept is typical of the *Pāñcarātra-Saṃhitās*, the Epics and Purāṇas deal quite extensively with the exploits of the *avatāras* Kṛṣṇa, Rāma, etc., and it is quite logical to regard the execution of one's *dharma*, rules for which were laid down in Manu etc., as the appropriate response to Viṣṇu's presence (as *antaryāmī*) in one's *ātman*. What could have been more natural than to connect the songs and poems of Nammāḻvār, many of which are directly dedicated to various temple images of Viṣṇu (the traditional figure is thirty-two temples), with the *arcâvatāra*?

The present passage alludes also to the pattern of the four *yugas*, without however developing it. Clearly the idea of an increasing corruption of humanity and religion implied in the *yuga* pattern runs counter to the most remarkable interpretation which the DSC provides for Viṣṇu's subsequent manifestations. He is presented here as struggling, we could almost say, experimenting, to discover the most effective means of saving the world, until he becomes the *arcâvatāra*[115] and reveals the Tamil Veda through the mouth of Nammāḻvār.

3.331. Later versions add interesting details to this conception. The GPPT states:

> (Viṣṇu) saw that he was not successful, since he belonged to a different class (vijātīya) [from men], and he sent out the Āḻvārs who were of the same class as men, like one catches a deer by setting up a decoy[116]. . .[117]

Taking this argument (and the metaphor) one step further, we would arrive at a conception in which Viṣṇu disguises himself as man.

3.332. Such an idea is in fact expressed by Vedântadeśika in his *Guruparamparāsāram*,[118] apparently deriving it from a verse in the *Viṣṇudharm (ôttara-Purāṇa)*.[119]

> 'Lord Acyuta in the *kali* age enters into various beings which were born already prior [to his entering them][120] and executes what he wants to achieve.'
>
> As is stated in this stanza, he performs once again a tenfold *avatāra* in the appearance of Parâṅkuśa, Parakālan̲, etc. Like the clouds absorb the [undrinkable] water of the ocean and then shower it down as rain upon which all beings live, he summarized in a language to which all people are entitled the most essential meanings of the Vedas and promulgated them.[121]

3.333. Maṇavāḷa mā mun̲i presents a somewhat similar version. According to him, Viṣṇu felt great pity for the souls in the world who are ill through separation from Him. Wanting them to be like the *nityasūris* in Vaikuṇṭha, he endowed them with a body and the senses, and revealed the Vedas to them. Moreover, indwelling Manu etc., he promulgated the *śāstras*, and for a less exclusive audience the sacred *mantra*. He was then more successful by speaking to men through the *avatāras*. But finally he decided to employ a means which was *sajātīya* with mankind; exploring the world in order to find such a means, he discovered Nammāl̲vār in the Tamil country. He revealed himself to him entirely, and as an outburst of that experience, the Āl̲vār sang his works.[122]

3.334. In the GPPV, the whole process is drawn out much further. After Viṣṇu had manifested himself as *vyūha* etc., but even as *arcā* in the hundred and eight *divyadeśams*, then in every village, and finally in every house, he still remained unsuccessful. Thus he chose to operate through the sages, and he ordered his companions, weapons, etc. to descend and be born on earth. After they were born, he entered into them.[123]

3.4. The significance of the Āl̲vār is thus defined through two, vaguely interconnected, structures both of which are firmly anchored in the soteriological concern of the heavenly Viṣṇu. The *guruparamparā* takes us from Rāmânuja via Yāmuna and Nāthamuni to Madhurakavi and Nammāl̲vār; in him, as the *aṁśa* of Viṣvaksena, we move from earth to the realm of Vaikuṇṭha. The particular juncture viṣvaksena: Nammāl̲vār is strengthened by the idea that also the other Al̲vārs are *aṃśas* of beings from Vaikuṇṭha. The motivation for these *aṃśâvatāras* however, is already derived from the second structure. Here Viṣṇu is envisaged as progressively revealing himself and the truth about himself, culminating in the *arcâvatāra* and the corresponding Tamil Veda. What appears to be a specifically Vaṭakaḷai device, viz. the idea that Viṣṇu not only uses the Āḻvārs as his instruments but also enters them in a kind of secondary *avatāra*, serves to bring the two patterns into a closer and more integrated relation.

By now a fair amount of individual pieces of interpretation have been discussed; there exists however another branch of Śrīvaiṣṇava literature in which these individual facets are dealt with in a more systematic manner, and we may turn now to these works.

4.00 *Nammāḻvār in the Theological Discussion.*

4.1. Śrīvaiṣṇava appreciation of the poems of the Āḻvārs expressed itself on a monumental scale in the exegetical literature, in the form of commentaries and systematic treatises, which evolved out of an intensive study of the *Prabandham*. The discussion of Nammāḻvār's *Tiruvāymoli* naturally constituted the centre. It is significant that the first commentary on the TVM was written by Kurukai ppirāṉ piḷḷāṉ who is said to have been born in Kurukūr and to have been requested by Rāmânuja to compose that work.[124] The present section will look at four such works in which theologians have discussed the significance of Nammāḻvār and his works. Nañjīyar (late twelfth/early thirteenth century) in the introduction to his commentary on the TVM, called the Nine thousand, provided the point of departure for these theological reflections; they are more or less repeated by Periyavāccān Piḷḷai (thirteenth century) in his Twenty-four thousand. The younger brother of Piḷḷai Lokâcārya, Aḻakiya Maṇavāla pPerumāḷ Nāyaṉār (early fourteenth century), deals with these issues in nearly a quarter of his systematic treatise *Ācāryahṛdayam*, which, in the early fifteenth century was commented upon by Aḻakiya Manavāḷa mā muṉi in his *Ācāryahṛdayavyākhyānam*.

4.21. Nañjīyar (and Periyavāccāṉ Piḷḷai) begins with a description of the devotion and mysticism of Nammāḻvār. He combined perfect learning with an ever-increasing zeal for Bhagavān, unable to bear any separation from him. Totally dedicated to the service of Viṣṇu, he became the standard of comparison for all other sages, and composed four works which are the outburst of his mysticism and settle all questions which the Vedas, Itihāsas and Purāṇas had left unanswered. These ideas are summarized in the form of a 'catechism'.

1) To which category (of literature) do these works belong? — They are the fundamental-and-foremost (pradhāna) works among those that expound the ends of man's life (puruṣârtha).
2) How did they originate? — (The Āḻvār) was made to speak them by the power of the extraordinary joy which was the result of his experiencing the qualities of Bhagavān.
3) What was the prerequisite (mūlam) [for their origin]? — They could originate because by the grace of Bhagavān he received a 'divine eye'[125] which was the prerequisite [of experiencing Viṣṇu's quallties].
4) How can one tell that this was so? — Because of the distinctiveness of sound-effects and words (svaravạcana-vyakti).[126]
5) How can one tell that they are authoritative scriptures (pramāṇam)? —Because all learned people who know the meaning of the Vedas accept them to be so, and because those meanings of the Vedas which must be known by people who have turned away from *saṃsāra* are found in them.
6) What is their central subject (pratipādya)?[127] — Viṣṇu who is the highest goal of man's destiny (prāpya).
7) Who is entitled to study them (adhikārī)? — Who realizes that he must reject all attachment to *saṃsāra* and perform service, of whatever kind, at the feet of Bhagavān.
8) Who is their audience (bhoktṛ)? — All those who wish to be liberated, are already liberated, and have eternally been liberated, and Viṣṇu himself, the husband of Śrī.
9) What was the purpose of creating them? — To make it known that to serve Bhagavān is the highest end of man's life (puruṣârtha).[128]

4.22. Nañjīyar now raises seven possible objections against the assumption that the Āḻvār's works are authoritative; rejecting them one by one, he then concludes that the same arguments used in disproving those objections make it all the more evident that the TVM etc. are definitely authoritative scriptures.

1) They are composed in a (vernacular) language which is prohibited (for brahmins). [Nañjīyar's first reason for refuting this objection is that such a prohibition of the vernacular for religious purposes does not apply to Vaiṣṇava matters. He refers to an episode in the *Matsyapurāṇa* as evidence: The brahmins Kaiśika etc. who had been singing songs in the vernacular in praise of Viṣṇu were banned by the king from his realm. Yama then reprimands the king, saying:]

'King! a brahmin must not sing in the vernacular, except when he praises Viṣṇu; therefore you have committed *papa* (in banning those brahmins).'[129] Secondly, if one applied this prohibition and (the corresponding) injunction in a purely formal manner to the language (of a religious work), it would follow as a corollary that (brahmins) could study the Sanskrit scriptures of heretics (like the Jains or Buddhists).[130]

2) It is found that these works are studied also by women, *śūdras*, etc. The Āḻvār rendered the meaning of the Vedas in Tamil out of his extraordinary compassion, so that even women, *śūdras*, etc. who are not entitled to study the Vedas can find salvation.
3) They are composed by a person who was born in the fourth *varṇa* which in the present *kali* age is excluded from *jñāna*. The Āḻvār had accumulated so much merit (in his former lives) that it was appropriate for Viṣṇu in a whole series of births to make him His subject;[131] he was the recipient of His uninterrupted grace; he was proficient in the *tattvas* and *hitas*[132] and had the talent to teach them; and he was superior to Vidura[133] etc.
4) They are of only local relevance (prādeśika) since they do not exist in other regions. This [Tamil] language has expanded the area where it is spoken to all those places where learned people abound; when eminent persons of a different mother-tongue hear about the unique characteristics of these [Tamil works], they lament: 'Alas! We were not born in the country where this language, which is the prerequisite for studying [these Tamil works], is in use.'
5) They are accepted by people who do not follow a Vedic life-style (avaidika). It only contributes to their fame that even *avaidikas* accept them when they see their excellence.
6) In many places they speak about *kāma* which is opposed to *śruti* and *smṛti*. *Kāma* appears here only in so far as it is bhakti, which in the Upaniṣads is called *vedana* and *upāsana*.[134]
7) (He discards other *puruṣârthas* like *kaivalya* because man's fulfilment is not found in them.)[135]

Nañjīyar adds that these works of the Āḻvār excel all other religious writing because their poetic (and musical) beauty and the lucid manner in which they display the qualities of Bhagavān give rise to spontaneous love and bhakti.

4.3. In Nañjīyar and Periyavāccāṉ Piḷḷai we can still notice a certain defensive and tentative attitude, at least when we compare this with the more daring interpretations which we discussed in section 3.00. The discussion which we find in the remaining two works is in character and interrelated with the latter attitude.

With the consolidation of the Teṉkaḷai a change in the self-awareness of Śrīvaiṣṇavism takes place; now an uncompromising and thoroughgoing re-evaluation of the Indian religious tradition is carried out. This results in the postulate of two different forms of religion, the superior one being that which is in perfect harmony with man's true nature. Nammālvār's works, the ultimate *pramāṇam* for that form of religion, have turned into self-sufficient axioms. The brief survey of the first *adhikaraṇam* of the *Ācārya-hṛdayam*, along with Maṇavāḷa mā muṉi's commentary, which follows, may illustrate some of the features of this later attitude.

4.41. The claim that the Āḻvār's works are superior scriptural authorities is made to rest on the superiority of Vaiṣṇavism. The key-terms are *karma* and *kaiṅkarya*, the first referring to Vedic forms of sacrifice and other expressions of religion, and the second to acts of worship and devotion ritualized in the temple. *Sūtra* (= s.) 26 distinguishes them with the following attributes: untrue, transient, in accordance with *varṇa*, and true, eternal, in accordance with *dāsya* ('servitude'). The commentator explains this: the latter is the expression of the soul's essential nature,[136] and thus not restricted by any external factors like *varṇa* etc. which obviously depend on a particular body. This implies also that *dāsya*, which defines the nature of a *śūdra*, is in his case the bodily realization of something that is essential to *all* souls.[137] S.27 describes the impelling force behind the performance of *karma* and *kaiṅkarya* as scriptural injunction and passion respectively. This is explained: any experience of Bhagavān creates love, and love in turn aims at serving the beloved, a service which constitutes the fulfilment of man's essence. Viṣṇu has made himself easily available to men, so that they can obtain that experience, in the form of the *arcâvatāra* (s. 29). This unique act of grace requires a unique human response which supersedes all other forms of ritual etc. (s.31). Mā muṉi spells out the significance of this *sūtra:*

> People who obey the rules of the *varṇâśrama* discard as forbidden all *dharmas* which are not appropriate for their own *(varṇa* and *āśrama).* Similarly people who have realized what is the essential character of their nature, discard and avoid all *dharmas* which are not in conformity with it.[138]

This means, because ritual service to Viṣṇu's *arcā* expresses something essential in man, it supersedes other forms of religion as preliminary and non-essential. Those who practise it are born from the inner meaning of the Vedas, and not the external words (s. 33), and are known as 'servants' or 'slaves',[139] viz, *bhaktas* (s. 34), who reject any other title or prestigious connection by lineage, ancestors, etc. (s. 35). Both groups (the true *bhaktas*, and the brahmins) look back to primordial founder-figures. Among the brahmins, Parāśara etc. are the exponents of the *gotras*, Vyāsa etc. of the *śākhās*, Bodhāyana etc. of the *sūtras*, and so on, but in the religion of *kainkarya*, Parâṅkuśa etc. are the heads of the *bhakta* lineage (s. 36). Like the study of the Vedas turns an Ārya into a true brahmin, to learn the TVM is the prerequisite for becoming a true *bhakta* and Vaiṣṇava (s. 37).

4.42. Having established a parallel religious system in which traditional Vedic religion is contrasted with Vaisṇavism as accidental and external, Nāyaṉār applies this to the Sanskrit and Tamil Vedas. There are many Vedas, in different worlds and ages (s. 39), and the distinction of a Tamil and a Sanskrit Veda is similar to that of a Ṛg, Sāma, etc. Veda (s. 40). The Tamil language is not the creation of Agastya,[140] but was only promulgated by him, being, like Sanskrit, eternal (s. 41). The following *sūtras* explore the parallelism of a Tamil and Sanskrit Veda (s. 42) for increasingly detailed features, through an increasingly ingenious and complex exegesis. S. 43 compares

4 Vedas	:	4 works of Nammāḻvār
6 *aṅgas*	:	6 works of Tirumāṅkaiy Āḻvār
8 *upâṅgas*	:	8 works in song form.[141]

The Sanskrit titles *ṛṣi*, *kavi*, and *muni* apply also to the Āḻvār, who like the famous Vedic *ṛṣis* Vyāsa etc. 'saw' the *śruti* (s. 47). When it is said in the *śrutiphalas* 'words of Caṭakōpaṉ', this is meant to specify the first reciter, parallel to Taittirīya etc. (s. 49). S. 50 provides the following comparison:

Ṛg	:	Tiruviruttam
Sāma	:	Tiruvāymoḻi
Yajur	:	Tiruvāciriyam
Atharva	:	Periyatiruvantâti.[142]

The *Sāma* is the expansion through musical means of the Ṛg;[143] similarly, the TVM elaborates, as songs, on the concise poems of the *Tiruviruttam*[144] (s. 51). Thus the TVM corresponds to the (Chandoga recension of the) Sāma-Veda (ss. 52-4). Referring to the complicated patterns of 'authorship' found in the Purāṇas (viz. who received it from whom and taught it to whom), Nāyaṉār points out that it is a unique feature of the TVM etc. to be the immediate and direct product of Viṣṇu's grace (ss. 55f) and his revelation of himself to the Āḻvār (ss. 55-7). Moreover, the *ṛṣis* obtained their knowledge after strenuous and lengthy *tapas* and *dharma*, while Nammāḻvār was thrown into mystical experience which gave rise to intense love and passion for Viṣṇu (s. 58). Also in other respects Nammāḻvār was superior to the Vedic *ṛṣis*, for example by his supreme *vairāgya* (s. 59), his not eating or drinking (s. 60), refusing to narrate 'useless' stories like that of Skanda's birth (s. 63), the complete consistency of his statements (s. 64),[145] etc.

4.43. In ss. 68 and 70, Nāyaṉār mentions two alternative interpretations of the TVM. Firstly, it could be considered an *upabṛṃhana*, an 'expansion', of the four Sanskrit Vedas; in this case it would correspond to the *Mahābhārata* which sometimes is regarded as the fifth Veda and whose Upaniṣad is the *Gītā*.[146] The second alternative is the schema discussed above (3.31/2). The phrase 'who rendered the Vedas in Tamil' can thus be explained as: who effected the transformation of the Sanskrit Vedas into the TVM for the *arcavatāra*.

4.44. The final group of *sūtras* (71-84) employs basically poetic means to point out the superiority of the TVM. Some examples may be mentioned here.

> Unlike an earthen vessel, the TVM is like a golden cup (s. 73).

While the earthen vessel retains, according to śāstric interpretation, the impurity of the person using it and thus cannot be used by anybody else, the golden cup can be shared among various people without any elaborate purificatory rites. S. 74 compares the TVM to a spouted vessel, which requires no effort whatsoever for the person who wants to drink water; the Vedas are here similar to the ocean whose salt water only the fish can drink.[147] Just as it would be sacrilegious to regard the *arcā* as mere metal, stone or wood (since through the *pratiṣṭhā* it becomes transubstantiated into Viṣṇu's body), the TVM is infinitely more than an ordinary literary work by a *śūdra* author (s. 75). If one looked at language alone, also the works of the heretics in Sanskrit could be accepted; or at birth alone, even Kṛṣṇa the speaker of the *Gītā* and Vyāsa the compiler of the *Mahābhārata* must be despised (s. 76). These three are compared further, for example, in s. 79: 'Could there be a resemblance between places smelling of fish and butter, and a place perfumed by *tulsī*?' Kṛṣṇa was born among cowherds, and Vyāsa's mother was called Matsyagandhā 'she who smells of fish'. Nammāḻvār on the other hand 'obtained the fragrance of the *tulsī*',[148] Viṣṇu's sacred plant.

> By the rise of the sun Bakulâbharaṇa the darkness within, which the sun cannot reach, was dispelled; the ocean of births which the sun Rāma[149] could not dry up, dried; and the lotus which is 'the house of enlightenment'[150] began to blossom, while it had not opened for the sun Acyuta. (s. 83).[151]

Finally, s. 84 connects the lowly birth of the Āḻvār with a grand interpretation of the history of grace:

> Like the Boar and the Cowherd (viz. Varāha and Kṛṣṇa) descended and were born in lowly families in order to raise up the earth and (elevate) his lineage, he descended low in order to raise those who were in a lowly position (viz. *śūdras*, women, etc.).

4.45. It is evident how closely the interpretation of Nammāḻvār and his scriptures is linked with a specific concept of man's religious nature. The older concept of man as (potential) *jñānī* is now practically replaced, not just complemented (as in Rāmânuja),[152] by that of the *śeṣa*: a being totally dependent upon another, Viṣṇu; knowledge consists in realizing that relationship and religion, in expressing it through acts of ritual service and love. The older religious tradition with its restrictions on who was allowed to become a *jñānī* had to appear élitist, preliminary, and external. What was more appropriate than having as scriptural authorities for this new religion a corpus of songs which had been composed by a person who by his very *varṇa* symbolized 'servitude', who was a *śūdra* saint, and who quite literally proved that salvation had now become possible at the very bottom of society? Moreover, Nāyaṉār could show with great ingenuity that Nammāḻvār's works, the central portion of those of all the Āḻvārs, were parallel, and in fact superior to, the Sanskrit Vedas; thereby he goes further than Nañjīyar who on the whole is concerned with showing that they do not contradict the Vedas.

The ĀH must, however, have been an esoteric treatise; its concise *sūtra* style in which a great variety of scriptural passages and whole arguments are alluded to merely through a word or a phrase, its complex arguments and feats of subtle exegesis — these features could hardly have made it a widely known work, since knowledge of it would depend on lengthy oral explanations. It was thus of particular importance that Maṇavāḷa mā mu̱ni, one of the most outstanding and revered theologians of the Te̱nkaḷai and a learned brahmin, wrote his detailed commentary on the ĀH. The theology based on the religion of the Ā̱lvārs and evaluated against the full background of Veda-inspired religion was thereby made available to a much larger audience.

4.5. These theological developments, particularly during the late fourteenth and the fifteenth centuries, must be evaluated in conjunction with the social history of Vaiṣṇavism in the South. Two important points may be mentioned here. Firstly, an *ācārya* called Tiruvāymo̱li Piḷḷai, who had been the disciple of Piḷḷai Lokâcārya and his younger brother Nāyaṉār (the author of the ĀH), went to Kurukūr and settled there. That this move was motivated by his great veneration for Nammā̱lvār is suggested by hagiography which credits him with the 'rescue of ruins'[153] there and with the reconsolidation of Nammā̱lvār's cult.[154] Among the disciples he attracted were Maṇavāḷa mā mu̱ni, born like himself in the Pāṇḍya country.[155] The latter studied the TVM along with its commentarial literature in Kurukūr.[156] Secondly, Maṇavāḷa mā mu̱ni became the leading figure in the organization and institutionalization of the Te̱nkaḷai. His 'activities involved a judicious combination of five kinds of strategics'[157] which were: the promulgation of Nammā̱lvār's works as fundamental scriptural authority, the organization of a network of local groups of 'disciples' who were totally dedicated to their *ācārya*, the stipulation and use of royal patronage, and the establishment of specifically Te̱nkaḷai control over a number of temples. Thus we could almost say that his commentary on the ĀH is the manifesto of an ideology which fought to materialize its religious premises in a new social organization.

5.00 *Nammā̱lvār in the Popular Imagination*

5.1. The picture that has been presented so far is typical of 'official', learned, *sāmpradāyika* Śrīvaiṣṇavism. The general structure of its doctrines and theology serves here as the context, but also the constraint, for the interpretation of an individual theme like that of the Āḻvār. But we must not forget that in a number of instances in the previous discussion our attention was drawn to something like a 'Kurukūr milieu' with its cult of the Āḻvār, and that particularly the Teṉkaḷai encompassed popular strata in the society. It is here that we find the Āḻvār envisaged and interpreted with a marked change in the idiom and along lines which differ from those of the *sāmpradāyika* position. Although considerable individual variation will be noticed, the common characteristic is that the various works discussed now are 'popular' in inspiration, which means, to be more precise, either that they employ purāṇic symbols, or that typically Tamil patterns are used.

5.21. We may begin by looking at a passage in which a particular theme is treated by recourse to the purāṇic idiom; the theme is the choice of Tamil as language of revelation. As we have seen above, the purely theological answer to that question has been that thereby 'all people' can come to know the meaning of the Vedas. The popular imagination is interested in a different kind of answer, as a passage[158] from the *Prapannâmṛta* (PA) shows.

5.22. [Nañjīyar asked his teacher Parāśara-Bhaṭṭa] 'For what purpose have Śaṭhakopa etc. ignored all other regions and were born in the Tamil country; did they compose all their works in Tamil and ignore the language of the gods; and how was it that Tamil became superior even to Sanskrit in the world?'

[Bhaṭṭa narrates this story in reply] 'Formerly the wedding of Śiva and Pārvatī was celebrated on Kailāsa; it was a feast for the whole world. Whoever lived in the threefold world, Brahmā and all the other gods, went there to participate in it. The crowds of gods, sages, and other people were filling the mountain densely, and this made the land in the North sink down, while the land in the South, not held down by any weight, moved upwards, like a ship [capsizing] in the ocean. On account of this, all the gods and sages got frightened.'

[Viśvakarmā suggests that Agastya 'in whom the three worlds rest' should go to the South and by his weight redistribute the load on the earth. Agastya is anything but pleased with this termination to his feasting, and he curses Viśvakarmā. Inevitably, the latter reacts with a curse of his own:] 'From now onwards, the Tamil language created by you will certainly become like the language of the Piśācas, and its grammar written by you will become greatly despised. Similar to the language of the Mlecchas, it will belong to the *śūdras*. Verily, the Tamil country will be a land of robbers[159] and deprived of brahmins, through my curse.'

[Agastya follows the advice of the gods and settles in the South, performing vigorous penance. Pleased with his *tapas*, Viṣṇu appears before him and rewards him:] 'The Tamil language will be everywhere. I shall cause my weapons, the conch, discus, etc., and the gods Viṣvaksena etc. to be born in the Tamil country. In the excellent town of Kurukā on the Tāmraparṇī, *I shall become* a true *bhakta* in order to render the *śrutis* into Tamil. *By me* and ten excellent Tamils born as my *aṃśas* literary works (amounting to) 4000 (stanzas) which contain all the meanings of the Vedas will be composed in the divine Tamil language.'

[Viṣṇu goes on to praise the unique efficiency of the Tamil Veda ('Sahasragīti', = TVM) and ends by saying:] 'Therefore a person deprived of the Tamil Upaniṣad will never obtain final salvation.'[160]

5.23. This *purāṇa*-like episode which Anantâcārya (late sixteenth century) derived from a source not known to me, assumes that we know about Agastya, the Vedic *ṛṣi* who turned culture-hero for the Tamils. We cannot enter here into a discussion of the various motifs which are combined in this legend — the Vedic *ṛṣi*, his association with Tamil, Śiva's marriage, the load on the earth, the curses, the Paiśācī language, *tapas* and its rewards. But the intention of the myth is clear: as a reward for the Vedic *ṛṣi's* penance (and in a sense, his saving the earth and the gods), his language, Tamil, becomes endowed with great sanctity and essential for man's salvation. The Āḻvārs, particularly Nammāḻvār and his Tamil Veda, are the means by which Viṣṇu fulfils his promise to Agastya. Anantâcārya utilizes popular *purāṇa*-inspired mythology to motivate and explain one particular juncture in the *sāmpradāyika* conception of the history of Viṣṇu's grace (see 3.2/3): why Tamil is chosen.

5.3. The previous passage contained two mysterious remarks: 'I shall become. . .' and 'by me. . .'; these remarks suggest that Viṣṇu himself is incarnated in Nammāḻvār. Such a concept contradicts the *sāmpradāyika* position, but is indeed put forward in a very elaborate manner by the local tradition of Kurukūr, which is found in the *sthalapurāṇa* of that temple (SPK). This version of the Āḻvār's life, possibly written after the fifteenth century,[161] differs substantially from the 'official' legends; its approach is based on the ritual significance of Caṭakōpaṉ and on purāṇic symbols.

5.31. The first two chapters of this *purāṇa* (viz. chs. 22f) deal very briefly with the events that led to Viṣṇu's taking abode in the temple of Kurukūr; the remaining eight chapters have Nammāḻvār as their theme. The story begins with Viṣṇu's *avatāra* as Rāma. Ananta had incarnated himself as Lakṣmaṇa, and Śrī had become Sītā. After killing Rāvaṇa (and discarding Sītā), Rāma withdrew to a lonely spot, giving Lakṣmaṇa instructions not to disturb him. When, for a legitimate reason, he did so, he was promptly cursed by Rāma to be reborn on earth as an insentient object, in fact, as a tamarind tree. Then Rāma calmed down and promised his younger brother

> Formerly I abandoned my faultless wife when she was pregnant; I shall (therefore) live at your feet in celibacy, by the name of Śaṭhâri, holding my hand in the *jñāna-mudrā*.[162]

Ananta-Lakṣmaṇa turned into the tree 'which does not sleep'; 'seeing this miracle, brahmins learned in the Vedas worship it/him with flowers, incense, perfumes, food, etc.'[163] Dharma became a *haṃsa* bird and, sitting on its branches, preached to all castes, including '*śūdras* filled with bhakti to Bhagavān'.[164] Now the scene is set for Rāma to fulfil his promise.

5.32. The king of Aṅga Vīravarman had a son Kāri; he married Ātmavatī the daughter of the Videha king. This couple was in fact a re-incarnation of Vasudeva and Devakī (Kṛṣṇa's parents) whom Kṛṣṇa had promised *mokṣa* at the beginning of the *kali* age and who had been incarnations of Kaśyapa and Aditi.[165] When Kāri had ruled as king for some time, he and his wife were driven away from their kingdom by enemies and eventually settled near Kurukūr to perform *tapas*. Although longing for a son, they remained childless. An ascetic sent them to Kuraṅgā (Kuṟuṅkuṭi) where Viṣṇu abided as Pūrṇa in the temple. Pūrṇa, seeing the couple worshipping him, remembered his promises to Ananta-Lakṣmaṇa and Vasudeva. Therefore he told them: 'I myself will become the son of you two.'[166] Ātmavatī became pregnant and gave birth to a son who was named Śathakopa.

5.33. Being a *kṣatriya* (!)[167] boy, various ceremonies like the *cūḍā* and *muñja* (in his eleventh year) were performed on him. Then the boy went to study all the Vedas and *śāstras*. During this period of study he developed a profound mystical inclination, becoming 'deeply depressed and then again, filled with joy, acting as if drunk'.[168] The parents became worried, but were consoled by a brahmin who told them that their son was Viṣṇu himself who through his *māyā* acted previously like an ordinary human child, but now had simply withdrawn back to his own nature. The couple went with their son to Kurukūr, where Śaṭhâri settled under the tamarind tree, 'seated in the lotus-position and holding his hand in the *jñāna-mudrā*',[169] and 'surrounded by all castes'.[170]

5.34. The *haṃsa* served him as vehicle, and riding on it he went all over the world to defeat the *māyāvādins* (advaita-vedântins) and to establish his own doctrine. He went first to Śrīraṅgam, then to Kāñcī, to Vēṅkaṭam, and finally to Yādavâdri.[171] After that he rendered the whole Veda into Tamil[172] 'in order to save brahmins, . . . , *śūdras*, women, and those of the lowest castes'.[173] His *Drāviḍâgama* was so efficient that Yama lost all his victims from hell, and Śaṭhâri consoled him by handing over to him all the *māyāvādins*. Lakṣmī-Sītā became depressed because Viṣṇu-Rāma had left her and was observing *brahmacarya*. Śaṭhâri turned her into a garland of *bakula* flowers and wore it/her around his neck.[174] Then Śaṭhâri left the human world, but all castes came to worship his *vigraha*[175] under the tree, learning the Tamil Veda. The place was so powerful that even a wolf — a reborn Kirāta tribesman who had hunted and killed — found *mokṣa*.[176]

5.35. This extraordinary version not only envisages Nammāḻvār as an incarnation of Viṣṇu, but also manages to connect him with three[177] of the classical *avatāras*, viz. Vāmana, Rāma and Kṛṣṇa, and finally to fuse him with Rāmânuja. Some of the many lines of association and imagination which converged to produce this complex picture, may be traced here.

5.351. *As incarnation of Viṣṇu.* Already the DSC had made two suggestions: Pūrṇa of Kuraṅgā had promised Nāthanāyikā that he would be her son, and that the tamarind tree was Ananta incarnate. Furthermore, a verse of the *Harivaṃśa*[178] mentions that Viṣṇu's *avatāra* is preceded by Ananta incarnating himself. The Vaṭakaḷai (see 3.332 and 3.334) envisaged Viṣṇu as entering into Parâṅkuśa. Finally, there was the iconographic type (see Figure I) of the Āḻvār. To regard the tree as incarnation of Ananta could easily also evoke another type, that of Nārāyaṇa reclining on Ananta (see Figure II). What was missing to complete the parallel between both types was Lakṣmī (indispensable in the second type); the SPK version achieves this by having Śrī become the garland of *bakula* flowers.[179]

II Viṣṇu on Ananta, with Lakṣmī

5.352. *In Relation to Other* Avatāras. It is likely that the iconographic type II evoked Śrīraṅgam, the most important temple for the Śrīvaiṣṇavas at the time. There type II (represented by the temple sculpture) is interpreted as Rāma. To regard Lakṣmaṇa as ideal *śeṣa* is common in Śrīvaiṣṇava literature,[180] and the association of *śeṣa* and Śeṣa (=Ananta) is easy enough. The present version completes the parallel by envisaging the garland as Sītā. The connection with Vāmana is established by reference to the local mythology of TirukKuṟuṅkuṭi. The Sanskrit name of the temple is *Vāmana-kṣetra*, and 'kuru' which *inter alia* means 'short, small', is interpreted as Dwarf (=Vāmana). Since Pūrṇa in Kuraṅgā was thus a manifestation of Vāmana, it followed that his birth as Kāri's and Ātmavatī's son, evoking Vāmana's birth by Kaśyapa and Aditi, could suggest that the latter parents were in fact reincarnated in the former.[181] A connection between Aditi and Kṛṣṇa is suggested in the *Mahābhārata*,[182] and thus also Vasudeva and Devakī could be fitted into the structure. In this manner the SPK succeeded in associating the Kurukūr temple with the three, from the point of view of the worship of the most important *avatāras*.

5.353. *As Rāmănuja.* Two themes attributed in the present version to Nammāḻvār are associated with Rāmânuja in the *sāmpradāyika* writings: the journey to the four places, ending with Yādavâdri, and the establishing of a doctrinal system which defeats the *māyāvādins*.[183] We may note that 'Rāmânuja' actually denotes Lakṣmaṇa, and that the pattern of Viṣṇu's companions incarnating themselves includes Ananta who becomes Rāmânuja.[184] This produced another iconographic type (see Figure III) in which

III Nammālvār

the element above the head symbolizes who the figure is in reality.[185] Thus regarding the tree above Nammāḻvār's head as Ananta, could also suggest that the person below it was in fact (an incarnation of) Ananta. Given the internal similarity between the two great teachers of Śrīvaiṣṇavism, a fusion of the two in the popular mind — which incidentally would remove the dichotomy of a Tamil and a Sanskrit strand within the tradition — becomes possible.

5.36. The present version has introduced also other significant changes. Firstly, any reference to Madhurakavi is avoided; I am, however, unable to explain this omission.[186] Secondly, Nammāḻvār is here a *kṣatriya*, not a *śūdra*.[187] It is difficult to explain what motivated this alteration, particularly since the text stresses in many places that the Tamil-Veda saves all castes, that all castes participate in the cult of the Āḻvār, and that all castes live together in harmony in Kurukūr. It may have been the inner logic of the purāṇic symbolism imposed on the life-story of the Āḻvār; after all, Rāma and Kṛṣṇa were *kṣatriyas*.[188] Hagiography depicts Kāri as powerful 'king', particularly in the later versions,[189] and Vaiṣṇava temple ritual employs a royal symbolism (on this see below). Thirdly, the SPK depicts the early life of Nammāḻvār as moving along ordinary lines; only when he has started to study does he become a mystic. In this case it seems possible to trace the motivation behind this alteration. In one place[190] the text mentions that his parents watched the various *bāla-krīḍās* of the boy and played with him. This suggests that the author was aware of popular poems in Tamil, like the *Nammāḻvār-piḷḷait-tamiḻ*,[191] which assume a setting in which a mother plays various games with her child. The treatment of the Āḻvār's childhood in the SPK provides precisely that setting.

5.4. We can at this point turn conveniently to other such popular works in Tamil. The generic name for them is *prabandham*;[192] unlike the *purāṇa*-inspired symbolism discussed above, these *prabandhams* have their roots in ancient strata of Tamil culture.[193]

5.41. The genre *piḷḷaittamiḻ* contains a sub-genre called *tālēlō* ('lullaby'); the anonymous *Nammāḻvār-tiruttālāṭṭu*[194] belongs to that category. It narrates the life-story of the Āḻvār, along lines similar, for example, to the PA, in the form of a cradle song. Moreover, in lines 282-300 it provides a very concise summary of the TVM thereby making the saving knowledge of the Tamil Veda available to women in the most direct manner.

5.42. The *Kurukai-mālai*[195] composed by Rāmaratna Kavirāya (eighteenth century?)[196] speaks in a few stanzas about Nammāḻvār. His remarks show an interesting fluctuation between the *sāmpradāyika* and the more unrestrained interpretations of the Āḻvār as *bhakta* and as Viṣṇu himself.

(Āḻvār as Viṣṇu's *prapanna*:)

Viṣṇu . . . loves Kurukai; to him went for refuge he who defeated the

caṅkam in Maturai with his threefold Tamil [viz. poetry, music, dance].[197]
(Viṣṇu dwells in the Āḻvār's heart:)
Kurukai which touches with its two *vimānams* made of pure gold the sky and shines forth like the earrings of the sun, is the home of Viṣṇu who loves to dwell in the palace which is the heart-lotus of Māraṉ who [wears] *makil* flowers that are fragrant . . .[198]
(Āḻvār = Viṣṇu:)
Kurukai which was praised by him of TirukKōḷūr (=Madhurakavi) by saying: 'That splendour alone which wears the *vakuḷa* flowers around his neck is Viṣṇu'.[199]

5.43. The fertile and unrestrained popular imagination is able to move away from the *sāmpradāyika* position even further than any of the sources discussed in the present section did, as the *Makiḻ-Māraṉ pavaṉi-kuṟam*,[200] an anonymous poem perhaps of the seventeenth to nineteenth century,[201] shows. In accordance with the general conventions of this literary genre,[202] Caṭakōpaṉ is presented as a beautiful and rich king who walks in procession through the town; a girl watching him falls in love with him. Consulting a *kuṟatti*, a tribal woman talented in palm reading, she is told that Māraṉ will come to her and unite with her.[203] Naturally, it was possible even on the conventional premises to envisage Nammāḻvār, as the son of Kāri the lord of Kurukūr, as walking in royal splendour through the town.[204] But to imagine him as lover runs counter to the whole interpretation analyzed so far, viz. of the Āḻvār as a *saṃnyāsī*. However, even this theme is not as far-fetched as it might appear at first sight. Firstly, his own poetry is pervaded by a strong bhakti-eroticism; secondly, the *bakula* flowers evoke amorous associations[205] and significantly Makiḻ-Māraṉ, 'Māraṉ who wears the *bakula* flowers' is used in this work as the Āḻvār's name. Thirdly, and this is probably the most important factor, it is conventional in Śrīvaiṣṇava Tamil poetry to describe the beauty and fascination of Viṣṇu who, like a king, is carried in procession through a town (as the *utsava-vigraha*) in terms of the attraction a girl feels who is watching the procession.[206] Thus the tendency to identify the Āḻvār with Viṣṇu himself had to lead to this form of treatment which was customary for Viṣṇu.

5.51. In various places we have so far drawn attention to the ritual context within which the Āḻvār was interpreted and which appeared to be useful for our analysis. Here we shall illustrate this from some details of the cult of Nammāḻvār as practised in Kurukūr. Permanent and seasonal *pūjā* to the Āḻvār *vigraha* is stated to be identical with that given to Viṣṇu. During the annual *janmôtsava*, the celebration of the Āḻvār's birth, on the fifth day of the festival, the Viṣṇus from nine surrounding temples are brought before him. They watch the various rites performed in his honour and pay their obeisance to him, and then those songs which the Āḻvār had composed in honour of those nine temples are recited.[207] Finally the Āḻvār, seated on a *haṃsa-vāhana*, is carried through the town, the nine Viṣṇus following him in the procession.[208]

5.52. This *janmôtsava* is more than merely an interesting local custom, because behind it we can detect a fascinating solution to a typical socio-religious conflict situation. Kurukūr is the centre, with Śrīvaikuṇṭham in second place, of what is known as the *navatiruppatis*, the 'nine sacred places'; it is from these temples that the Viṣṇu *utsava-vigrahas* are brought to the Āḻvār. A closer look at these temples reveals that the Āḻvār functions as the unifying factor of otherwise separate and heterogeneous elements. Two of the temples appear to belong to *brahmadeya* villages, and a further two to non-brahmin settlements;[209] these are Tullaivilli-maṅgalam and Varaguṇa-maṅkai, and Kuruk'-ūr and Kōḷ-ūr respectively. In Śrīvaikuṇṭham, Viṣṇu is called Kaḷḷapiraṉ, 'lord of the Kaḷḷar' — the Kaḷḷar are a prominent low-caste group in the area — and the *sthalapurāṇa* of the temple suggests a local Kaḷḷar-brahmin alliance.[210] Today a Kaḷḷar is trustee not only of that temple, but also of Varaguṇa-maṅkai and TirupPuḷiṅkuṭi. To complicate matters further,[211] the Puḷiṅkuṭi temple still bears witness to a period in its history when non-brahmins were not allowed inside. There is no Nammāḻvār shrine in the temple; a window in the *garbhagṛha* wall allowed those prohibited to enter to look inside on the *mūla-vigraha.* Thus when the nine *vigrahas* are brought to the Āḻvār, this festival, in which all castes participate (as also the SPK so frequently pointed out), transcends and unifies different local attitudes towards caste.

6.00. *Nammāḻvār in Kāvya-style Poems*

6.1. The previous sections, but particularly the last one on popular imagination, have shown how the interpretation of the Āḻvār and his works developed through the association of different symbols (mythical, ritual, iconographic). But it is in the Sanskrit poetic style of the *kāvya* that a technique has been perfected by means of which different symbols are combined, to interpret each other, in most concise statements. Often misinterpreted as mere verbal trickery,[212] this poetic technique is nevertheless of great potential for theology, as ought to become evident from the following. Without doubt the greatest exponent of this theological *kāvya*-poetry in Śrīvaiṣṇavism is Veṅkaṭanātha (fourteenth-century),[213] who probably as a result of the expansion of the Teṉkaḷai (see 4.5), became regarded by Śrīvaiṣṇavas who maintained a more orthodox position than the Teṉkaḷai as the fountain-head of the Vaṭakaḷai.

6.2. A superficial look at the vast literary output of Vedântadeśika will discover little which deals directly with Nammāḻvār. His *Dramiḍôpaniṣat-tātparyaratnâvalī*, a hundred and twenty stanzas summarizing the TVM, seems insignificant when compared with the vast exegetical literature of the Teṉkaḷai.[214] But a more detailed analysis shows that most of his writing is permeated, in some form or other, by references and allusions to, and ideas taken from, the *Prabandham*. The expression of his appreciation of Nammāḻvār which will be discussed now is therefore by no means merely rhetorical and isolated within the context of his works.

6.3. The (Śrīraṅga-nātha) *Pādukāsahasram* (PS) is a *mahākāvya* of one thousand and eight Sanskrit stanzas in praise of the sandals which Bharata accepted from Rāma and carried on his head as a sign that Rāma even in his exile continued to be the king; moreover, in Śrīraṅgam the ritual includes a stylized form of the sandals (and the carrying of them) known as *caṭakōpam*.[215] The second section plays with the similarity of the names *caṭakōpam* and Caṭakōpaṉ, and the *kāvya* technique produces an extraordinarily complex symbolism. I shall first give a literal (though hardly comprehensible) translation of the more important verses.

6.31. In order to make acceptable to Śrī's lover even those who have remained outside the *Dramiḍôpaniṣad*, Śaṭhakopa whose *ātman* is the sandal, must have descended (and taken on bodily form) of his own accord. (22)

Indeed, o jewelled sandal! that sage, in carrying your name 'Saṭhakopa' displayed a respectable form so that the lineage of those born from the foot to which you have resorted could find respect-and-pride in it. (23)[216]

O jewelled sandal! by the sage and by you — both of you being known by the name 'Śaṭhakopa' — two things became a blessing for all: by him the *śruti* and by you its meaning.(24)

That sage Śaṭhakopa who moved up to the ultimate state of *śeṣaness* which was raised by seven storeys, was defeated by you through wearing his name. (26)[217]

O sandal! the language of Agastya which was born in eternity and (descended) by its free will comes out of your mouth, — you who have Śaṭharipu as your body, and comes before the ancient *śrtis*. (29)[217a]

6.32. We may unpack this highly complex symbolism in the following manner. Since the Āḻvār is not the main subject matter of the whole *kāvya*, the emphasis is on the sandals also rhetorically, which means that for poetic reasons they are praised as 'superior' to the Āḻvār. Abstracting from this, the following can be considered to be Vedântadeśika's interpretation of the Āḻvār. The sandal under Viṣṇu's foot symbolizes perfect *dāsya*, servitude and humble submission, and thus the essential nature of the soul. Since it is the innermost message of the Vedas that the soul's nature is *śeṣatva* and that *kaiṅkarya* is the means to actualize it, and since the Vedas are brought to men by Viṣṇu himself, the sound which the sandals make when Viṣṇu approaches the worshipper can be taken as a metaphor for the recitation of the Vedas. On the second level, the sandal is envisaged in its stylized, ritual form as *caṭakōpam*. The *pūjāri* brings it from the inner shrine to the devotee and places it on his head; thereby the *bhakta* expresses in a ritualized manner, in an act of *kaiṅkarya* ('touching with one's head the feet of Viṣṇu'), his essential nature as Viṣṇu's *śeṣa*. The sandal here comes to him as the medium by which he can actualize what is potential in him and what the sandal (as a symbol) is already: Viṣṇu's totally devoted and dependent servant. On the third level of symbolism, Nammāḻvār is attributed with everything said so far about the sandals and the *caṭakōpam*. He is the ideal *śeṣa* and servant, the bodily manifestation of the sandal, carrying it on his head[218] and granting self-respect and prestige to the *śūdras* who were born from Viṣṇu's feet. His words are the Tamil rendering of the Vedas which as the *Dramiḍôpaniṣad or °saṃhita* became a blessing for all, because they were the 'sounds' of his who, belonging to the lowest caste, at the 'foot' of humanity (or bottom, as we would say), serves as its 'sandal'. Like the *caṭakōpam* the Āḻvār is brought to all people in his poetry through which they are enabled to actualize their potential essence and what he is fully: *śeṣas* of Viṣṇu.

6.33. The content of this poetic play of the imagination corresponds, I believe, in essence to what the *Ācāryahṛdayam* etc. state. But it was significant that Vedântadeśika expressed his ideas in poetic symbols and not in theological statements, for obviously the former allow much more easily for a variety of interpretations than the latter. A brief look at a modern Vaṭakaḷai commentary on these stanzas may be of interest here; this is the *Pādukāsahasra-paricaryā*[219] by Uttamūr Vīrarāghavâcāryar, one of the most eminent living theologians of the Vaṭakaḷai. On v. 23 he says:

> That he carried your name made it clear that you hold in esteem that lineage (of *śūdras*), because you consider it the offspring of the feet of His which you protect; it also was for the sake of accomplishing your function towards people. Earth and *śūdras* were born from His feet; earth is the realm of orthodox religion which brings happiness to all people, and the *śūdras* assist, by performing their duty, all members of the other *varṇas*. By becoming a *śūdra*, the Āḻvār helped the brahmins by means of his poetic work which was for all.[220]

On v. 24 he comments that the purpose of the Tamil Upaniṣad was to make people realize that the Vedas are a blessing, and on v. 29 he rejects the claim that the Tamil Veda is, like the Sanskrit Vedas, eternal in the sense of having no beginning in time; Tamil, he says, was the creation of Agastya. All this seems to suggest that the primary importance of the orthodox *varṇa*-system and the Sanskrit Vedas is maintained and the *śūdra* Āḻvār and his Tamil Upaniṣad is placed in a subservient rôle. I find it however difficult to read this in Vedântadeśika's own stanzas.

6.4. Practically all major works of the Teṉkaḷai are in Tamil or *Maṇippravāḷa*,[221] while the cultivation (also) of Sanskrit is commonly associated with the Vaṭakaḷai.[222] But given the prestige of Sanskrit and the attractions of the *kāvya* style, and we may presume, the reputation of Vedântadeśika which is based on these two factors, it is not surprising to find that also the Teṉkaḷai has its *kāvya* in honour of Nammāḻvār. This is the *Nakṣatramālikā* (NM) which Jīyar Nāyaṉār, a grandson of Maṇavāḷa mā muṉi,[223] composed around 1500 A.D. This Sanskrit poem in praise of Nammāḻvār, consisting of twenty eight stanzas in various metres (which is the characteristic of the genre *mālikā*), contains in each stanza the name of *nakṣatra*, lunar mansion. It is a masterpiece of ingenuity, full of complex sound effects and elaborate symbolism.

The *śleṣas* involving the *nakṣatra* names are by no means out of place in this poem in honour of the Ā<u>l</u>vār, because its symbolism interprets the Ā<u>l</u>vār in terms of the moon. V. 9 says

> the lovely moonshine which is friendly to the (night-) lotuses, (viz.) the people who have taken refuge (with him, *prapanna*).

V. 11 describes the Ā<u>l</u>vār as 'nectar-ocean of compassion', alluding thereby to the pan-Indian connection of the moon and nectar.

Further aspects of the symbolism underlying the poem can best be illustrated through a visual representation (see Figure IV). From vs. 1-14 the length of a verse increases by one syllable (per

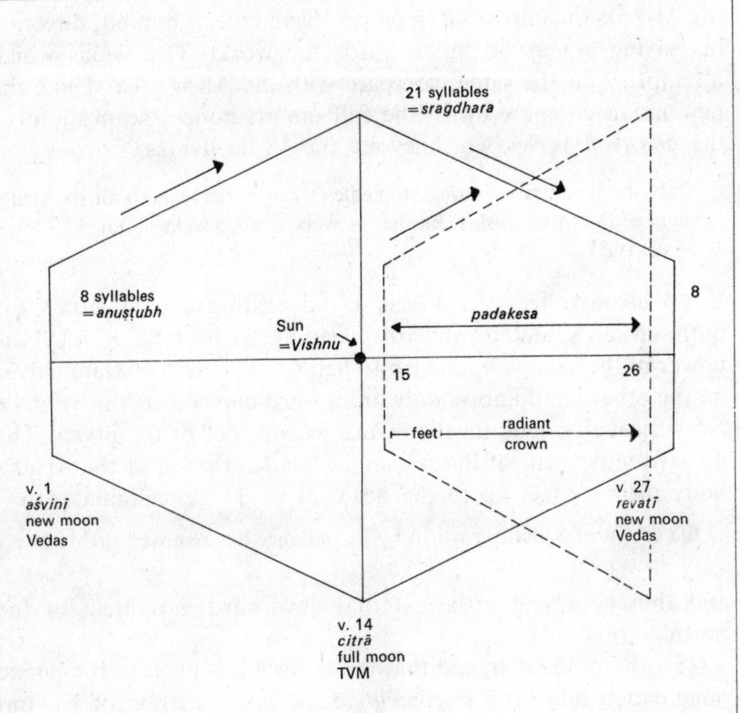

pāda); v. 1 is in the *anuṣṭubh* metre, of 8 syllables per *pāda*, and v. 14 in *sragdhara* of 21 syllables. The same metres are repeated in reverse order for the second half, vs. 15-27. Stanza 14, thus the structural centre, relates to the full moon *(citrā nakṣatra)*, and we may note that the metre *sragdhara* 'who wears a garland' echoes the 'who is fragrant from the *bakula* flowers' in the same stanza. The light of the moon is metaphorical for *Viṣṇu's* saving grace. Already v. 7 says

> (Nammāḻvār) who on account of the 'divine eye' of his knowledge made the Highest Light visible which [in itself] cannot be perceived.[224]

Accordingly v.14, in its central portion, says.

> Śaṭharipu who does not interrupt, even for a moment, his prostration before the feet of the Unique Light who . . . desires to protect all beings and things, whose nature is what the Vedas aim at [expressing], and who shines forth in the company of Śrī.[225]

Thus just as the full moon is the complete reflection of the sun, the Āḻvār is the mirror upon which Viṣṇu reflects himself, directing his saving grace via him towards the world. The Vedas which attempt to do the same, compare with the Āḻvār's TVM like the new moon compares with the full moon: notice the position of the *anuṣṭubh* verses which evoke the Vedic hymns.

> Only the Upaniṣads among all Vedic (scriptures) speak about the Ornament of the three worlds; but he, in every word, speaks about the Primal Man. (v.5)

V. 4 characterizes the Vedas as advocating a path that leads both upwards and downwards, leading to heaven, and by the power of the same *karma*, also to hell.[226] The path of Nammāḻvār on the other hand knows only an upward movement; this is made clear through poetic means in the second half of the poem. The upward movement of the *pādâkeśa*, the description of the Āḻvār's body from its feet up to the head, in vs. 15-26, culminates in

> the crown of Śaṭharipu which by its radiance has removed the darkness of sin (v. 26),

and thus counteracts the external downward movement of the poem.

6.5. It could be argued that these ingenious plays of the poetic imagination add little *in content* to the interpretation of Nammāḻvār found in the works previously discussed. This may be the case, but other factors will support the great importance of these works. They illustrate to us in a clear and direct way a kind of thinking which could be detected as underlying also many of the other texts analysed: a more or less free play of associations, and an imagination typical of poetry. Nammāḻvār's works are regarded as displaying Viṣṇu's qualities in their poetic beauty; truth for the Śrīvaiṣṇavas is Viṣṇu, one of whose qualities is beauty which in turn gives rise to love in anyone experiencing this beauty. Similarly any statement about the Āḻvār would, in the ideal, express the truth as and through beauty. When the medium of Sanskrit is chosen, the *kāvya* is clearly the most appropriate means of communicating that beauty in poetic terms. More prosaic considerations can be added; only the medium of Sanskrit could ensure that the religion of Southern Vaiṣṇavism, which was so intrinsically connected with the local vernacular Tamil, became available to other regions of India, and that the movement avoided a complete discontinuity in relation to the pan-Indian religious heritage. The Vaṭakaḷai is certainly interested in the second point.

7.00. *Evaluation and Summary*

7.1. The beginning of all those complicated developments which we have traced in the previous pages lies in the Tamil poetry of Caṭakōpaṉ. Its aesthetic appeal and religious fervour, set within an institution (Madhurakavi and a bardic tradition) and a local cult (*vigraha* of Caṭakōpaṉ under the tamarind tree), attracted people from different *varṇas*, including brahmins (Nāthamuni and his descendants). With the consolidation of a particular *sampradāya* (Rāmânuja and his disciples and teachers), the Āḻvār and his works found a definite place within it. His works were regarded (and treated, in the commentaries) as Tamil renderings of the four Vedas, and their position within the universal history of revelation and Viṣṇu's grace was defined. At the same time hagiography provided not only a full life-story of their author but also moulded him as the ideal mystic and teacher.

It appears, however, that parallel to these developments in the *sampradāya*, Kurukūr, the Āḻvār's birthplace and centre of the initial cult, maintained its own local tradition (eventually expressed in the *sthalapurāṇa* and in the *janmôtsava* rituals), influencing the *sāmpradāyika* developments (Kurukai kkāval appan, Kurukai ppirāṉ piḷḷān), attracting Tiruvāymoli Piḷḷai and Maṇavāḷa mā muṉi, who reinforced the local cults and made the town the starting-point of the consolidated Teṉkaḷai.

A whole range of works, in Tamil and Sanskrit, popular and learned, and spanning the centuries up to the present day[227] illustrates the attraction and power of the *śūdra* and his Tamil Veda as a religious symbol. Since his works are in Tamil, it is nevertheless not surprising that Śrıvaiṣṇavism as such[228] did not succeed in conveying its appreciation of the Āḻvār to regions of India other than Tamilnadu and neighbouring areas in Mysore[229] and Andhra.[230]

7.2. We may turn now to a few practical corrolaries of the belief that the *śūdra* Caṭakōpaṉ revealed in Tamil the ultimate truth of the Vedas. Doctrinal issues were discussed in the vast exegetical literature; Tamil and Maṇippravāḷa works on theology in either *kaḷai* will constantly refer to his works as *pramāṇam;* Śrıvaiṣṇava ritual (daily *pūjā*, *dīkṣā*, wedding, funeral, etc.) includes many of his hymns. When Viṣṇu's *vigraha* is carried in procession, one group of Śrıvaiṣṇavas recites the TVM before, and another group of brahmins the Sanskrit Vedas behind, the icon. The *janmôtsava* of the Āḻvār has been described in 5.5.

7.3. The scope of the present study does not permit us to look in detail at the general Śrīvaiṣṇava attitude towards caste and *varṇa*. It seems, however, clear that quite universally the restriction of saving religious knowledge and of the access to it to a limited number of castes/*varṇas* is rejected: salvation is available to all regardless of their social position. This does, however, not imply that this 'social position' itself is thereby discarded. Theologically the problem lies here in the question to which extent earlier revelations which, after all, are also by Viṣṇu, particularly the *dharma*-scriptures, can be ignored. I shall at least highlight the problem as it presented itself to the early Śrīvaiṣṇavas, by referring to one particular case. Aruḷāḷa pPerumāḷ Emperumāṉār, a (senior?) contemporary of Rāmânuja, was, according to hagiography, a *saṃnyāsī* and *vedântī*. Defeated by Rāmânuja in a philosophic discussion, he converted to Śrīvaṣṇavism and became his disciple. He then wrote a work entitled *Ñāṉasāram*[231] (to which, significantly, Maṇavāḷa mā muṉi added a kind of commentary).[232] Here we read for instance,

> Regard as refuge for all people but the feet of Viṣṇu! What could be the use of distinguishing four *(varṇas)* among human beings who are all

born with the (same kind of) body, consisting of a combination of the five elements![233]

Viṣṇu's feet alone are lineage and family for his servants, like all the names and colours of the rivers on earth vanish when they have run into the ocean.[234]

Hagiography says that the author of these remarks was quite prepared to live out his ideas: he abandoned the various insignia of brahmin-and *saṃnyāsa*-hood (upavıta, tridaṇḍa, śikhā). But Rāmânuja considered this a grave offense and had him perform the expiatory rites prescribed for such a breach of orthodox behaviour.[235] In theory the Teṉkaḷai and Vaṭakaḷai split over the same issues; but even when we ignore other factors which appear to have played an equally important rôle in the schism (factors like social prestige, royal patronage, and control over temples), in practice the differences are certainly much less pronounced than one would expect from certain statements made in the *Ñāṉa-sāram* or *Ācāryahṛdayam*.[236]

7.4. Stein,[237] in a 'historiographical critique', has claimed

. . . if one seeks to understand Hinduism in relationship to the political system, that is, as an aspect of ideology, then it must be recognized that it often provided for considerable instability. The power of political legitimation was vested with local Brahmans responsible to no superiors, and the religion was characterized by a basic discontinuity between relatively high-caste (Brahman and non-Brahman) participants in Vedic sect activities and the mass of Hindus involved in highly localized, non-Vedic, folk religious affiliations.

Note the 'often' here; while it is certainly true that this is the situation envisaged in the orthodox tradition, it does not appear to apply to the particular case we have been studying. In fact we can formulate the great achievement of the movement which evolved out of the *śūdra* and his Tamil Veda in terms of the passage quoted. It succeeded in providing considerable stability and in overcoming the basic discontinuity between the different castes and their religious cults by harmonizing them in one structure, under the symbol of the Tamil Veda.[238] Stein himself has pointed out[239] 'the competence of local institutions in early South Indian society to manage all aspects of local life in a wide variety of ethnic and ecological contexts.' At the beginning of this paper I drew attention to the *vaḷa-nāṭu*. If it could be shown that any of the important personalities mentioned here (e.g. Nammāḻvār himself,

Tiruvāymoḻi Piḷḷai, Maṇavāḷa mā muṉi) had participated in such a local or regional institution which allowed for practical inter-caste communication, we could argue that this kind of institution provided the model for, or at least the psychological experience underlying, the Śrīvaiṣṇava community. That Nammāḻvār calls himself a *nāṭaṉ* and *vaḷa-nāṭaṉ* could be a strong indication for it.

7.5. We may conclude the present analysis[240] by looking at the principles which we have found underlying the approach of the authors which have been discussed here. For a brahmin like Nāthamuni to accept Madhurakavi's claim that the TVM was a Tamil rendering of the Vedas was truly remarkable. Once the Śrīvaiṣṇava system had been established (Rāmânuja's achievement), the axioms were given which made the further defense and interpretation of that claim relatively easy. From the premise that Viṣṇu is the personal absolute, man his *śeṣa*, and *kaiṅkarya* the means of liberation, Nammāḻvār's writing could easily be proved to be superior to the Vedas. The difficulties arose when this belief wanted to express itself in social terms. Not merely a vague 'orthodoxy' stood in the way of this, but in a sense Rāmânuja himself. Relatively little could be achieved by a common-sense approach ('religion must correspond to man's inner nature', 'all human beings are entitled to salvation'), and a different direction was chosen: socially operative symbols. Nammāḻvār as *ṛṣi*, *saṃnyāsī*, and *ācārya* (as found in the hagiographic accounts), as Viṣṇu-like temple icon (*sthalapurāṇa* and folk literature), as 'full-moon' or 'sandal' (Sanskrit *kāvyas*) — these are some of the symbols we have encountered. Purāṇic themes and patterns of Tamil poetry were employed to place these symbols in a meaningful, and thereby appealing, context. These associations of symbols and their balanced and harmonious interplay are clearly aesthetic factors, which is directly born out by the *kāvyas* we have discussed. Whether seen as an ideology or a social reform programme, the beliefs concerning Nammāḻvār appealed, and were made to appeal, not as philosophical, rational arguments, doctrinal statements, common-sense expressions, but by virtue of their symbolic, and that means predominantly aesthetic, value.[241]

BIBLIOGRAPHY OF MAIN SOURCES

TVM *Tiruvāymoḻi* edited with commentaries in 10 volumes, under the title *Bhagavadviṣayam*, by V.M. Kōpālakiruṣṇamācāriyar and A.V. Narasimmācāriyar (Tamil and Grantha characters). Triplicane, 1925-30;
contains *inter alia*: *Ārāyirappaṭi* (6000) by TirukKurukai ppirāṉ piḷḷāṉ, *Oṉpatiṉāyirappaṭi* (9000) by Nañjīyar, *Iruppatiṉālāyirappaṭi* (24000) by Periyavāccāṉ Piḷḷai, *Dramiḍôpaniṣattātparyaratnâvalī* by Vedântadeśika, and the various *taṉiyaṉs* in praise of the Aḻvārs and their works.

Knct *Kaṇṇi nuṇ ciṟu ttāmpu* edited with commentaries by S. Kiruṣṇasvāmi Ayyaṅkār (Śrīsūktimālá malar 17) Tirucci, 1956 (Tamil and Devanagari);
contains *inter alia* commentaries by Nañjīyar, Periyavāccāṉ, and Aḻakiya Maṇavāḷa pPerumāḷ Nāyaṉār.

Prabandham text only: edited by K. Kōpālācāriyar, Ceṉṉai, 1971;
with modern commentaries by K.P.B. Aṇṇaṅkarācāriyar (Lāñcī) and U. Vīrarāghavācāryar (Madras).
TVIR = *Tiruviruttam* by Nammāḻvār.

DSC *Divyasūricaritam* edited by A.M. Śrīnivāsācārya, Kāñcī, 1953 (Telugu characters)
the following manuscripts have also been consulted: Government Oriental Manuscript Library, Madras, R 4558 and D 12150.

GPPT *Guruparamparāprabhāvam*, Teṉkaḷai (by Piṉp' Aḻakiya Perumāḷ Jīyar) edited by S. Kiruṣṇasvami Ayyaṅkār (Śrīsūktimālā malar 23), Tirucci, 1968 (Tamil characters).

GPPV dto., Vaṭakalai (by the Third Brahmatantrasvāmī) edited by K. Śrīnivāsācāriyar, Ceṉṉai, 1968 (Tamil characters).

PTMA *Periyatirumuṭiyaṭaivu* (by K.K. Nāyaṉ, son of a disciple of Maṇavāḷa mā muṉi), included in the edition of the GPPT.

PA *Prapannămṛta* (by Anantâcārya) edited by Rāmanārāyaṇâcārya, Beüares, 1966 (Devanagari characters).

ĀH *Ācāryahṛdayam* edited by K.P.B. Aṇṇaṅkarārāccriyar with the *vyākhyānam* of Maṇavāḷa mā muṉi (vol. I of *Śrīmad-Varavaramunĭndra-grantha-mālai*), Kāñcī, 1966 (Tamil characters);
edited with a Tamil translation of the *vyākhyānam* by B.R. Purushothama Naidu, parts 1-2, Madras University, 1965 (Tamil characters, very useful because it traces the majority of quotations in the *sūtras* and commentary).

SPK *Sthalapurāṇa* of Kurukūr chapters 22-31 in: *Navatiruppatimāhātmyam,* edited Śrīnivāsācārya, Śuṇḍappāḷayam, 1909 (Grantha characters);
chapters 16-18: *sthalapurāṇa* of Kōḷūr, chapters 1-5: dto. of Śrīvaikuṇṭham. The whole work claims to belong to the *Brahmăṇḍa-Purāṇa.*

PS *Pādukāsahasra* edited by U.T. Vīrarāghavācāryar, Madras, 1970 (Tamil and Devanagari characters), including *inter alia* the editor's own Sanskrit commentary and Tamil annotations.

NM *Nakṣatramālikā* edited by K.P.B. Aṇṇaṅkarācāriyar (1) pp. 110-112 in *Stotramālā*, Kāñcī, 1969 (text only, in Devanagari characters); (2) pp. 48-66 in *Nityănusandheya-stotramālā*, Ceṉṉai, 1968 (text in Tamil characters, with Tamil commentary by the editor).

NOTES

1. IX, 31f: . . . *na me bhaktaḥ praṇaśyati* // *māṃ hi* . . *vyapāśritya ye 'pi syuḥ* . . . *striyo, vaiśyās tathā śūdrās te 'pi yānti parāṃ gatim* // But compare for example XVIII, 44-8 where the *śūdra* is expected to perform his specific *dharma karma* and said to find thereby his perfection (saṃsiddhi).
2. Thus v. 32 is only ancillary to the main point Kṛṣṇa makes in v. 33; it is added more for rhetorical effect than to serve as a definite statement about the *śūdras* in relation to *mokṣa*; in a similar manner, IX, 26 can be regarded more as a rhetorical than a theological justification of village religion. There are some traces in the *Gītā* (for example II, 45f; 52f) of an antagonism to the older Vedic tradition.
3. *Brahmasūtrabhāṣya* (translated by G. Thibaut, *Sacred Books of the East*, vol. 34, Oxford, 1890) *ad* I, 3, 34-8 deals with this problem, The passage quoted (Thibaut p. 229, *ad* 38) concludes Śaṅkara's discussion.
4. It is said, for instance, that he proclaimed from the *vimānam* of the temple in TirukKōṭṭiyūr the *aṣṭâkṣaramantra*, making it available to all people, although his teacher there had made him promise to keep it secret; or that he became extremely angry with his wife when she treated the low-caste *bhakta* Tiruk-Kacci Nampi in a disrespectful manner. But see below (7.3) on his attitude towards Aruḷāḷa pPerumāḷ Emperumāṉār.
5. *Śrībhāṣya*, where the *sūtras* are numbered 32-39 (translated by G. Thibaut, *Sacred Books of the East*, vol. 48, Oxford, 1904, pp. 337-47).
6. This objection is raised *ad sūtra* 39 (Thibaut pp. 345f). By postulating that *brahman* (=Viṣṇu) can only be known from revelation (see *ad* I, 1, 3, Thibaut pp. 161-74), he must exclude the *śūdras* from this knowledge, since he cannot violate the deep-rooted premise that *śūdras* are excluded from the Vedas.
7. See Thibaut (vol. 48) pp. 343-7; liberation defined as insight into the unreal nature of the world, and thus also of bondage, would be possible for the *śūdra* without direct knowledge of the Vedas.
8. J. van Buitenen, *Rāmānuja on the Bhagavadgītā* (Delhi, 1968), p. 17, suggests that the *Gītābhāsya* is later than the *Śrībhāṣya*; p. 18 he says that the former work reveals Rāmânuja as 'the priest of the temple of Śrīraṅga'.
9. *Gītābhāṣya* (edited by K.P.B. Aṇṇaṅkarācāriyar, vol. I of *Rāmânuja-grantha-mālā*, Kāñcī, 1970), p. 144; his comment consists of a simple paraphrase of the original. Van Buitenen (op. cit., p.26) is correct in rejecting the rather extreme contrast which Kumarappa (*Hindu conception of the deity* . . ., pp. 305ff) sees between the two passages from the two *bhāṣyas*. After all, van Buitenen says, such a vague statement can also be interpreted simply to mean that devotion helps a *śūdra* to be reborn in a higher *varṇa* and from there to obtain *mokṣa*.
10. There are many more works in Sanskrit and Tamil dealing with Nammāḻvār which were not available to me. Even the following list, derived from catalogues etc., will be far from exhaustive. G. Oppert (*Lists of Sanskrit Manuscripts in Private Libraries of Southern India,* vol. I, Madras, 1880, vol. II 1885) includes: three *stotras Parâṅkuśapādukā-pañcāśat* (No. 5084), *Śaṭhakopa-sahasranāmam* (No. 6442), and *Śaṭhavairivaibhavaprabhākara* (No. II 2887); two *kāvyas Śaṭhârivyutpattidīpikā* (No. 4125) and *Bakulâbharaṇacāṭu* (No. 5637); a

caritra Śaṭhavairivaibhavadīpikā (No. 5665). The editor of the *Kurukaimālai* (see note 195 below), pp. xif, mentions four Tamil works: *Māraṉ-alaṅkāram, Māraṉ-akapporuḷ, Pāppāviṉam,* and *Māraṉ-kōvai*. No. 17 of the *Tiruñāna-muttiraikkōvai* (published in Alvartirunagari) is a *Śrī-Parâṅkuśa-nāṭakam* by Śeṣakavi. Śrīvaiṣṇava theology discusses problems of caste for example in the many commentaries on the *Gītā*, but particularly with reference to v. XVIII, 66 which as the *caramaśloka* figures as the third *rahasyam* — the *rahasya*-literature is vast.

11. It has, however, been suggested (for example by B. Stein, 'The state and the agrarian order in medieval South India', in: *Essays on South India*, ed. B. Stein, Asian Studies at Hawaii No. 15, Hawaii, 1975, p.80) that the *nāṭu* as an institution predates 1000 A.D. in the Cōḻa country.
12. The relevant material has been collected and discussed by K.V. Subramanya Aiyer, 'Largest provincial organisation in ancient India', in: *Quarterly Journal of the Mythic Society*,. Bangalore, vols. 65 (1954-5) pp. 29-47, 70-98, 270-86 and 66 (1955) 8-22.
13. No date is suggested for the particular inscription mentioned below; others, which use often identical phraseology, are ascribed to the period mentioned *(passim)*.
14. Subramanya (p. 284) identifies the two.
15. The inscription is from *South Indian Inscriptions* (Texts), vol. 7, General, No. 129; see Subramanya p.71.
16. *Cāturvarṇa-kulôdbhavam . . . cen tamiḻ vaṭa kaḷai terint' uṇarnu. .* ; see Subramanya p. 70.
17. On these two institutions see in particular N. Karashima, 'Allur and Isamangalam', in: *The Indian Economic and Social History Review*, Delhi, vol. 3, No. 2 (1966) 150-62. *Sabhā* belongs to brahmin, *ūr* to non-brahmin villages,
18. Stein, op. cit., p. 80.
19. This is the name he himself used; among Śrīvaiṣṇavas he is much more frequently referred to by the honorific title Nammālvār', viz. 'our saintly lord'.
20. Four are traditionally ascribed to him, but only two, viz. the TVM and TVir, have *śrutiphalas* which mention his name. For details on this Āḻvār and his works see F. Hardy, 'Emotional Kṛṣṇa bhakti' (D. Phil. thesis, Oxford, 1976, manuscript), pp. 379-442; on p. 339 I have suggested the 7th or early 8th century A.D. for him. As will be seen below, my treatment of the saint's 'life-story' differs from the approach illustrated by W. McLeod's excellent study *Gurū Nānak and the Sikh religion* (Oxford, 1968). My interest lies in the religious *interpretation* underlying the legends, something unfortunately ignored by McLeod. On the other hand, it is clearly impossible within the limits of the present study to pursue in a systematic manner how such legends evolved and by which devices this interpretation is expressed in them. Such a study will have to look at the hagiography of all twelve Āḻvārs and, preferably, also of the Nāyaṉārs.
21. TVM III, 6, 11.
22. TVM VII, 2, 11; IX, 2, 11; X, 3, 11.
23. TVM IV, 7, 11, VIII, 3, 11, and 6, 11 respectively.
24. TVM X, 3, 11; the *sthalapurāṇa* (SPK), 28, 67 — 29, 16, calls this *tuṟai* (bathing ghat) Śrīśaṅkha-tīrtha, connecting it with Viṣṇu's conch.

25. TVM I, 1, 11 and frequently elsewhere. The etymology of this name is difficult (compare Hardy, op. cit., p. 319); Prof. T. Burrow suggested (in a personal communication) that it might be *śaṭha* 'naughty' and *gopa* 'cowherd', = the young Kṛṣṇa. The GPPV (p. 18) explains the name from *kopa* 'hatred → 'drive away' (= nirākarittavar) and a bodily humour called 'śaṭha'; the Sanskrit dictionary of Monier-Williams does not know such a meaning for the word *śaṭha*, but the *Madras Tamil Lexicon* gives, without source, for *caṭam*[2], as No. (5), 'evil humour of the body that destroys the innate wisdom of the soul at birth'.
26. TVM II, 6, 11; V, 10, 11; IX, 9, 11. Māṟaṉ is an ancient Tamil name, for example of a Pāṇṭiya king in *Puṟanāṉūṟu* 55: ? < māṟu 'enmity, death, etc.'
27. TVM IV, 7, 11; 10, 11.
28. TVir 100; TVM X, 2, 11.
29. TVM IV, 5, 11; V, 2, 11. Kāri is an ancient Tamil name, for example of a chieftain in *Cirupāṇāṟruppaṭai* 95, 100: < karu 'black'.
30. TVM III, 6, 11, IX, 2, 11; II, 8, 11; V, 6, 11, X, 4, 11.
31. TVM IV, 10, 11.
32. TVM III, 6, 11.
33. TVM X, 3, 11.
34. See Hardy, op. cit., pp. 321f.
35. Already DSC IV, 16 mentions Kāri as Nammāḻvār's father. Āṇṭāḷ, the daughter of Periyâḻvār, signs her poems as Viṭṭucittaṉ Kōtai, which means, she places her father's name simply before her own.
36. The commentaries *ad* TVM II, 8, 11, etc. treat *Vaḻuti vaḷa nāṭu* simply as a geographical area, but not as an institution; *nāṭaṉ* is interpreted (also by the hagiographers) as 'king' of that area, but the word could equally well refer to a 'member of the *nāṭu* (institution)'. Stein (op. cit., p. 71) speaks of 'the important role of those in control of *nādu* localities (*nāttār*) in the affairs of Brahman and non-Brahman villages'. 'Nāṭṭār' is the plural of a related *nāṭṭaṉ*.
37. TVM IV, 10, 11. Tamil *makiḻ* and Sanskrit *ba/vakula*, *ma/mukula* and *makura* denote the pointed-leaved ape flower, *mimusops elangi*. The symbolic value of this flower is difficult to evaluate, since it does not seem to figure in the *akattiṇai*. But note that *Makiḻttāraṉ* denotes Kāmadeva, and the name Makiḻ-Māṟaṉ (see 5.43 below), playing on that name, occurs in an erotic poem. In Sanskrit poetry, the *bakula* has definite erotic associations; see Ingalls (Harvard Oriental Series No. 44) pp. 111, 507: noted for its heavy scent, it was made to blossom with wine from a girl's mouth. In the drama *Mālatī-Mādhava* of Bhavabhūti, Act I, prose between verses 20 and 21, the hero made a garland of *bakula* flowers taken from a tree growing in the courtyard of Kāma's temple.
38. Already Yāmuna (*Stotraratna* v. 5) alludes to it in the phrase *bakulâbhirāma* (see note 58 below); as such, the name occurs first in DSC IV, 87. It is difficult to imagine that this name, in the context of Sanskrit works, did not evoke some of the associations mentioned in the previous note.
39. TVM IV, 10, 1f. 8f mention Ātippirāṉ; the Āḻvār probably knew the local temple god by that name. *Polintu niṉṟa pirāṉ* occurs only in v. 5, and could have evolved as a proper name of the god in later times. The *sthalapurāṇa* (SPK chs. 22f) mentions two Viṣṇus, one called Ādinātha, and the other Ādi-varāha. The Varāha figures also in the hagiography: see DSC IV, 34. SPK

(ch. 22, 62-8) narrates a story which is meant to exemplify an etymology of *polintu niṉṟa* 'who came to stop after moving about'.

40. V. 8 'nakka pirāṉ', Skt. < *nagna*.

41. V. 4 'iliṅkiyarkkē', < Skt. *liṅga*. The commentaries interpret *liṅga* here as one of the technical terms of logic, and the derivate as 'followers of the doctrine of inference'. This seems forced to me, motivated merely by an attempt to avoid repetition of the same meaning for the *iliṅkatt'* at the beginning of the next stanza.

42. *Kulan tāṅku cātikaḷ nāliluṅ kīḻ iḻintu, ettaṉai nalan tāṉ ilāta Caṇṭāḷa Caṇṭāḷarkaḷ ākilum, . . . maṇi vaṇṇarkʼ āḷ enrʼ uḷ kalantār aṭiyār tam aṭiyār emm aṭikaḷē.* See Hardy, op. cit., pp. 510-13; 562f, on similar statements by other Āḻvārs; none of them reject the *varṇa*-structure as such, but maintain the superiority of *any bhakta* over a non-*bhakta* brahmin.

43. V. 2: . . .eṉ collāl yāṉ coṉṉav iṉ kaviy eṉpittu ttāṉ collāṟ ṟāṉ ṟaṉṉai kkīrttitta Māyaṉ...

44. V. 5; for a more detailed discussion of this song see Hardy op. cit., pp. 398-400.

45. The name is found in the *śrutiphala*, v. 11, of the song.

46. The poetic form is that of a *tiruvāymoḻi*; there are allusions in the phrases e.g. to TVM IV, 10; it is structured like a song dedicated to a temple, but Namm-āḻvār figures here in the poetic slot conventionally reserved for the temple-god.

47. *Nampi* as such is an honorific title (rendered in Sanskrit as *Pūrṇa*); it can refer to a 'temple priest' (Āṇṭāḷ refers to her father as *nakar nampi*, XIII, 10) or a 'temple god' (compare TirukKuṟuṅkuṭi Nampi below). The latter sense, referring to Nammāḻvār's *vigraha* in Kurukūr, seems intended here.

48. . . . nāṉ maṟaiy āḷarkaḷ puṉmaiy āka kkarutuvar ātaliṉ, aṉṉaiy āy attaṉ āy eṉṉaiy āṇṭ' iṭun taṉmaiyāṉ Caṭakōpaṉ eṉ nampiyē.

49. The contrast of *avv-aru maṟai* and *ivv-ulakiṉil* is pronounced: while 'those difficult Vedas' are something alien and remote, the TVM concerns 'this world here'.

50. . . . aruḷiṉāṉ avv-aru maṟaiyin poruḷ.

51. . . . Vētiyar Vētattiṉ uṭ poruḷ. . .

52. For example PTMA (p.11) says that his *tiruvārātaṉam* was the Āḻvār. Already the GPPT (p.83) mentions that he 'had a *vigraha* of the Āḻvār consecrated as his *arcā*'. Madhurakavi himself said (v.2) 'I do not know any other deity'; this could still refer to Viṣṇu, but the previous and following phrases in the poem praise Nammāḻvār, and thus the later commentators interpret it quite literally as 'who had no other deity but the Āḻvār'.

53. For example GPPT p. 101; PTMA p. 12;GPPV p. 51;PA 107, 19ff.

54. See PTMA p. 13.

55. The Veda of a thousand *saṃhitās* is the Sāma-Veda; this purāṇic theme was developed in the idea that there existed a thousand *śākhās* of this Veda, with a thousand Upaniṣads (see for example M. Winternitz, *A History of Indian Literature*, Calcutta, 1927, p. 163). The *Chāndogya-Upaniṣad* belongs to this Veda.

56. *Taṉiyaṉ* of the TVM: *Śrī-Śaṭhakopa-vāṅmayaṃ sahasra-śākhôpaniṣat-samāgamaṃ namāmy ahaṃ Drāviḍa-Veda-sāgaram.*

57. Second *taṉiyaṉ* on the TVM: *aru maṟaikaḷ antâti ceytāṉ.*

58. *Stotraratna*, v. 5: *mātā pitā . . . yad eva . . mad-anvayānām ādyasya naḥ kulapater bakulâbhirāmaṃ śrīmat-tad-aṅghri-yugalaṃ praṇamāmi mūrdhnā.*

59. A *taniyan* verse on Nammālvār's fourth work, the *Periyatiruvantâti*, is ascribed to Rāmânuja. The author encourages in that verse his heart to recite the name of Māran.
60. V. 1 of the *iRāmānuja-nūrr' antâti* (included in Kōpālācāriyar's edition of the *Prabandham*): *pā mannu Māran ați panint' uyntavan*.
61. V. 19: *Māran vilaṅkiya cīr neri taruñ cen tamil āranamēy enr' in-nī nilattōr ari tara ninra*. Various other stanzas of the work refer to the Ālvār and his Tamil Veda: 18.20.29.46.54.60.64.
62. The GPPT breaks off four generations after Rāmânuja which suggests the latter half of the thirteenth century as the date for its composition. In at least twelve places, the DSC is quoted and mentioned as the source; the DSC breaks off with Rāmânuja. I find it therefore difficult to make sense of the suggestion that the DSC was written *c*. 1400 A.D. (see J. Carman, *The Theology of Rāmānuja*, New Haven, 1974, p. 49 with note 1, p. 283).
63. Corresponds as pure Sanskrit to Nammālvār's Kurukai (see note 21); the etymology of the pure Tamil form, Kuruk' ūr, seems to be 'village of the storks (kuruku)'. DSC IV, 2 (quoted PA 103, 15), however, derives it from *Kaurava*, descendant of Kuru. But note that the SPK (see 5.31 below) alludes to a *haṃsa* bird.
64. *Vedyo Veda-śikhā-vidbhiḥ*. 'Heads of the Vedas' for 'Upaniṣads' is common in Śrīvaiṣṇava writing; the whole expression, more frequent as *Veda-vedya*, alludes to *Gītā* XV, 15.
65. Cāturvarṇya-bhavā nityaṃ prapannā yatra jāgrati.
66. The reading of this verse is difficult; it seems to be: *dharma-sampad-ārjava-lampaṭāḥ*.
67. One *ms*. reads °*naṭêndra*, and PA (103, 17) °*nāthêndra*! This is clearly a misunderstood *nāṭan*.
68. See notes 29 and 35 above. The names of the ancestors in the second to sixth generation are pure invention; GPPT (p. 74) provides Tamil replicas of the names, but spoils the number seven by rendering *Pāṭala-locana* twice, viz. *Ceṅ-kaṇṇar* 'he with red eyes' and *Cen-tāmarai-kaṇṇar* 'whose eyes resemble red lotuses'.
69. The GPPT (p. 74) specifies it to be Vaṇparicāram, and gives her father's name as Tiru vāl mārpan.
70. That means: Viṣṇu in TirukKuruṅkuṭi, a temple *c*. 35 km SW of Kurukūr and another 35 km N of Vaṇparicāram (near Nagarkoil). Kuraṅgā is a sanskritized form of the name.
71. *Ādideśa Kuraṅgêśo Viṣvaksenaṃ tad-ātmajam*. The contradiction with v. 20 *putras tava bhaviṣyāmi* remains unresolved also in later works.
72. A full date is given in v. 30; there are many similar verses, showing some variants of the date, quoted in Śrīvaiṣṇava works, e.g. GPPT p. 77, GPPV p. 17, PA 103, 56; PTMA p. 5. Incidentally these verses suggest something like the fourth millennium B.C. for the Ālvār.
73. *Nirnidra*, which appears to refer to the fact that the tree does not close its leaves during the night.
74. The idea that Tamil is the vernacular language spoken all over the world is expressed also in later works.

75. Since the work concludes with Nampiḷḷai in the fourth generation after Rāmânuja, a date of *c.* 1275 A.D. may be assigned to it.
76. Arccā-rūpam āṉa Āḻvār vikrahattaiyum ēṟiy aruḷa ppaṇṇi avarukku nitya. . . utsavaṅkaḷaiy ellām mahôtsavam āka . . naṭatti kkoṇṭu . . (p. 83.) *Mahôtsava* could refer to the ritual practice, still continued today, of treating the Āḻvār like an *arcā* of Viṣṇu himself.
77. This episode is intended to explain the origin of a Tamil poem called *Caṭakōpar-antâti*. This poem is popularly ascribed to Kampaṉ, the author of the famous Tamil *Rāmāyaṇa*, and PA 105 indeed mentions *Kamba* as the name of that *caṅkattār*, but is completely ignorant of the allusion to the classical *caṅkam* (<*saṅgha*) in the GPPT, because it translates *caṅkappalakai* as *śaṅkha-pīṭha*! On the *Caṭakōpar-antâti* see K. Zvelebil, *Tamil Literature*, Leiden, 1975, p. 185.
78. Written *c.* 1500 A.D., and based *inter alia* on a much longer version (in 12000 *granthas*) by the author's teacher; the longer version was not available to me.
79. P. 18.
80. Ibid. We can notice an increase over the centuries in the preoccupation with formalized instruction and initiation: DSC IV, 43 says that by the grace of Viṣṇu the Āḻvār knew the *tattvas*, *śāstras*, and Vedas; GPPT p. 79, in some mss. only, has a passage in which Viṣṇu sends Viṣvaksena to teach him the *mantras* etc.
81. TVM III, 3, 2.
82. 'My . . .' is a common way of referring to Viṣṇu of a particular temple, showing that what follows (here: 'On whose chest Śrī lives') is already used as a proper name.
83. Thus the local guide-books.
84. The poem is about a girl (as also the ones discussed in 2.64 and 2.65); but since the commentaries treat this poetic girl-figure as a symbol of the Āḻvār's emotions (see Hardy, op. cit., pp. 342.345.543 etc.), there was no difficulty in applying individual statements made in such poems to the Āḻvār's 'life-story'.
85. TVM V, 5; compare III, 9, 2: 'My Father who abides in Kuṟuṅkuṭi'.
86. TVM VI, 7, 1.
87. See Hardy, op. cit., pp. 320-2.
88. For details on this figure, the 'general of the heavenly armies', see S. Gupta, 'Viṣvaksena the divine protector', in: *Wiener Zeitschrift für die Kunde Südasiens*, vol. 20, 1976, pp. 75-89. Since religious knowledge is understood as 'protection' (see DSC IV, 42 quoted above), the heavenly general is not out of place here.
89. *Padmâsanôpaviṣṭaṃ Para-pada-yugale niviṣṭa-caitanyam / para-tattva-bodha-mudraṃ paramâcāryaṃ Parâṅkuśaṃ vande //* Quoted PA 104, 17.
90. Until Madhurakavi aroused his interest in the outside world.
91. P. 80.
92. DSC IV, 37 actually uses the word *saṃnyāsa* (and *heya* 'what must be avoided').
93. I have styled it 'emotional bhakti', see Hardy, op. cit. *Prapatti* is however different from this type of bhakti.
94. PA 104, 89, and (as variant) DSC IV, 47.
95. The earlier Āḻvārs do not yet exemplify this form of bhakti fully, but prepare the ground for Nammāḻvār. Earlier Hinduism does not know 'emotional bhakti' in the sense defined.

96. 'Tentative' because we have to rely to a large extent on the much later hagiographers who project the situation at their own time back into that of the Āḻvār.
97. Māyōṉ himself is Viṣṇu, but by the time of Nammāḻvār this northern mythical figure had already passed through a period of at least 500 years of Tamil treatment. See Hardy, op. cit., pp. 167-378.
98. Instances of a tension between the Āḻvārs (and also the Pāñcarātra) and the brahmin establishment are alluded to in the *Prabandham* (see Hardy, op. cit., pp. 511-3.562f), in Yāmuna (see J. van Buitenen, 'On the archaism of the *Bhāgavata-Purāṇa'*, in: *Kṛṣṇa: myths, rites, and attitudes,* ed. M. Singer, Chicago, 1966, pp. 27-9), and in the hagiography of TirupPāṇ-Āḻvār.
99. GPPV p. 6 states this explicitly, quoting the stanza and mentioning that it was incorporated by Garuḍavāhana in his DSC; there it is found as I, 93, concluding the first canto. According to the PTMA (p. 26), Ācci was a disciple of Maṇakkāl Nampi, Yāmuna's teacher, and thus he probably lived in the late tenth or very early eleventh century.
100. In Southern Sanskrit, *ava-tṝ* is used in both meanings, 'descend' and 'be born'.
101. *Nirdiṣṭā Madhuripuṇā dayâkareṇa Śrīraṅgâdiṣu bahu-dhāmasu kṣamāyām // nityās te śubha-guṇa-sūrayo 'vatīrṇāḥ saṃsāre* . . . DSC I. 93 has the third *pāda* as: 'liberated, they once again were born as the sages.'
102. Clearly used in its general sense, 'appearance, manifestation', and not in the technical, *advaita*, sense.
103. These don't seem to fit in here.
104. DSC I, 85-92.
105. GPPT (p. 6) 'They descended and were born, in various *varṇas*, in the Tamil country which is constituted by the land between those rivers, as is said in *kalau khalu*. . .' Vedântadeśika, in his *Guruparamparāsāram* (ed. with a Tamil commentary by Narasimmācārya, Madras, 1920, pp. 34-9) quotes the same verses in the same context.
106. XI, 5, 38-41; see Hardy, op. cit., pp. 682-4.
107. DSC IV, 53 states *Gaṇesaḥ Kumudo nāmnā* which seems to refer to a Vaiṣṇava replica 'Kumuda' for the Śaivite 'leader of the *gaṇas*'; this is, however, a rôle more typical of Viṣvaksena and that might explain the confusion in later works which replace Kumuda by Garuḍa (for example GPPT p. 77), although thereby the pattern Garuḍa-Periyāḻvār is upset.
108. GPPT p. 74, comp. GPPV p. 6 and *Parâṅkuśapañcaviṃśati* v. 2 (*Stotramālā*, p. 108, edition as NM (1).
109. PTMA p. 5.
110. 'Karma' refers to the Saṃhitās and Brāhmaṇas (the *pūrva-mīmāṃsā*) and 'brahman' to the (Āraṇyakas and) Upaniṣads (the *uttara-mīmāṃsā* or Vedânta).
111. Alludes to *Gītā* VII, 15; XVI, 20 etc.
112. Ghaṭīyantra-ghaṭa-nyāyān nirayôtpatti-gāminaḥ.
113. DSC I, 72-83.
114. DSC IV, 67-70.
115. On the development of the *arcâvatāra*-concept and its treatment in Tamil culture and Śrīvaiṣṇava literature see my paper 'Ideology and cultural contexts of the Śrīvaiṣṇava temple' in *The Indian Economic and Social History Review*, vol. XIV, No. 1 (1977), 119-51.

116. *Pārvai* 'that which is attractive in appearance' - *mirukam* 'animal used as a decoy'. Maṇavāḷa mā muṉi (p. 2 of his commentary on the ĀH) uses the expression, in the same context, *iṇakku ppārvai* '(putting on) a matching disguise'.
117. P. 6.
118. Usually included in his *Rahasyatrayasāram;* see note 105.
119. 108, v. 50 (thus the editor).
120. *Pūrvôtpanneṣu bhūteṣu teṣu teṣu . . . anupraviśya.* This means, unlike the *avatāras*, these are human beings who were born in the normal course of *saṃsāra*, into whom Viṣṇu then enters.
121. Pp. 34-6. Compare GPPV p. 5 where the same stanza is quoted and explained.
122. Introduction to the AH-*vyākhyānam.*
123. GPPV pp. 4-6.
124. PTMA p. 27; GPPT pp. 340f.
125. Alludes to *Gītā* XI, 5-8.
126. This seems to mean: both poetic form and content are unique, completely lucid with reference to Viṣṇu's qualities, one of which, after all, is 'beauty'.
127. For a more detailed discussion of the 'subject' of the TVM see the commentaries *ad* VII, 9.
128. Vol. 1 of TVM, pp. 36 and 42.
129. Hari-kīrtiṃ vinâivânyad brāhmaṇena . . bhāṣā-gānaṃ na gātavyam.
130. Compare ĀH s. 76 below, and *Drāmiḍâmnāya-saṅgati* (vol. 1 of TVM, p. 101) v. 8.
131. This refers to TVM II, 7, 6, a difficult stanza. We cannot enter here into the exegetical problems; some commentators had suggested that Viṣṇu 'descended' for the Āḻvār's sake in many of his lives.
132. One of the five *arthas*, referring to the means by which liberation can be obtained.
133. Son of Vyāsa and a *śūdra* woman, *aṃśa* of Dharma.
134. Knowledge of *brahman* has to be bhakti, since *brahman* is Viṣṇu; the former is called *vedana* in the Upaniṣads, and is identified with *upāsana* 'worship'. On this see *Śrībhāṣya ad* IV, 1, 1 (Thibaut pp. 715f). Since the eroticism in Nammāḻvār's poetry is part of his bhakti, the element of *kāma* can thus be given Upaniṣadic justification.
135. Vol. 1 of TVM, pp. 39f and 42f (slightly shortened and rearranged).
136. *Atmāvukk' uḷḷa vēṣam ākaiyālē satatâika-rūpam āy yāvat-ātmâ̄nuvarttiy ākaiyālē* (p. 19). The statement depends on the concept of 'śeṣa', on which see below (note 152, etc.)
137. *Ad* s. 31, the commentary quotes from the *Āpastamba-Dharmasūtra* the following definition of a *śūdra*: *śuśruṣā śūdrasya itareṣām varṇānām* 'obedience to the remaining three *varṇas* is the *śūdra's* (dharma)'; *Gītā* XVIII, 44b speaks of *paricaryâtmakam karma* 'work whose nature is service'. Relating the ideas of 'obedience' and 'service' to Viṣṇu, they denote then a universal human *dharma.*
138. If one takes this remark literally, the 'discarding' would be a necessity, since it would be unlawful to practise the *dharma* of another *varṇa* (comp. *Gītā* III, 35).
139. *Aṭiyār* and *toṇṭar*, very frequently used in the *Prabandham.*
140. On this Vedic *ṛṣi*, cultural hero of the Tamils who is often regarded as the 'creator' of the Tamil language, see below 5.2 and 6.31, v. 29.

141. The commentator says that these refer to the works of the remaining eight Āḻvārs (although ten remain); but it seems preferable to interpret it as referring to the eight works in *tirumoḻi* form (all found in Book I of the *Prabandham* but excluding the *Tiruccantaviruttam*, which is not a *tirumoḻi*), because this also avoids the difficulty of speaking of *upâṅgas* written supposedly *before* Nammāḻvār — the hagiographers are unanimous in placing four Āḻvārs in an earlier period than Nammāḻvār.
142. Already the DSC IV, 73-8 made this equation.
143. This refers *inter alia* to the melodies of the *Sāma-Veda* (which in its actual text uses *Ṛg-Veda* hymns), to additional words called *stobha*, etc.
144. Indeed various editions of the *Prabandham* (as the one 1971) mention for each song in the TVM a corresponding poem in the TVir which sometimes makes sense.
145. This alludes to the great difficulties Śrīvaiṣṇava exegetes had in harmonizing the two facts of Jaimani's *pūrva-Mīmāṃsā* negating any form of personal absolute and the *Brahmasūtras* quoting supposedly the same Jaimini's theistic views.
146. The commentator, *ad* 68 quotes from the *Viṣṇu-Purāṇa Vedān adhyāpayāmāsa Mahāvhārata-pañcamān*; as personal revelation to Arjuna, the *Gītā* is clearly the *anta* of this fifth Veda; already Nañjīyar suggested such a comparison between the Āḻvār and Arjuna (see note 125).
147. A favourite simile, found elaborated upon in s. 72; compare 3.332 above and NM v. 8.
148. TVM IV, 4, 3 and VIII, 9, 10. In his commentary on Knct v. 8, Nañjīyar went so far as to say that 'the compassion of the Āḻvār, who composed the TVM, with the world is greater than the mercy of the Lord of the Universe who proclaimed the secrets of the Vedas'. This he explained by saying that 'Viṣṇu had those entitled to the Vedas saved, (but) the Āḻvār spoke so that also those not entitled could find fulfilment' and 'the grace of Viṣṇu is restricted to certain places and times, (but) that of the Āḻvār is everywhere' (p. 172).
149. Refers to Rāma forcing the ocean into submission, when he wanted to cross over to Laṅkā.
150. Periyâḻvār V, 4, 2; - viz. the lotus of the heart.
151. The *sūtra* is a paraphrase of GPPT p. 76 (bottom).
152. See Carman, op. cit., pp. 190-3. We should note that the concept 'śeṣa' does not merely imply a being at the mercy, or in the clutches, of the *Śeṣī*, but also a definite element of personal enjoyment (and 'bliss', the *ānanda* experienced by the *jñānī*). Nañjīyar said (on Knct v. 8): 'solely to find pleasure is the nature of him who is the *śeṣa*: to be a *śeṣa* and to be one who is delighted are not different from one another.' (p.172)
153. PTMA p. 43.
154. PA 121, 45.46a: 'He pulled Śaṭhavairī out of a great tank where it had been sunk, and re-established (=re-consecrated) it in Kurukā as before. By means of great festivals he increased (the fame of) that great god.' SPK 30, 24-6 may refer to the same incident; v. 24a says that after the Āḻvār's death people 'kalebaraṃ khanitvā', dug out the body.
155. PTMA pp. 43f; Kuntikai and Kiṭāram are mentioned as the villages where Tiruvāymoḻi pPiḷḷai and the mā muṉi were born.

156. PTMA p. 44; PA 122, 24-6a.
157. Arjun Appadurai, 'Kings, sects and temples in South India: 1350-1700', in: *The Indian Economic and Social History Review*, vol. XIV, No. 1 (1977), 63.
158. PA 72f. The whole account of the Āḻvārs' lives is presented in the PA as a dialogue between Nañjīyar and Paṭṭar.
159. This could be an allusion to the Kaḷḷar (comp. 5.52 with note 210.)
160. PA 72, vs. 4-6; 10-4; 25b-8; 73, 4-7; 21.
161. It is difficult to date this kind of literature; fortunately, the PA (73, 28) refers to the *Brahmâṇḍa-Purāṇa* and the *Kurukā-māhātmyam*, and this might provide a *terminus ad quem* for the SPK, viz. sixteenth century. If it is legitimate to connect SPK 30, 24 with Tiruvāymoḻi pPiḷḷai (see note 154 above), the *terminus a quo* would be the late fourteenth or early fifteenth century.— The editor of GPPT (p. 424) mentions as source for a Sanskrit verse (No. 209) in the GPPT the SPK (where, however, I cannot trace it); all that this implies is that we are dealing with a *muktaka* stanza (just as the editor identifies other Sanskrit verses as 'Prapannâmṛta'!).
162. 24, 25b/26a.
163. V. 42.
164. 25, 40b.
165. This couple had twelve sons, called the Ādityas, among them Indra and Viṣṇu. See Sorensen (*An index to the proper names in the Mahābhārata*, reprinted Delhi, 1963) pp. 13f.
166. 27, 53b.
167. This is made quite clear, for example 27, 45a; 28, 15ff.
168. 28, 27.
169. 28, 54a.
170. 29, 29a.
171. 29, 37.
172. The names used are: *Drāviḍa-brahman, Drāviḍa-brahma-saṃhitā, Drāviḍāgama* (29, 48 . . . 50), etc.
173. 29, 49.
174. 30, 1-20.
175. 'Which had been dug out' (30, 24a).
176. Ch. 31.
177. A fourth *avatāra*, viz. that of Varāha, is connected with the *sthala* in ch, 23; comp. DSC IV, 34.
178. The verse is *nāga-paryaṅkam utsṛjya hy āgato. . .*; it is not included in the critical edition, but can be found in vol. II (ed. P.L. Vaidya, Poona, 1971, p. 172) as line 1034 of App. No. 20. This long passage is found also in Southern *mss.*, and Maṇavāḷa mā muṉi, *ad* s. 74 of ĀH, quotes the verse in a (Telugu) 4 variant.
179. Compare the Āḻvār's 'makiḻ mālai mārpiṉaṉ' (TVM IV,10,11) with 'Tiru vāḻ mārpaṉ'.
180. For example. Piḷḷai Lokâcārya's *Mumukṣuppati* s. 169.
181. The Ādityas belong to Vedic mythology, and thus Viṣṇu who is one of them is envisaged predominantly as Trivikrama who, in turn, is treated as the *Vāmanâvatāra* in the Purāṇas. See Sorensen, op. cit., p. 13, column b (bottom).
182. See *ibid.*, column b (top).

183. Compare the *Śrī-Rāmânuja-catuḥ-ślokī* (each verse refers to one of the places), and the *Dhāṭī-pañcakam*.
184. GPPT pp. 122f; PTMA p. 18; etc.
185. Illustrated for example by *vigrahas* of Garuḍa, Ananta, and Maṇavāḷa mā muṉi.
186. It is perhaps even more surprising that also the *sthalāpurāṇa* of TirukKōḷūr does not refer to Madhurakavi, although Viṣṇu there is said to be *pratyakṣam* this Āḻvār (it is common in *sthalapurāṇas* to relate a story about the individual figures which Viṣṇu 'faces' in a temple).
187. See note 167; compare the renderings of *nāṭaṉ* (which can be translated as 'lord of the region. . .') as *rājêndra* and *nāthêndra* (see note 67).
188. This is further strengthened by the Āditya theme; Indra after all is the epitome of *kṣatriya*-hood. This would also affect the line of identification Āditya→ Trivikrama → Vāmana.
189. GPPT p. 75 describes the great splendour and the festivities in Kurukūr when Kāri returned after his marriage, comparing the scene to the grand welcome given to Janaka when he returned to Ayodhyā. PA 103, 33-8 elaborates on it.
190. 28, 13f.
191. Edited *Tiruñāṉamuttiraikkōvai* No. 6, Alvartirunagari, 1946.
192. See K. Zvelebil, *Tamil Literature*, Wiesbaden, 1974, pp. 193-230.
193. The *piḷḷaittamiḻ* genres were cultivated by Periyâḻvār, Āṇṭāḷ, Parakālaṉ, etc. Religious love-poetry was developed by the Āḻvārs from the *akam* poetry of *caṅkam* literature.
194. Tanjore Saraswati Mahal Publications No. 43, 1951 (with notes and introduction). Also: *Tiruñāṉamuttiraikkōvai* No. 1, 3rd edition, Alvartirunagari, 1967. The editor of the first-mentioned edition suggests the thirteenth century for this work, but his only evidence for this is that the work does not refer to Vedântadeśika! (p.4).
195. Edited with Tamil commentary *Tiruñāṉamuttiraikkōvai* No. 24, Alvartirunagari, 1957.
196. Suggested by the editor, p. xvii.
197. On the 'defeat of the *caṅkam*' see 2.4. with notes.
198. On the 'heart-lotus' see note 150.
199. Madhurakavi did not state it as such, see 2.13 with note 52. The statement attributed to him here plays with an idea found, for example, in Paṭṭar's *Śrīguṇaratnakoṣa* vs. 4 and 13, viz. that Śrī is the symbol or characteristic sign by which the personal absolute can be recognised.
200. Edited *Tiruñāṉamuttiraikkōvai*, No. 7, Alvartirunagari, 1932.
201. This is the period during which the genre is said to have been productive; see K. Zvelebil, *Tamil Literature*, Wiesbadeñ, 1974, pp. 197, 201, 213, 224-6, and Leiden, 1975, pp. 254-7.
202. The present poem is a mixture of two genres: *pavaṉi* (a variant of *ulā*) dealing with the procession, and *kuṟam* which presents the fortune-teller.
203. Stanza 65: 'Māṟaṉ with the *makiḻ* flowers, who is attractive to women, tomorrow will come and unite with you'; stanza 75: 'to-day he will join you'.
204. The 'great festivals' celebrating the birth etc. (see note 76) of the Āḻvār would involve, during the later medieval period, processions in which the *vigraha* is accompanied by dancing girls, courtesans, etc. Compare also PA 105, 5-11.
205. See above note 37.

206. This is treated in detail in my paper mentioned in note 115, in the section on 'Viṣṇu as lover'.

207. DSC IV, 86 simply mentioned that the Āḻvār spent his time praising those eight (the older figure) Viṣṇus; GPPT p. 82 mentioned that all Viṣṇus came from the 108 sacred places, and PA 104, 5off repeats this. Moreover, the PA version says that 32 were granted the special favour of having a song composed by this Āḻvār dedicated to them.

208. A similar custom takes place in Nāṅkūr which involves, I think, twelve Viṣṇus from neighbouring temples.

209. See N. Karashima, op. cit., and 'The power structure of the Chola rule', vol. 2 of *Proceedings of the Second International Conference Seminar of Tamil Studies*, Madras, 1968, p. 236, note 16.

210. See pp. 142-9 of my paper mentioned in note 115, and compare *ibid.* D. Hudson, 'Śiva, Mīnâkṣi, Viṣṇu — reflections on a popular myth in Madurai', pp.107-18. This paper deals with a temple festival involving another Visṇu temple associated with the Kaḷḷar, viz. the Aḻakar temple in Tirumāliruñcōlai.

211. Obviously, the few selective facets which I mention here are not meant to serve as a complete syn- and diachronic picture of the sociological situation in these nine temples. The festival mentioned here would reveal its full significance only when seen in relation to that complete picture.

212. Compare Ingalls, op. cit., pp. 49-53, for a general (positive) evaluation of *kāvya*-style.

213. I am preparing a study of his *stotras* which illustrate this type of poetry. Other works in *kāvya*-style are his *Yādavâbhyudaya*, *Subhāṣitanīvi*, *Haṃsasandeśa*, and also his drama *Saṅkalpasūryôdaya.* He composed, however, also a number of Tamil poems, collected in the *Deśikaprabandham.* Earlier Śrīvaiṣṇava *ācāryas*, like Kūratt' Āḻvāṉ and Paṭṭar, also wrote elaborate Sanskrit poems.

214. A commentary on the TVM, called *Nigamântaparimala,* is sometimes mentioned; but even if this were correct, the work is lost.

215. The *Madras Tamil Lexicon* defines it: 'metal head-cover on which Viṣṇu's sandals or feet are engraved, and which is placed over the head of worshippers'. The etymology of the word itself is difficult; if we accept the meaning 'evil humour. . .' for *śaṭha* (see note 25), it could be: *śaṭha* + *gopam* 'that which protects from the *śaṭha* humour which destroys knowledge'.

216. *Pāda-ja* 'born from the foot', a paraphrase of *śūdra*, alludes to the *Puruṣasūkta.*

217. To bear somebody's name is an act of bhakti, but also of acknowledging defeat — Aruḷāḷa pPerumāḷ (see note 235 for sources) took on the name 'Emperumāṉār' (one of the common Tamil names of Rāmânuja) when defeated in a theological discussion by the latter. Thus the statement here is a paradox; TVM III, 7, 10 mentions that the Āḻvār considers himself the servant of the servant of. . . Viṣṇu, viz. in the eighth position of a hierarchy of *bhaktas.*

217a. Dramiḍôpaniṣan -niveśa-śūnyān api Lakṣmī-ramaṇāya rocayiṣyan / dhruvam āviśati sma pādukâtmā Śaṭhakopaḥ svayam eva. . . // 22
niyataṃ maṇi-pāduke dadhānaḥ sa munis te śaṭhakopa ity abhikhyām / tvad-upāśrita-pāda-jāta-vaṃśa-prapattyai param ātatāna rūpam // 23
muninā maṇi-pāduke tvayā ca prathitābhyāṃ śaṭhakopa-saṃjñayâiva / dvitayaṃ sakalôpajīvyam āsīt prathamena śrutir anyatas tad-arthaḥ // 24
yaḥ sapta-parva-vyavadhāna-tuṅgāṃ śeṣatva-kāṣṭhām abhajat. . / tasyâpi

nāmôdvahanāt tvayâsau laghukṛto 'bhūc Chaṭhakopa-sūriḥ // 26
. . .kumbhī-sūnor . . . svaira-bhāṣā / nityam-jātā Śaṭharipu-tanor niṣpatantī mukhāt te'prācīnānāṃ śruti-pariṣadāṃ pāduke pūrva-gaṇyā // 29.

218. TVM X, 6, 5: '(His) pair of feet are on my head' is alluded to in PS v. 920.

219. This name refers to the Sanskrit commentary; the same author also wrote a Tamil commentary, included in the edition.

220. Tamil notes, p. 47; on v. 24: Sanskrit comm. p. 48; on 29 dto p, 55.

221. All the works by Piḷḷai Lokâcārya and his younger brother, and by Maṇavāḷa mā muṉi (except for a short poem on Rāmânuja) are in Tamil and Maṇippravāḷa.

222. In fact, the name itself means *inter alia* 'Northern art', and as in note 16 above, 'Sanskrit'. Moreover, in the Tamil geographic awareness, *vaṭa* refers to the area of Kāñcī, Vēṅkaṭam, etc.

223. His Sanskrit name is Abhirāmavara; PTMA p. 49.

224. *Prajñā-dṛśônmiṣitayā . . jyotiḥ paraṃ yad an-idaṃ tad idaṃ cakāra.* On 'divine eye' see note 125.

225. Natyā na ty-aga-kārī kṣaṇam api cid-acit-trāyakâmeya-kāme chandaś-chanda-svarūpe mahasi Kamalayā bhāsamāne 'samāne /.

226. See *Gītā* II, 42-5.

227. Thus we have the *Parâṅkuśa-pañcaviṃśati* (edited *Stotramālā* pp. 108-110) by Vādhūla Varada-Nārāyaṇa (after sixteenth century); member of the Kantāṭai family of Śrīraṅgam and thus descendant of one of the most influential disciples of the mā muṉi, he expresses in this Sanskrit poem the sentiments required for the act of *prapatti* (*ākiṃcanya* etc.). — Devarāja Bhārati (resident of Kurukūr) completed in 1926 a *Śrī-Caṭakōpa-tivya-carittiram* (edited *Tiruñāṉamuttiraikkōvai* No. 3, Alvartirunagari, 1929) in 1191 lengthy Tamil stanzas.

228. It was the achievement of the *Bhāgavata-Purāṇa* to render the religious spirit of the Āḻvārs in Sanskrit and thereby caused something like a religious revolution in Northern India; see Hardy, op. cit. (1976), pp. 554-607; 608-20; 676-90.

229. A pamphlet issued by the Śrī-Kalki movement (Bangalore, c. 1920) mentions that Śrī-Kalki (=M. T. Narasimhiengar, born 1867 in Melkote, Mysore) translated the whole TVM into Sanskrit and wrote an elaborate commentary in Kannaḍa on it. The 'Universal Religion' of Śrī-Kalki, who 'has proclaimed Himself *God-Incarnate*', is meant for the whole world: 'His Magnanimous Glory Divine has been proved in extending the privileges of attaining Salvation to all souls in All Worlds. He invites and welcomes all souls — irrespective of race or nation, caste or creed, kind or sex, and grants Salvation to all that are devoted to Him, by pardoning them for their past sins.' As scriptural basis for this message the pamphlet gives something like an English rendering of TVM III, 7 (see 2.12).

230. On the interaction between 'Telugu warriors' and Śrīvaiṣṇava sectarian leaders see the paper by A. Appadurai. — The first printed edition of the TVM with its commentaries was in Telugu characters.

231. Included in the same volume as ĀH, along with the *pramāṇa-yojanā*.

232. This *pramāṇa-yojanā* provides (on the whole) Sanskrit verses as parallels to the statements of the Tamil stanzas.

233. Stanza 14: *pūtaṅkaḷ aintum porunt' uṭaliṉār piṟanta cātaṅkaḷ nāṉkiṉōṭum caṅkatam ām pētaṅ koṇṭ' eṉṉa payaṉ peṟuvīr evvuyirkkum Intirai kōṉ taṉṉ aṭiyē*

kāṇuñ caraṇ. The Sanskrit verse quoted by Maṇavāḷa mā muṉi to substantiate the statement is said to be from the *Paramâikântidharmam*.

234. Stanza 15; the Sanskrit verse quoted by Periyajīyar for it is also quoted by him *ad* ĀH s. 35 where it is said to be from the *Paramâikântidharmam*. The first half reads: *ekântī vyapadeṣṭavyo nâiva grāma-kulâdibhiḥ Viṣṇunā vyapadeṣṭavyas tasya sarvaṃ sa eva hi* ||

235. GPPT pp. 185-9; 203f; PTMA p. 28; PA 25f.

236. The PTMA records who of the *ācāryas* was a brahmin, and gives details like his *gotra*, *śākhā*, *sūtra*, etc. — Maṇavāḷa mā muṉi acknowledges *ad* ĀH s. 31 that certain saintly people continue to perform the *nitya-karmas* (permanent rites enjoined by *śruti* and *smṛti*); he excuses them by saying that 'it is solely because of their compassion which desires that the world, by following their example, will not be lost'. That means, a life more orthodox than intended or permitted in the Teṉkaḷai is justified in order not to offend the pusillanimous and in order to show to the non-Teṉkaḷai people that those orthodox forms of behaviour do possess a value.

237. Op. cit., note 11, p. 86.

238. Stein made the statement quoted above in the context of the investigation, whether the notion 'feudalism' can be applied to the structure of medieval South Indian society. The 'discontinuity' pointed out by him serves as one element in his conclusion that 'feudalism' is not a useful notion. It would be an interesting point to investigate whether this notion 'feudalism' can be applied to the social structure of the Śrīvaiṣṇava community which, as we have seen, has overcome this discontinuity and which is held together by strong sentiments of 'discipleship', 'service', and loyalty.

239. Ibid., p. 73.

240. Interesting material for comparing the Śrīvaiṣṇava attitudes towards caste with those of a similar, though later, movement is provided by W. McLeod, 'Caste in the Sikh panth', in: *The Evolution of the Sikh Community*, Oxford, 1976, pp. 83-104. McLeod speaks of a vertical and a horizontal aspect of caste. The second is of no relevance in the context of man's salvation, viz. his access to the media of grace, and thus there was no need to reject it (above all, caste-rules for marriage). The vertical aspect, however, implying a value-judgement and hierarchy, was rejected by Gurū Nānak and his disciples because it restricted the access to grace to certain groups of people.

241. I wish to express my thanks here to the Central Research Fund, University of London, whose grant made it possible for me to visit many of the Śrīvaiṣṇava temples in Tamilnadu during the summer of 1975, and to Dr. K.K.A. Venkatachari for his kind assistance.

Islamization in Nineteenth Century Bengal

RAFIUDDIN AHMED

St. Catherine's College, Oxford

That community solidarity could be achieved despite internal differences was demonstrated by the successful mobilization of the rural Muslims in Bengal by the mullahs and the political elite in the late nineteenth and early twentieth centuries. There is no reason to suppose that the internal social and cultural differences that divided the community gave way to a more homogeneous system under the impact of the religious reform movements, but there is evidence of important changes in the ideas and attitudes of the ordinary people which enabled the élite, at a later stage in the history of Bengali Muslims, to appeal to their religious sentiments and to mobilize for political ends the sentiment of social solidarity born out of them. The activation of religious sentiment among the Bengali Muslims was the achievement of the reform movements, notably the Faraizi and the Tariqah-i-Muhammadiya, better known as the Wahabi movement. They were fundamentalist in their religious orientation and endeavoured to purge popular Islam in Bengal of its native accretions. Despite their activities over several decades the Islam of the masses remained very different from the fundamentalist interpretation of its doctrines and principles, and looked not very different from what they had been practising for ages. Between them and their Hindu neighbours there were obvious doctrinal and social differences which marked them out as different social entities, but the rural Muslims continued to cling to many popular rites and ceremonies. What was important then was not the religious change effected by the reform movements but the momentum they generated in the rural Muslim society and brought about a measure of unification between diverse social and cultural groups who constituted the Muslim community in Bengal.

Religious Debates

One of the immediate consequences of the rise of Islamic reform movements was the aggravation of social and religious tension in the rural areas of the province. This was both inter-communal and intra-communal. While the inter-communal tension at the earlier stage was primarily of an agrarian character and was more in the nature of a zamindar-tenant struggle, intra-communal tension was mostly religious and more often concerned with the beliefs and attitudes of the people.

The tension generated in Bengali Muslim society by religious propaganda and counter-propaganda gave rise to social conflicts which did not remain confined within the bounds of religious polemic, but often had serious repercussions on the state of relationship between different social groups within that society. In some cases the groups sought the aid of the British Government, or even of the Hindu zamindars, to harass their opponents. A typical example of such harassment was reported from a Murshidabad village in 1875. It concerned the visit by a reformist maulavi in the area. When the intended visit came to the notice of the village mullahs, they conspired to put the maulavi into trouble. In an application filed with the local police officer they accused him of sedition and requested the Government to take action against him: '(We feel that) he has come with an evil intention. . . .', they complained to the police; 'It looks as if he has secret links with the *Badshah* (Emperor) of Delhi; otherwise why should he come here. He is the leader of the devils . . . His only aim is to spread sedition in Bengal . . . It looks as if the Company (i.e., the Government) may suffer as a result.'[1]

It is paradoxical perhaps, but true nonetheless, that such tension and conflict, occasioned by the rise of the reform movements, ultimately assisted in the achievement of community solidarity among the Bengali Muslims. Reformist propaganda and the counter-propaganda by the village mullahs contributed to increased religious activity and discussion in traditional Muslim society. In the same Murshidabad episode, referred to above, when the Government apparently took no action against the reformist preacher despite the application made by the traditionalists, the village mullahs finally decided to debate and discuss the religious questions with him, and the result was a massive public debate attended by the village people. The real implication of such a confrontation may be appreciated if one takes into consideration the peculiar devotion of the rural masses to their religious leaders. For the Islam of the Bengali masses had been virtually a mullah monopoly; it was to him that the rural people turned for advice and suggestion whenever necessary. His authority to act as the sole interpreter of the Islamic doctrines never came under critical scrutiny by a rival group nor were the existing social and religious practices and institutions seriously questioned. The mullah himself was never inclined to bring about any material change in the system — he did not have the knowledge required for doing so. The reformist challenge of the nineteenth century did not shatter the foundations of mullahism from rural society but did cause a breach in its ranks, producing in consequence much religious debate and confrontation between, and amongst, the rival maulavis.

The religious tension generated by the activities of the rival maulavis resulted in an increase in the religious activity of the society as a whole. In the midst of the tense social and religious environment maulavis belonging to all shades of opinion made efforts to vindicate their own views and repudiate those of their rivals, and in that process published materials, initially of a polemical nature, trying to enlist support for their own sides.[2] This was in itself an important departure from the traditionalist spirit of blind obedience to the pirs and maulavis. At the social level this had the immediate effect of increasing interaction between the peoples of different localities and different social groups. This increased social activity helped in the formation of common attitudes and the development of a common identity.

Bahas or Religious Disputations

The frequent religious debates, or *bahas* meetings, between rival religious groups represented an entirely new pattern of religious activity in the rural society in as much as they reflected the growing interest of the illiterate public in social and religious matters and provided them with a venue for social communication, a thing virtually unknown to them in the pre-reformist period.

It is almost impossible to give more than a fragmentary account of the *bahas* meetings held in Bengal during the late nineteenth century. The local government officials apparently took interest only in those meetings which threatened to disrupt public peace and order in a locality,[3] but since these local incidents had very little impact on the country as a whole, they hardly found any mention in government records dealing with inter-communal rioting, or other similar incidents.[4] We have, however, the details of some of the *bahas* meetings in the pages of the contemporary religious literature. Despite the exaggeration and inaccuracies from which they might suffer, these accounts constitute a very important source material through which to get an insight into some of the most interesting features of these religious debates which were so characteristic of the late nineteenth century Bengali Islam.

Saif al-Momenine, for example, is one such religious work that gives an interesting account of a religious debate held between a reformist preacher and the local maulavis of Murshidabad village (in 1280 B.S.).[5] The pomp and grandeur that marked the occasion was indeed remarkable: 'The debate was celebrated with great eclat; whoever saw it was gratified. For two to three days there was a fair as at *baruni*; there was so much fun and so many people came, how can I describe it; you will all understand what I mean: it was as if suddenly a city sprung up in the middle of a jungle.'[6] An interesting feature of the *bahas* meetings was the presence of the law-enforcing authorities, the police and the village *Chaukidar*, in the midst of the contending parties. The scene of the Murshidabad *bahas*, as described in *Saif al-Momenine*, provides an example of such presence and brings in view of the reader the total picture of a *bahas* meeting: 'The *Pir* (the Hanafi Maulavi) came to the garden (the venue of the meeting) and took his seat on the eastern side quite happily. The other party too was no less (clever). They too came forward and occupied seats on the western side. The *darogah* (the Sub-Inspector of Police) took position on a chair on the northern side (of the *Pandal*), and the *jamadar* (Sergeant of Police) on the southern side. The *barkandazes* (police constables) with huge spears in their hands, and eyes fixed on the public (took position on all sides) according to arrangements. The *Chaukidars* (Village police) constantly moved about the *bahas* venue. The *barkandaz* and the *chaukidars* always kept on shouting warning signs to the public (to scare them from committing disturbances).'[7]

This precaution, which obviously gives the picture of a real battle scene, had to be taken to guard against any outbreak of violence. Popular enthusiasm on such occasions was difficult to contain within the bounds of law. The rival groups were often so determined to win a *bahas* that they were prepared to use force against each other if arguments failed. Such confrontations would continue to inflame relations between the parties for a very long time, no matter who won the battle of the day.

A *bahas* meeting reported from Jamalpur illustrates the pernicious effects that some of these gatherings had on the rural society. In this case, the *bahas* between the traditionalist maulavis and the reformists, according to the reports of the District Magistrate of Bogra, 'ended with the use of most filthy language by both parties. Since then each party is trying to outbid the other. Two madrassas have been started in the locality, one by the *Hanafis* and the other by the Rafi *Yaddains*. . . . The feeling of the two sections. . . had grown so bitter that they both applied to me for protection.'[8] A similar meeting, scheduled to be held between the same two parties in 1905, had to be prohibited by the government for fear of serious disturbance in the area.[9]

Although the *bahas* meetings discussed a variety of questions concerning the interpretation and significance of various social and doctrinal points over which the rival maulavis differed,[10] the two questions that excited the utmost interest during the period and formed the subject-matter of frequent *bahas* meetings, were, first, the question of the legality of holding congregational prayers of *Jumah* and *'Id* in India under the British; and, secondly, the importance of *mazhab* (religious schools) in Islam.[11]

The Faraizis had declared that congregational prayers of *Jumah* and *'Id* could not be held in the country as it was not *dar-ul-Islam*.[12] This challenge to a well-established practice, considered essential by orthodox Islam, was central to the Faraizi-Taiyuni conflict in Bengal in the late nineteenth century when Keramat Ali openly denounced what he termed as the Faraizi extremism on such issues.[13] The two groups confronted each other in a number of *bahas* meetings to determine the issue, which, however, remained unresolved until the very end of British rule. According to Muin ud-Din Ahmad Khan, the Faraizis commenced holding congregational prayers only after the British had relinquished power to the Indians in 1947.[14]

The first reported *bahas* between the Faraizis and the Taiyunis was held in 1867 in Barisal which was particularly concerned with the question of congregational prayers.[15] Most other questions of a doctrinal sort which were discussed at that meeting were sorted out quite amicably,[16] but the issue of congregational prayers proved to be the main stumbling block on which no consensus could be reached.

The two parties met again formally to discuss the question of prayer in 1879 at Madaripur in the district of Faridpur. The meeting, discribed as the *Battle of Jumah* by Nabin Chandra Sen, Sub-divisional officer of Madaripur at that time,[17] was reportedly attended by more than five thousand people from all walks of life, and the proceedings of the meeting continued for more than seven hours, but without arriving at any decision. One more similar debate between the Taiyunis and the Faraizis was recorded some time later from Daudkandi in the district of Tipperah. The Faraizi soruces claimed that their leader Abdul Jabbar pushed his point successfully and scored a victory over the Taiyunis[18] at the *bahas*, although this does not seem to have resulted in a total stoppage of Jumah prayers by the Bengali Muslims: on the contrary, a Taiyuni religious tract claimed that the Muslims all over Bengal had already started offering their *Jumah* prayers regularly at the direction of Keramat Ali and his disciples.[19] It may be assumed that it was the Faraizis alone who continued to oppose the practices, and even under the moderate leadership of Naya Miyan and Saijuddin Khan Bahadur, who professed total allegiance to the British Government,[20] they did not retreat from their stated principle.

Surprisingly, although the Faraizi prohibition of congregational prayers was supposed to concern all the traditionalist Muslims of the country, the theologians of the older school did not make any serious attempt to fight the Faraizis on this question, as they had done over others, nor did this find much mention in the religious tracts published by them. The conflict over this important question thus remained primarily confined to debates between the Taiyunis and the Faraizis, although it is true that the Taiyunis had by now identified themselves far more closely with the older school than with the reformed sects. A possible explanation for the apathy of the older theologians to the Faraizi prohibition of congregational prayers could be that such prohibition did not have much effect on the members of the traditional society, and since this prohibition did not enjoy the support even of the other reformed groups the older theologians were content to let it be debated by the rival reformed groups between themselves, while concerning themselves with those questions that affected their immediate interest.

The question of *mazhab*, or school of Islamic law, was perhaps the single most important doctrinal point that engaged the attention of the traditionalist theologians and induced them to come to the *bahas* meetings readily. For them conformity to one of the four *mazhabs* was an essential principle of Sunni Islam. Those who, like the Tariqah members, repudiated the concept of *mazhab* were considered by them as not really belonging to the Islamic faith. Their attitude in this respect was summarized by a reformist *puthi:* 'the traditionalists regard the reformists as a new *mazhab*, but this new *mazhab* was not recognised by the original *mazhabs*, and since they thought that all *mazhabs* outside the recognised four were really *la-mazhabi* (without *mazhab*), the reformists were unIslamic.'[21]

Both the Faraizis and the Taiyunis were, juristically, believers in the Hanafi school of law.[22] The Tariqah movement, (and its later off-shoots, such as the *Ahl-i-Hadis* and the *Rafiyad-dains*), on the other hand, did not consider itself bound to conform to any of the four schools.[23] It was therefore the *Tariqah* preachers who came into direct conflict with the traditionalist theologians over the question of *mazhab*. They decried the traditionalists for having called them by the opprobrious appellation of *la-mazhabi*. '. . .you call (us) *la-mazhabi*', argued a reformist Puthi, '. . .but there were no such divisions at the time of the Prophet. . . . It is only your attitude that has turned (the reformists) into *la-mazhabis* in your eyes.'[24]

It is important to note that to the traditionalist maulavis in the rural areas *mazhab* had a special significance, and this was specifically related to the question of their own spiritual authority in the society. To the rural maulavis *mazhab* was an institution from which they derived their authority to interpret the law of Islam: 'If it is essential to have a spiritual guide', argued one traditionalist Maulavi, 'why then should it not be necessary to belong to a *mazhab*?'[25] The question of the doctrinal importance of *mazhab*, which it is doubtful if many of them understood, was clearly of comparatively less consequence than that of the preservation of spiritual authority of the maulavi over his religiously devoted but otherwise ignorant flock.

Most *bahas* meetings, held between the Tariqah preachers and the tradionalists during the closing years of the nineteenth century, devoted particular attention to this all-important question of *mazhab*. Typical of such meetings was the one held in a Murshidabad village around the year 1270 B.S. Inviting his opponent to comment on the importance of *mazhab*, the reformist maulavi asked if he (the tradionalist maulavi) considered it obligatory to belong to a school of Muslim *mazhab*: '(Tell us) if the four *mazhab* is *Farz* or *Sunnat*, or is it *Nawfal* or *Wajib*? . . . Is conformity (to *mazhab*) blissful, and non-conformity sinful?'[26] In reply the traditionalist maulavi characteristically observed that it was obligatory to follow one of the religious schools. The Tariqah preacher then asked: 'If it was obligatory to follow *mazhab*, why (are you all) not believers in one *mazhab*?'[27] After a great deal of discussion the reformist maulavi summed up his views by suggesting that the holy scriptures of Islam did not enjoin upon Muslims to be party to any *mazhab*, and as such it was unnecessary to do so.[28]

Such inconclusive meetings, as most *bahas* meetings turned out to be, did not often produce any positive result. On the other hand, in most cases they served to inflame mutual relations between the contending parties for a long time.[29] But the interest in religious matters they generated among the illiterate Muslims was enormous. More important, the preachers often used such occasions to appeal to the masses to fashion their lives in accordance with the precepts of Islam notwithstanding the differences amongst the theologians.[30]

An interesting feature of the *bahas* meetings was the presence of respectable members of the society as adjudicators, invited by the consent of both the parties. Their task was to listen to the debate and give their own verdict. In one such debate, held between the Hanafis and the reformists (*Rafiyad-dains*) at Salar village in the district of Murshidabad, the judges gave their verdict in support of *mazhab*.[31] How far such decisions affected the attitude of the people who attended these meetings is difficult to assess. The author of *Adellaye Hanifiya*, however, claimed that the decision at Salar 'exposed the evil designs' of the reformists, and encouraged many to desert their ranks and join the Hanafi school.[32]

It is, however, quite significant that although these meetings were concerned with the doctrinal principles of Islam, not all the adjudicators were Muslims. More often than not they were chosen from among the members of other communities. There could well have been an European Magistrate or a Hindu Munsiff of the locality, if the *bahas* was held in the vicinity of a town, or just a Hindu notable of the locality.[33] This was obviously done with a view to avoiding any unnecessary controversy that might have resulted from a decision given by a Muslim Judge, who, in theory, could not have been an impartial adjudicator in such matters. But this procedure did not always have the desired effect. In 1899 The *Mihir-o-Sudhakar*, a Calcutta Muslim organ, expressed deep resentment at the selection of Hindu officials to preside over Muslim religious meetings and decide their outcome. Such a decision, the paper observed, 'could not be held by the Muslim community as final.'[34]

But the *bahas* meetings must not be viewed solely as religious meetings. It was not as if the inarticulate public attended these meetings merely 'to seek the truth'. As it happened, often these meetings were attended by people in their thousands from all walks of rural life.[35] Their interest in such meetings was more than religious, and it is doubtful if any significant proportion of those who attended them understood much about the technical and legal details of what was discussed by the maulavis. Many of them were apparently concerned with the 'victory' or 'defeat' of their own party, no matter what was discussed, and they obviously enjoyed themselves when 'famous maulavis are pitted against each other to argue some knotty points of law and practice.'[36]

The story of a debate when a clever maulavi, in an obvious attempt to out-manoeuvre his rival, asked if his opponent knew the exact meaning of an Arabic passage that literally translated 'I have no idea', may be cited as an instance.[37] The rival maulavi had no option but either to give the correct meaning of what was asked, or to confess his inability to do so, for the public were in no mood to hear his explanations. And the meaning, when given, was so misconstrued by the clever maulavi as to give the ordinary public an impression that the rival really did not know the answer to the question asked. The meeting consequently broke up with the 'victory' of the former and the defeat of the latter, although all indications suggest that the defeated maulavi was the more learned of the two.[38]

It is difficult for us to verify the authenticity or otherwise of such a debate, for we have to rely on the information supplied by the very mullahs who participated in such meetings. But we have evidence of more than one such meeting, where the object seemed to have been either the harrassment of the rivals, or to obtain for themselves some pecuniary advantage from the public by staging a false *bahas*.[39]

For the rural populace, *bahas* meetings were not merely occasions for religious discussion and debate. They offered the opportunity for social gathering and festivity. The author of *Saif al-Momenine* thus fondly recalled the details of some of the events that marked the occasion of the *bahas* meeting at Murshidabad: '(They) engaged themelves in the preparation of food with great enthusiasm. Cases of rose water, *attar* (fragrance) and *Sorma* had already been stored in the rooms. (And) so were folded betel leaves of various kinds mixed with the spices of different kinds in a number of *dalis* (baskets) . . . . Various kinds of food and curry were cooked. Countless people visited (the venue) and had their meals there. What a scene. . . . The two villages took the guise of two bazaars of happiness. The shop-keepers were happy and so were the buyers. Happiness filled the hearts of all in both the bazaars.'[40]

Thus, despite the violent character of some *bahas* meetings they contributed directly to increased social communication beween the people of different localities and villages by bringing them together on a particular occasion. This was bound to reduce the barriers that divided them from each other, and help diminish the tension in society by providing avenues for the regulation and control of existing conflicts. This is evidenced by the fact that some years later the different religious groups agreed to a formal compromise and resolved to work together for the well-being of the community as a whole.[41]

Public debates on such vital questions as the legality of prayers under the British, the desirability of *jihad* etc., were not merely of theological interest, but had a profound impact on the minds of the ordinary people. Although they did not, in many cases, understand the technical and legal details of the arguments, the very fact that such questions were publicly discussed by the contending maulavis was bound to affect their minds and help to transform their attitudes towards their rulers as well as towards the neighbouring communities. In that sense the *bahas* meetings served as an instrument of social mobilization in rural society and were more effective in their appeal than even the missionary work undertaken by individual preachers. This was more so because one of the primary concerns of the contenders at such meetings was to bring the message of Islam to the masses and to counter what they thought to be the mis-representation of the tenets of Islam.

Despite a certain amount of sectarian tension in society greater efforts were now directed by all concerned towards organized religious activities and discussion in an effort to change the face of Islam in rural society; the initiative for fresh reform was no longer limited to the reform movements alone. The traditionalist theologians fought a rearguard action against the reformists, confronting them in *bahas* meetings in an attempt to defend the foundations of the traditionalist system, but were quick to perceive the importance of immediate religious reform in the society. Already in the middle of the nineteenth century men like Maulana Siddiq Ali had spelled out the desirability of some positive action in this regard.[42] The need for reform was further accentuated on account of the confusion caused in the traditionalists' ranks by reformist propaganda. A counter-purificatory campaign was therefore set in motion in the Bengali Muslim society at the initiative of the more enlightened mullahs by the seventies of the nineteenth century. This campaign not only aimed at defending the traditionalist system but equally at re-shaping the older institutions and ideas.

There was thus a remarkable unanimity of action between all the religious groups devoted to the cause of the Islamization of the ordianry Muslims. 'At the present day', wrote H.H. Risely, in 1901, '. . . the efforts of the reformers are directed mainly to the eradication of the superstitious practices not sanctioned by the Koran and to the inculcation of the true principle of the religion.'[43] He cited a government official to say that 'in cities almost every mosque has its school, and the smaller villages in rural tracts are regularly visited by itinerant maulavis. The propaganda is facilitated by the circulation of cheap religious books which give the ordinary prayers in Arabic with the explanation of the meaning (in Bengali).'[44]

The increased religious activity of the muslim preachers may be conveniently studied under three principal heads: (a) publication of religious tracts; (b) Urban impulse; and (c) *Waz Mahfils* and *Anjumans*.

Publication of religious tracts

More than anything else it was the cheap religious tracts, commonly referred to as *nasihat namahs* (Manuals of religious instruction) that reflected the growing spirit of reform and change in the Bengali Muslim society. A real understanding of the rural Muslim mind in the late nineteenth century is impossible without a study of these *nasihat namahs*. In the history of the development of theological studies this literature had obviously very little importance. None of the writers claimed any originality of thought or interpretation, nor was it their intention to produce literature for its own sake. The religious tracts were artless, simple and direct.[45] They took no note of the social and cultural changes that had resulted from the impact of the West, nor did they concern themselves with the adjustment or modification of the orthodox principles of Islam so as to make it compatible with the modernist trends in society. The two important issues with which most of the *nasihat namahas* dealt were, first, how to transform the ideas and attitudes of the ordinary Muslims so as to bring them in conformity with what were considered to be the basic tenets of Islam, and, second, how to remould their life style so as to make it congruent with those tenets. In other words, Islamization of the masses was the key-note of this literature. There was virtually nothing in the life of a Muslim that did not come under the purview of the *nasihat namahs* published during the period. The basic theme of this literature, and this was characteristic of all such works that are extant, was the total rejection of all known local and alien customs and practices with which the average life of a rural Muslim was so closely associated.

Nasihat namahs were not altogether unknown in Bengali Islam prior to the publication of the works under discussion. There was a vast corpus of religious literature in medieval Islam dealing with the faith of the ordinary believer.[46] Its aim, like that of the literature we are considering, was to transmit to the Bengali speaking audience a basic knowledge of the laws and principles of Islam.[47] But, unlike the latter literature, most pre-reformist works give one the impression of confused religious ideas and practices, the details of many of which would appear to the majority of the orthodox Muslims as sacriligeous. Recent researches have described this phenomenon in pre-reformist religious literature as an attempt at 'synthesis' between the ideas and practices that were of local origin with those that came from outside.[48]

The most interesting feature of the pre-reformist literature was the very thin line of distinction in the treatment of the Hindu gods and goddesses with those of the Muslim faith, and the distinction between the two often seemed so blurred that to an average rural Muslim the difference was hardly intelligible. Muslim Prophets were thus often compared, and likened, to the Hindu deities and *avataras*, and the Hindu gods glorified in the same fashion as were the Muslim heroes.[49] A striking example of this class of literature is provided by the works of Sayyid Abdus Sultan (1550-1648?), a Muslim religious leader, who composed nearly a dozen didactic *puthis* in Bengali in an attempt to educate the Muslim masses.[50] His most notable work, *Nabi Vamsa*, was designed to provide a detailed account of all the Islamic prophets, from Adam to Muhammad, for the benefit of the ordinary believers, who were at that time deeply devoted to Hindu epics, particularly the Bengali version of the *Mahabharata*.[51] But the picture drawn by Sayyid Sultan in his attempt to turn the Muslim masses away from un-Islamic beliefs and practices was not what the orthodox society would have approved of. It represented a localized version of popular Islam, with Brahma, Vishnu, Maheswar, Bamana, Rama, Krishna, Adam, Sish, Noah, Abraham, Moses, Jesus and finally, Prophet Muhammad, all having their due place in it.[52] This attempt at 'Hinduization of the Islamic faith' brought upon Sayyid Sultan, and others of his kind, considerable opposition from the orthodox section of the society,[53] but apparently this trend continued until challenged by the reformists in the nineteenth century.

A few *nasihat namahs*, like Afzal Ali's (sixteenth century) *Nasihat Namah*, Shaikh Paran's (1550-1615?) brief composition dealing with '130 obligatory observances', Nasrullah Khan's (1560-1625?) *`hariat Namah*, Muhammad Khan's (1580-1650?)

Maqtual Hossain, Shaikh Muttalib's (1595-1660?) *Kifayat al Musalli*, and Abdul Karim Khondker's (seventeenth century) *Hazar Masail*, did attempt to present the monotheistic fundamentalist Islam to the public,[54] but the overwhelming tendency on the part of the authors of such works was to present Islam to the masses in a more familiar garb.

Now there is no reason to suppose that the authors, many of whom were religious leaders of the people, were ignorant of Islam or its laws and principles. On the contrary, they seemed quite aware of the censure they invited upon themselves by their popular interpretations of Islam.[55] Some of them hesitated to translate religious works into Bengali, which was despised by the orthodox Muslims as a Hindu language.[56] According to Dr. Muhammad Enamul Huq, the primary reason that induced the authors of pre-reformist *nasihat namahs* to 'write in the language of the masses' was to make things easily intelligible to them.[57]

In brief, it was the popular interpretation of Islam that distinguished the compositions of the pre-reformist authors from the latter works. While thus the former attempted to propagate 'Tauhid' in a familiar garb to the people, the latter *nasihat namahs* sought to reject all such compromise with local ideas and practices, and instead attempted to present Islam in its pristine form. They symbolized the uncompromising tendencies of the latter period. Even the traditionalist mullah, who fought a rearguard action against the reformist preachers for the latter's scathing criticism of some of their cherished practices, now showed an incredible hostility to all forms of local associations and their *nasihat namahs* had almost the same characteristics as those of the reformist works of the period. The differences between the two more often concerned details, and where it was found that certain practices, such as incantations, could not be rejected outright, care was taken to islamize the whole institution so as to bring it in line with the Isalamic practices.

The *nasihat namahs* were basically didactic works and often dealt with the obligatory duties of Muslims. *Ketab Kasf al-Huq Tasnif*, for example, thus urged its readers: 'Have faith in (the oneness of) Allah first. Then have faith in the angels. Next have faith in the Book of Allah. Next have faith in the Prophet of Allah. The *Koran* and the *Hadis* are both equally important.'[58]

Ketab Najat al-Islam gave elaborate details of the principal observances that a Muslim was required to perform after he had understood the basic principles as enunciated in *Ketab Kasf al-Huq Tasnif*: 'There are five obligatory observances in Islam. First *Kalam* (the *Kalimah*, declaration of faith); second, *Namaz* (prayer); third *Roza* (fasting); fourth, *Zakat* (giving of alms); and fifth *Haj* (pilgrimage to Mecca).'[59]

There were other *nasihat namahs*, again, that dealt with more specific questions, such as the importance of Friday prayers or the importance of pilgrimage. *Ketab Ahkam-i-Jumah*, for example, devoted itself entirely to a discussion of the importance of Friday prayers, with frequent references and quotations from the Prophetic Traditions.[60] The author urged his readers to try to understand the real significance of prayers and follow them in practice. This was obviously a response to the Faraizi prohibition of congregational prayers. But, at the same time, the author seemed much concerned at the apathy of the people about such vital observances as the Friday prayers.[61]

The *nasihat namahs* were generally unanimous in condemning the existing un-Islamic beliefs and practices in the society and their emphasis was invariably on leading a truly pious life, which was interpreted as a life based on the strict observance of the essential practices of Islam.[62] *Namaz*, or prayer, particularly, was considered so vital that almost all the *nasihat namahs* made efforts to drive home to the ordinary reader its real significance. '*Namaz* is the point of distinction between the infidels and the Muslims', proclaimed one author; 'Be it known to all (that) a *be-namazi* (one who neglects his prayers) is a friend of the infidels.'[63] A second author went further and decried those who did not say prayers as *be-namazi Malaun* (one who has turned infidel). His advice to those who had a *be-namazi* wife in his house was: '*Be-namazi* wife in any house (must not be tolerated). The scriptures make it imperative that she should be divorced. Divorce that evil (therefore) and drive her out. . . .'[64]

However, as indicated earlier, the primary purpose of the *nasihat namahs* was to inform the public of the detailed rules of Islamic laws and observances and to try to induce the people to act in conformity with them. But a truly pious life that would ensure a blissful heavenly life obviously did not depend merely on the observance of the obligatory rules and practices, such as *namaz* and *roza*; in addition a pious Muslim was also required to ensure that none of his acts violated the basic code of conduct as enjoined in Islam. *The nasihat namahs*, therefore, had to make sure that all such rules and laws that should guide the life of an average Muslim were clearly explained to him and consequently an entire set of *nasihat namahs* dealing with social and religious questions, including the rules of marriage and divorce, and relationship between man and woman, was composed.

Typical of this class of *nasihat namahs* was one *Bedar al -Ghafilin* by Munshi Samir al-Din. This voluminous work contained information on almost every subject that concerned the life of a Muslim. These included prayer, fasting, *Bakr-Id*, giving of alms, rights of women in Islam, money-lending, life in heaven, rights and duties of children etc.[65] Abdul Sattar's *Dafi-al-Sharur* similarly dealt with such social and religious questions as are important in the life of an ordinary believer.[66] *Khulasat al-Nikah* by Maulavi Tajuddin Muhammad is another work that discussed particularly the rules of marriage according to Islamic law and asked its readers to abide by them.[67]

The true import of this literature lay in its being a valuable aid to the religious preachers in their task of Islamization of the masses. They imparted religious education to the ordinary people through this literature, which also made them understand their differences with others. This was one reason why the authors of the later *nashiat namas* took particular care to emphasize the the distinctiveness of Islam from Hinduism and to assert its superiority. In the didactic literature of the pre-reformist era too there is evidence of this tendency, but this could not be pressed very far because of the authors' desire to teach people in the language they understood. The later *nasihat namahs*, true to the spirit of the time, were openly intolerant of Hinduism, and often displayed an aggressive want of courtesy towards other religions. One author went so far as to suggest that the Hindus were the real 'untouchables in the society' and 'anyone coming very close to a Hindu must have ablution immediately (afterwards)'.[68] Efforts were made to undermine the Hindu gods and goddesses and establish the comparative greatness of Islamic heroes. In fact, anything associated with Hinduism came to be looked down upon as evil, and the term itself was generally used in an abusive sense in all such literature.[69]

Closely connected with this attitude was the desire to find an altogether new language in which to write these works. These were written mostly in a mixed jargon, widely known as 'Islami Bangla' or 'Musalmani Bangla' on account of the presence in it of numerous Arabic, Persian and Urdu words. This was again in marked contrast with the earlier literature, whose mode of expression was as 'Sanskritic' as the work of any contemporary Hindu author.[70] Dr. Suniti Kumar Chatterji characterized it as the 'Maulavi's reply to the Pandit's *shudhabhasa* (chaste language)',[71] and emphasized that many of the words used in the literature had no relevance to the dialect commonly used by the Muslims in the villages.[72] But the real significance of the Islamization of the Bengali language lay in the mullah's attempt to reject all that was considered of local and Hindu origin.

The endeavour to develop a distinct Muslim variant of the Bengali language was part of the drive to establish a separate identity for Muslims. The authors of the *nasihat namahs* used Bengali reluctantly and sought to modify its character by a wholesale introduction of more and more Arabic and Persian words. One author expressed himself quite candidly when he explained: 'Much of the information contained in that *Kitab* (the religious work on which the author's present work was based) must not be rendered into Bengali. As such, all Arabic Persian and Hindi (i.e. Urdu) words have been left in their original forms (without being translated into Bengali).'[73] The author of *Ketab Ahkam-i-Jumah* (the Importance of Friday Prayers) also had the same confession to make when he wrote his work in Bengali. 'Somehow we were born in Bengal', he wrote; 'Most people do not understand the meaning of Arabic and Persian. That is why I write this *Kalam* (holy book) in Bengali. Try to follow the injunctions of Islam (from this). Try to learn the religious doctrines from this Bengali (work) and manage to learn the truth about God and Prophet somehow.'[74]

The Urban Initiative

Quite consistent with the ideas and thoughts as presented in the rural *nasihat namahs*, but different in style and language, was another type of religious literature published by the educated Muslims. Explaining the reasons for such publications, the author of *Zubdat al-Masail* wrote that although the mullahs of late had rendered into Bengali the rules and laws of Islamic observances, many did not like those works for their style and language. This made it necessary to publish such works in 'simple Bengali' for the benefit of the common people.[75]

Incidentally, *Zubdat al-Masail* by Mohammed Naimuddin was the first of its kind in chaste Bengali that has come to our notice. Written at the request of a Muslim zamindar of Atiya, in Mymensingh, the book is a compendium of the essential tenets of Islam in the form of a catechism. The author claimed to have written this on the basis of authoritative works on Islam.[76] Its popularity may be gauged from the fact that eight editions of the book were published during the lifetime of the author himself.[77] Among other works of the author the most important was his Bengali translation of the *Koran*, done, part by part, between 1892 and 1908 — the first work of its kind ever undertaken by a Bengali Muslim.[78]

Closely following on the heels of *Zubdat al-Masail*, other similar works were published by the educated Muslims. Shaikh Abdur Rahim's *Hazrat Muhammader Jivana Charita O Dharma Niti* (1883), Yaqinuddin Ahmed's *Islam Dharmaniti* (1900), Samiruddin Ahmed's five volume *Muhammadiya Dharmasopan* (1902), Nawab Syed Nawab Ali Choudhuri's *Id ul-Azha* (1900) and *Maulid-i-Sharif* (1903), Shaikh Abdur Rahim's *Namaz Tattva* (1898), *Haz Bidhi* (1903), are a few of such works that were particularly aimed at the less educated public. It is doubtful, however, if they achieved great popularity with the rural people, who were deeply devoted to the *nasihat namahs* produced by the mullahs.[79] The urban works, particularly because of their language and style, were bound to have very limited impact on the rural public; they were better suited for those who were relatively more educated and could appreciate the chaste Bengali of the town.

The importance of these urban compositions lay in their revelation of a sudden awareness amongst the educated Muslims of the need for reform and Islamization of large sections of their society, a task so far undertaken primarily by the maulavis and the mullahs. A pamphlet issued in Bengali by Khan Bahadur Maulavi Abdul Majid Chaudhuri, zamindar of Mohipur in the district of Rangpur (who was also the president of the Rangpur Branch of the Central National Mahomedan Association), on the occasion of the foundation of a Muslim Mission in 1902, explained this new phenomenon purely in terms of religious necessity. It was argued that as all the works on Muslim theology were either in Arabic or Persian, it was important that these should be rendered into Bengali and communicated to the illiterate Muslims by the Islamic preachers.[80]

It must be emphasized however that the interest and initiative taken by the educated and the well-to-do Muslims in the matter, also represented a desire on their part to establish contacts with the rural and illiterate masses through the intermediacy of the religious preachers and religious literature. The need to do so was made imperative by the growing communal rivalry and tension in the country. In no sense was this a parallel movement to that initiated by the mullahs and the reformists in the rural society, for the urban leaders had usually to rely on the semi-literate mullahs to act as their contact men with the villagers and they therefore recruited them, thus establishing a partnership, rather than rivalry, between themselves and the mullahs.

The urban effort in the religious propaganda was unmistakably influenced by the reform movements, despite the fact that the latter's violent activities did not receive any support in urban areas. It was more directly influenced by the activities of men like Sir Sayyid Ahmad Khan (1817-1898)[81] in north India, and Syed Amir Ali (1849-1928), and Khan Bahadur Abdul Latif (1828-1893) in Bengal.[82] These men were primarily guided in their task of social reform by considerations other than religious; they were more concerned with the remoulding of the Muslim society so as to make it adaptable to the changing circumstances.[83] Sir Sayyid Ahmad Khan was more interested in the re-interpretation of Islam in the light of the knowledge derived from the West, and was never very keen either to Islamize the masses or to attend to their problems. He was an aristocrat himself and his thoughts and ideas, like those of Syed Ameer Ali and Khan Bahadur Abdul Latif, revolved round the interests and needs of the Muslim upper class.

Syed Ameer Ali was not a religious reformer but a scholar. He hardly knew any Bengali[84] and did not write in that language. His works were addressed to the western and western-educated Indian Muslim readers, upon whom he endeavoured to impress the past literary and artistic glories and achievements of the Muslims.[85] His Islam had very little to do with the religion of the masses and there was hardly anything in it that was of immediate concern to the Bengali Muslims. Likewise, there were many other Muslim thinkers in contemporary India, men like Maulana Shibli Nomani (1857-1916) and Chirag Ali (1844-1895), who made significant contributions to the study of Muslim thought and theology, but in the context of the Islamization of the Muslim masses this was of little immediate value in Bengal.

Quite different from the individualistic traditions of the religious scholars and thinkers was the religious seminary founded by the scholars of the Waliullahi School at Deoband in 1867. Its principal aim was 'to conserve traditional theological learning in general and certain elements of the teachings of the school of Wali Allah in particular.'[86] The Deoband school, through its pupils, exercised greater direct influence on the masses than did the religious scholars. As a theological seminary of repute it attracted students from all over India, including Bengal. Even the later Faraizis were known to take recourse to the Deoband for the religious training of their preachers.[87] But greater still was the influence exerted by the Calcutta and Hooghly Madrassas. Niether of them was a religious seminary of the Deoband type; they were merely schools or colleges for the teaching of Islamic *Fiqh* literature and the oriental languages. The graduates that came out regularly from these Madrassas found employment as religious teachers in rural Madrassas and Maktabs, as well as *Imams* in mosques.[88] Although trained in the traditional Islamic way, they had also been exposed to the modernist impact in the towns and it is through them that some of this stimulus spread to the rural areas.

Sir Thomas Arnold has pointed out that the spread of education itself had a direct bearing on the question of Islamization, for it led, according to him, 'to a more intelligent grasp of religious principles and an increase of religious teachers.'[89] There is no evidence to link this enhanced interest in religious matters to any political pursuits on the part of the educated Muslims, although it may well have served their interests through being manipulated by them whenever possible.

A basic feature of the new urban religious literature was its overwhelming tendency to glorify Islam and its history almost in the same vein as the earlier reformists did. Their purpose was to present Islam to the ordinary people in its golden image, emphasizing the lofty ideals for which Islam stood and the glories that it helped to create. This was the theme of Nausher Ali Khan's *Bangiya Musalman* (1890), as well as of Kaikobad's *Asrumala* (1895), and his epic poem *Maha Samasan Kavya* (1904).[90] Books of this kind were written and newspapers published in an attempt to educate the masses as well as to inspire them with a confidence that was to play a vital role in the development of self-consciousness among the Bengali Muslims.

The desire for religious reform among the educated Muslims was also induced by the activities of the Christian missionaries who were making a great deal of effort to propagate their faith among the local population.[91] The uneasiness felt by the educated Muslims at missionary propaganda could be seen from the pages of contemporary Bengali Muslim newspapers and religious tracts.[92] *The Sudhakar*, a Calcutta Muslim newspaper, while expressing its grave anxiety at the reports of large-scale conversion of Muslims to Christianity, particularly in the district of Jessore, indicated its determination to counter Christian missionary propaganda by the formation, in Calcutta, of a Muslim society known as the the Islam Mission Fund. Muslims who knew any Arabic and Persian were invited by the paper to join the group and save Islam.[93] Dr. Anisuzzaman notes that the same motive of counteracting Christian influence induced a group of Calcutta Muslims to write a book on Islam, known as the *Islam Tattva*, during this period.[94]

There is no quatitative evidence to determine the extent of conversion from Islam to Christianity in Bengal. But we do find the names of a few notable Mulims in the list of converts and would-be converts, indicating that the missionary movement had achieved some success in its campaign.[95] It does not seem, however, that the rate of conversion assumed any significant proportion at a time when the Muslim preachers themselves were actively engaged in the task of Islamization throughout the mofussil areas of the province. The uneasiness felt by the educated Muslims about Christian missionary activities seemed more a reaction to the nature of the missionary propaganda rather than to any large-scale conversions. The missionaries not only launched a campaign of conversion aimed at the ordinary Muslims but published propagandist literature that was hostile to Islam. On many occasions they used extremely objectionable language in describing the Prophet and the heroes of Islam, even casting aspersions on the personal character of the Prophet. 'Muhammad's character', wrote the author of *Satya Dharma Nirupan* (Exposition of the True Faith), 'was worse than his religious teaching. It is doubtful if there is any other person who can equal him in licentiousness. . . . Not content with his wife and mistresses, he even took other men's wives. . . . He did not respect age or relationship in gratifying the cravings of the flesh. He was a notorious robber.'[96]

Such utterances were not confined to the publications addressed to the educated Muslims alone. The missionaries published books in Musalmani Bengali aimed at the rural Muslims and made efforts to win converts and discredit Islam.[97] This evoked sharp criticism from the educated Muslims as well as the ulema, who produced religious literature designed to strengthen the cause of Islam and counter the Christian missionary propaganda.

No one played a more prominent role in the anti-missionary crusade in Bengal than Munshi Meherullah (1861-1907) of Jessore. In his first treatise on Christianity, entitled *Kshristiya Dharmer Asarata* (Hollowness of the teachings of Christianity), published in 1886, Meherullah drew attention to the intolerance exhibited by the missionaries; he wrote: 'In the contemporary world there is a tendency amongst the preachers of different religions . . . to boast about the greatness of their respective faiths. But no other people can slander more, and show more contempt for others' faiths than the preachers of Christianity.'[98] Three years later, in a letter to *The Mihir O Sudhakar*, he criticised the educated Muslims for their inability to deal with the missionary threat and wrote that it 'was useless to hold sham religious meetings (to protest against the missionary propaganda) . . . Men who whilst professing Islam can put up with the abuse of the Prophet are not worthy of the name of Musalman.'[99]

Unlike Abdul Latif and most other contemporary Calcutta Muslim leaders, Munshi Meherullah belonged to the masses by circumstances of his birth and residence.[100] Born in Jessore in the year 1861 he had little formal education. He came from a family of poor means and lost his father at an early age. He had therefore to earn a living when, under ordinary circumstances, he should have been studying in a Madrassa. Although he missed the opportunity to attend school for any considerable length of time, Meherullah learnt enough Arabic, Persian and Urdu (and acquired a good command over Bengali, in which he published all his religious works)[101] to undertake the work of a religious preacher. He began his career as a tailor in Jessore town but soon found himself deeply committed to religious preaching which, in course of time, turned into a passion. His career as a preacher actually started in protest against the activities of the Christian missionaries in the Jessore area. He encountered them in a number of open religious debates, or *bahas*, at the beginning of his missionary work but soon found it more important to impart basic religious training to his own ignorant co-religionists than chasing the missionaries down the small towns and *bazaars* of rural Bengal. In other words, he chose to strengthen the religious foundations of his own society in an attempt to counteract the growing influence of the Christian missionaries. He sought to achieve this through three principal means: active missionary work in the rural areas to educate the people; publication of religious tracts in the vernacular; and the establishment of religious associations, or anjumans. In his great task of Islamization he found willing allies in the ranks of Keramat Ali's disciples, notably Pir Shah Abu Bakr of Furfura.[102] He also established close contact with the so-called '*Sudhakar* group' Calcutta — a group so named for its very close association with the Muslim newspaper *Mihir o Sudhakar*.[103] The *Sudhakar* group, which included men like Shaikh Abdur Rahim (1859-1931), Muhammad Reazuddin Ahmad (1862-1933), and Pandit Reazuddin Ahmad Mashadi (1859-1919), was already engaged in the production and publication of religious tracts in Bengali for the religious education of the Muslim masses.[104] They found an extremely useful collaborator in the person of Munshi Meherullah, and their partnership continued uninterrupted for a long time.

What made Munshi Meherullah's role particularly significant in the context of the late nineteenth century Bengali Muslim society was his close contact both with the educated classes as well as the masses in the countryside. He could be seen as frequently at the educational conferences held in the towns and cities as in the *waz mahfils*-religious meetings-in the rural areas. He thus had the distinct advantage of acting as an effective link between the educated and the illiterate and between the urban Muslims and their rural co-religionists.

Meherullah's treatises on Islam encompassed a wide variety of subjects.[105] His primary concern, as indicated earlier, was to counteract the growing anti-Islamic propaganda of the Christian missionaries and to establish the greatness of Islam. This induced him to write works primarily of a polemical nature, arguing against Christian missionaries and sometimes even against the Hindus. In *Kshristiya Dharmer Asarata* Meherullah was openly critical of the missionaries and the doctrines of Christianity and sought to prove that Christianity as such was based on poor foundations. His *Hīndu Dharma Rahasya O Devlila*, on the other hand, was intended to be a reply to the alleged anti-Muslim writings by the Hindu critics of Islam. But side by side with these polemical writings he published materials of a decidedly didactic character which were intended for the religious instruction of the uneducated rural Muslims.[106] He was particularly keen to see Islam restored as a living force in the daily life of ordinary people, not just as a dogmatic set of beliefs and practices, which also made him something of a social reformer (he bitterly criticized the upper classes for their reluctance to allow widow-remarriage).[107]

Waz Mahfils and Anjumans

However, it was Meherullah's initiative in establishing the Islamic anjumans in the rural areas and in the holding of peaceful religious assemblies, *waz mahfils*, that represented his abiding contribution to the process of Islamization of the Bengali Muslim community.[108] The first anjuman which he helped to establish in Jessore in about the year 1887, known as *Islam Dharmattejika* (Regenerating Islam), was certainly not the first anjuman in Bengal, and it is most likely that Meherullah was influenced in undertaking this activity by the example of other similar organizations, notably Syed Ameer Ali's National Mahomedan Association (founded in 1877).[109] But what made his effort particularly significant was the special role his anjuman was intended to play: unlike the Mahomedan Association or other similar bodies, Meherullah's anjuman was primarily a religious body, founded with the obvious intention of propagating Islam and publishing religious materials.

Meherullah's efforts at the religious training and teaching of the masses thus represented a significant break with the tradition initiated by the earlier reformists, whom he encountered in a number of *bahas* meetings. In ideas and practices he belonged to the tradition of Maulana Keramat Ali but never formally joined his movement. He was thus technically a traditionalist. But his desire for reform in the Muslim society, in the direction of Islamic orthodoxy, made him radically different from the traditionalist mullahs who were, on the whole, hostile to innovation requiring a certain amount of liberalization and modernization of the existing social values and practices. Like Sir Sayyid Ahmad Khan, Meherullah wanted to bring about a fundamental change in the attitude of the community towards Islam and both equally recognized the value of modern education for achieving this end and actively encouraged Muslims to acquire modern learning in both the arts and sciences.

Meherullah's biographer, Asiruddin Pradhan, claimed that Meherullah initiated a movement in Bengal that resulted in the foundation of religious anjumans and the holding of *waz mahfils* all over the province.[110] We do not have details of any such anjuman founded in the wake of Meherullah's *Islam Dharmattejika*. However, there were several Islamic anjumans, founded independently of the activities of Meherullah, which were engaged in the propagation of Islamic doctrines. The author of *Dughdo Sarobar* (1298 B.S.), Mirza Yusuf Ali, mentioned the existence of two Islamic anjumans, one in Rajshahi district and the other in the district of Rangpur, in the late nineteenth century. Explaining their objects he wrote that they 'intended to propagate (among the Muslims), both to the elderly and the young, as well as to the children, the real meaning of Islam, the obligations enjoined by the *Koran*, and the meaning of the *Koran*, or the *Tafsir*. (They) are determined to do this in the mosques, in village bazaars, (and) in every populated place. In addition to this, they will publish translations of religious works in Bengali and will print booklets for the benefit of the Muslim community.' 'Both the Associations in North Bengal', wrote the author, 'are desirous of uniting (the Muslims of all Bengal) into a common brotherhood.'[111]

It is beyond question that though their number may not have been very great, such anjumans played a key role in the creation of Muslim self-consciousness in rural Bengal. As one early twentieth century Muslim lawyer observed: '. . . the influence of the anjumans has been in some ways entirely beneficial to the community; it has enabled the individual *rayat* to adopt a more independent attitude towards the petty oppression of the local zamindars . . . it has resulted in closer observance of religious forms and an abolition of practices not in strict conformity with Moslem orthodoxy.'[112]

With the backing of such organized bodies religious preachers were better able to communicate the message they were carrying to the ordinary public and this was often done through organized *waz mahfils*.[113] The importance of these assemblies was that instead of open religious debates, as with *bahas*, they were more concerned with the peaceful propagation of the principles of Islam. By the closing years of the nineteenth century more and more preachers joined in the campaign and frequently addressed such meetings all over the country.[114]

But *waz mahfils* did not concern themselves only with the propagation of Islam and asking the audience to follow the injunctions of the *Koran*, although this was ostensibly their primary purpose. Munshi Meherullah often used such occasions to enlist public support for modern education, asking his audience to establish schools and madrassas in the villages.[115] The *mahfils* were ordinarily expected to be addressed by eminent personalities, but it was not unusual for men of humble status to preside over such meetings. In many instances men from far off places, as far as Northern India, would be invited to address the religious gatherings.[116]

Popular enthusiasm on such occasions was very considerable and people in their thousands came to attend these meetings and hear the religious leaders speak on various subjects. The meetings often ended with a clarion call to the audience to try to get back their lost glory by changing their habits and style of living. Giving details of a rural *mahfil* meeting, an anonymous writer noted the great enthusiasm that the *mahfil* meeting occasioned among the ordinary public. He pointed out the beneficial effects that these meetings had on the rural population. A *mahfil* arranged by the author himself, and attended by the neighbouring Muslim villagers, created such enthusiasm in the area that every single village in the locality subsequently started organizing them. He wrote: 'As arranged, the meeting continued for three days. More than three thousand people attended every day. The *waz* had real effect this year. As a result the Muslims villagers in seventeen or eighteen villages suddenly found a new lease of life. . . . The Maulavi (the preacher who was invited to preside over the meeting) founded an anjuman, known as the 'Anjuman Mafidul Islam', in our village. . . . It was decided, on behalf of this association, to establish a *Maktab* in the village. Two or three paid, and four or five unpaid *waez* (preachers) were also appointed.'[117] Consequently, claimed the author, 'our locality, which had hitherto been shrouded in irreligiousness, was now lit with the dazzling ray of the sun of Islam.'[118]

This statement, although obviously exaggerated, illustrates popular interest in *mahfil* meetings. Like the *bahas* meetings, they not only made the public increasingly conscious of their Islamic identity, but worked, both directly and indirectly, to strengthen the bonds of unity between the people of different localities. In addition, they acted as a channel for the quick dissemination of the educated Muslims' ideas in the rural areas through the instrumentality of urban religious preachers, who often used such occasions to propagate the cause of modern education and such other matters that directly concerned the community.[119]

An important preoccupation of the nineteenth century Bengali Muslim society was with religious activity. It would be wrong to expect this activity to have produced any dramatic change in the fundamental social and religious conceptions of the rural Muslims. Indeed all evidence tends to suggest that this did not happen. What was significant, however, was the mass awakening it brought about, and the wider social and religious contacts between the Muslim villagers of the different localities it established. The results of this stimulated religious instinct could be seen in the establishment of new religious institutions and organizations in remote mofussil areas, in the publication of numerous religious tracts, and, finally, in widespread religious debates and *waz mahfils*. That they still retained many of the older customs (which in fact most Muslim villagers in Bengal still do), contrary to the injunctions of orthodox Islam, does not in any way contradict our basic argument that intensified religious and social activity in late nineteenth century Bengali Muslim society immensely contributed to the social mobilization of the rural Muslim population in the province. At the beginning of the nineteenth century there was virtually nothing that could have roused the apathetic Muslim peasantry of Bengal to united action. They were like several separate caste groups in the rural hierarchy, with their social and cultural activities and contacts remaining restricted primarily within the bounds of their own groups and localities. The reform movements, particularly the efforts at Islamization, brought them out of their old environment and helped in the process of achieving horizontal solidarity within the lower strata of the community. By the closing years of the century the conflict between the opposing religious groups of Muslims lost its intensity and eventually became transformed, under changed circumstances, into harmony, based on a recognition of the inter-dependence and the ultimate unity of interests and values of Bengali Muslims. Conflict and tension indirectly worked as mobilizing and integrating forces generating a sense of *communitas* across social divisions.

Side by side with social mobilization and social integration, increased religious and social activity also resulted in gradual changes in the ideas and attitudes of the rural people. This process was more significant, in may respects, than even the *jihad* movement of the Tariqah-i-Muhamadiya, which wanted to conquer India by force from the British; the aim of the later movement was to conquer the soul of the ordinary Muslim by bringing his thoughts and ideas into line with the orthodox faith. Whether they succeeded in their principal task, i.e., Islamization of the soul, is doubtful, but they did transform his social world.

NOTES

1 Anonymous, *Saif al-Momenine*, Calcutta 1875, p. 10.

2 See Muhammad Mallick, *Akhbar al-Marifat*, Calcutta 1283 B.S. / 1876, pp. 12-36; also Abdul Qadir, *Akhbar-i-Pir-i-Najdi*, Calcutta 1874, pp. 3-4, & *passim*.

3 See, for example, the report of the Magistrate, Jamalpur, quoted in *Census of India 1901*, vol.VI:I, p. 175; see also *The Mohammadi*, 31 March 1905.

4 Some of these *bahas* meetings were reported in the Police and Judical Proceedings of the Government of Bengal, but with little details on the occurrences.

5 *Saif al-Momenine*, *passim*.; also Muhammad Naimuddin, *Adellaye Hanifiya*, Karatia 1905, *passim*.; Abdul Qadir, *Akhbar-i-Pir-i-Najdi*, pp. 12-13.

6 *Saif al-Momenine*, p. 5.

7 Ibid., p. 19; also Muhammad Naimuddin, *Adellaye Hanifiya*, p.27; S.M.Zamiruddin, *Meher Charita* Calcutta 1909, p. 49.

8 Quoted *Census of India 1901*, vol.VI:I, p. 175.

9 *The Mohammadi*, 31 March 1905.

10 The *bahas* at Barisal (1867) between the Taiyunis and the Faraizis, for example, discussed among others such questions as (a) the relationship between faith and work, (b) the method of initiation into the mystic orders, and (c) the legality of holding congregational prayers in India under the British. see Maulana Keramat Ali, *Hujjat-i-Qati*, pp. 85ff, quoted M.A. Khan, *History of the Faraidi Movement in Bengal 1818-1906*, Karachi 1965, p. 92; also *Saif al-Momenine*, pp. 20-4.

11 See *Saif al-Momenine*, pp. 24-35; Muhammad Mallick, *Akhbar al-Marifat*, p. 3 Muhammad Naimuddin, *Adellaye Hanifiya*, p. 25.

12 See Nazimuddin, *Jumah* (non-dated *Faraizi Puthi*): the author analyses the Faraizi viewpoint on congregational prayers and challenges the view that Bengal could be called *dar-al-Islam* under the rule of the British.

13 For orthodox reaction to Faraizi prohibition of congregational prayers, see Abdul Qadir, *Akhbar-i-Pir-Najdi*, p. 22; Abdul Kader, 'Bangla Shahitye Shadhinata Sangramer Rup' *Mah-e-Nau*, Dacca, Bhadra 1365 B.S./1958; Maleh Muhammad's *Ketab Shahi Ahkam-i-Jumah*, Dacca 1876, gives a traditionalist interpretation of the importance of Friday prayers.

14 M.A.Khan, *The Faraidi Movement*, p. 101.

15 Ibid., p. 92.

16 Ibid.; *Shorter Encyclopaedia of Islam*, Leiden 1953, p.217.

17 Nabin Chandra Sen, *Amar Jivani*, vol.III, Calcutta 1317 B.S. 1910, pp. 150ff.

18 M.A.Khan, *The Faraidi Movement*, p. 58.

19 Abdul Qadir, *Akhbar-i-Pir-i-Najdi*, p. 22; also Abdul Aziz, *Tariqah-i-Muhammadiya*, Calcutta 1283 B.S./1876, p.9; Abdul Aziz claimed that the Tariqah preachers succeeded in 're-introducing' *Jumah* all over Bengal by the closing years of the nineteenth century.

20 Nabin Chandra Sen, op.cit., p. 149; also *Census of India 1901*, vol.VI:I, p. 174.

21 Fakir Maleh Muhammad, *Ketab Kasf al-Huq Tasnif*, Dacca 1876, p. 43; also Muhammad Mallick, *Akhbar al-Marifat*, p. 10.

22 Aziz Ahmad, *An Intellectual History of Islam in India*, Edinburgh 1969, pp. 1-11; M.A.Khan, *The Faraidi Movement*, pp. lxxiv, lxxv, and *passim*; also Abdul Qadir, *Akbhar-i-Pir-i-Najdi*, p. 3.

23 Aziz Ahmad, op.cit., p. 11; also M.A. Bari, 'A Comparative Study of the Early Wahhabi Doctrines and the Contemporary Reform Movements in Indian Islam', D.Phil, Oxford, 1953, Chapters I & II.

24 Fakir Maleh Muhammad, op.cit., pp. 43-4.

25 *Saif al-Momenine*, p. 25; also Muhammad Mallick, op.cit., p. 13.

26 *Saif al-Momenine*, p. 24.

27 Ibid., p. 25.

28 Ibid., pp. 30-1.

29 Muhammad Naimuddin, *Adellaye Hanifiya*, p. 25; also *Census of India 1901*, vol.VI:I, p. 175; *The Mohammadi*, 31 march 1905.

30 S.M.Zamiruddin, *Meher Charita*, p. 50; also *Saif al-Momenine*, p.56.

31 Muhammad Naimuddin, *Adellaye Hanifiya*, p. 125.

32 Ibid., p. 16.

33 At the Salar *bahas* for example all three judges, selected unanimously by

the parties concerned, were Hindus; see Muhammad Naimuddin, *Adellaye Hanifiya*, p. 28; also *The Mihir O Sudhakar*, 10 November 1899.

34 *The Mihir O Sudhakar*, 24 November 1899.

35 Muhammad Naimuddin, *Adellaye Hanifiya*, p. 18; also *Saif al-Momenine*, pp. 17, 19.

36 *The Imperial Gazetteer of India* (New Series) vol. VII, Oxford 1908, p.240.

37 Abdul Awal Khondker, *Islami Jhanda*, Calcutta 1884, pp. 3-4.

38 Ibid.

39 Popular reaction to such acts of deception by the unscrupulous mullah, when made known to them, was one of deep shock and regret. See Abdul Qadir, op.cit., p. 12; also Abdul Karim, *Muhammadan Education in Bengal*, Calcutta 1900, p. 55.

40 *Saif al-Momenine*, pp. 12-17.

41 See Rajat K.Ray, 'Social Conflict and Political Unrest in Bengal 1857-1927' (forthcoming), p. 93; also S.M.Zamiruddin, op.cit., p. 56.

42 See, for example, *Siddiq Alir Puthi* (trs. from Sylheti-Nagri by Himmat Allah), Golachipa 1281 B.S./1875, pp. 13-15; Siddiq Ali, it may be noted, was converted to Islam in the mid-nineteenth century. Formerly known as Sree Goher Kishore Sen, Siddiq Ali claimed in his *Puthi* that his growing doubts about Hinduism induced him to seek the truth and accept Islam. His *Puthi* gives detailed information on the socio-cultural life of rural Bengali Muslims in the mid-nineteenth century. It was first published in Sylheti-Nagri, but later translated into Bengali by a disciple, Himmat Allah.

43 *Census of India*, 1901 vol.I: I, p. 37.

44 Ibid.; also T.W.Arnold, *The Preaching of Islam*, second edition, London 1913, pp. 286, 7.

45 M.A.Hai and S.A.Ahsan, *Bangla Sahityer Itivritta*, Dacca 1964, p. 32; also Q.M.Husain, 'Bengali Literature', S.M.Ikram and P.Spear, (eds), *The Cultural Heritage of Pakistan*, Karachi 1955, pp. 140-1; and Anisuzzaman, *Muslim Manos O Bangla Shahitya*, Dacca 1964, *passim*.

46 For details, see Enamul Huq. *Muslim Bangla Sahitya*, second edition, Dacca 1965, pp. 66-9, 71-3, 140-210; Munshi Abdul Karim and Ahmad Sharif, *A Descriptive Catalogue of the Bengali Manuscripts in Munshi Abdul Karim's Collection*, Translated with an introduction by S.Sajjad Husain, Dacca 1960, Introduction; Asim Roy, 'The Social Factors in the Making of Bengali Islam' *South Asia*, No. 3, August 1973, 28-30.

47 See Muhammad Khan, *Maqtul Husain*, in Enamul Huq, *Muslim Bangla Sahitya*, p. 190; also Sayyid Abdus Sultan, *Shab-i-Miraj*, in Enamul Huq, op.cit., pp. 141-2, 160-1.

48 Asim Roy, op.cit., pp. 29-34; also Munshi Abdul Karim and Ahmad Sharif, op.cit., Introduction.

49 Enamul Huq, op.cit., pp. 147-51.

50 Among his works the following may be mentioned: *Nabi Vamsa*, *Shab-i-Miraj*, *Rasul Vijaya*, *Wafat-i-Rasul*, *Iblis Namah*, *Jnan Pradip*, *Marfati Gan*.

51 See Enamul Huq, op.cit., pp. 147-60.

52 Sayyid Abdus Sultan, *Nabi Vamsa*, in Enamul Huq, op.cit., p. 147.

53 Sayyid Abdus Sultan, *Shab-i-Miraj*, and Shaikh Abdul Muttalib, *Kefayet al-Musallin*, in Enamul Huq, op.cit., p. 161, 198.

54 Enamul Huq, op.cit., pp. 147-50; also Munshi Abdul Karim and Ahmad Sharif, op.cit., p. xxvi.

55 See note 53 above.

56 Muhammad Khan, *Maqtul Husain*, and Shaikh Muttalib, *Kefayet al-Musallin*, in Enamul Huq, op.cit., pp. 190, 198-9.

57 Enamul Huq, op.cit., pp. 147-50; also Munshi Abdul Karim and Ahmad Sharif, op.cit., p. xxvi.

58 See Fakir Maleh Muhammad, *Ketab Kasf al-Huq Tasnif*, p. 50; also Tajuddin Muhammad, *Khulasat al-Nikah*, Calcutta 1281 B.S./1875, p. 35; Muhammad Maniruddin, *Hujjat-i-Salihin*, Barisal 1876, p. 6; Ahmad Hesabuddin, *Khulasat al-Nasihat*, Dacca 1876, p. 32; Anwarul Islam, *Islam Jyoti*, first edition, 24 Parganahs, 1904, *passim*.

59 Abdul Hamid, *Ketab Najat al-Islam*, Calcutta 1276 B.S./1870, p. 22; Munshi Maleh Muhammad, *Jarurat al-Islam*, second edition, Calcutta 1281 B.S./1874, pp. 2-12; Fasihuddin, *Minhaj al Islam*, Calcutta 1876, pp. 78ff.

60 Maleh Muhammad, *Ketab Shahi Ahkam-i-Jumah*, pp. 2-76.

61 Ibid., p. 61, *passim*.

62 See Abdul Sattar, *Dafi al-Sharur*, Calcutta 1877, pp. 2,30; Muhammad Danesh, *Nurul Imaner Puthi*, Calcutta 1876, pp. 4,52,56.

63 Munshi Samir al-Din, *Bedar al-Ghafilin*, Calcutta 1879-80, p. 31.

64 Abdul Sattar, *Dafi al-Sharur*, p. 6.

65 See Munshi Samir al-Din, *Bedar al-Ghafilin*, Preface, and *passim*.

66 Abdul Sattar, *Dafi al-Sharur*, pp. 6,16,21,26,30,31,34,73.

67 Tajuddin Muhammad, *Khulasat al-Nikah*, *passim*.

68 Muhammad Shah, *Gulzar-e-Momenine*, Calcutta 1911-12, p. 36.

69 Ahmad Hesabuddin, *Khulasat al-Nasihat*, p. 12; also Muhammad Mallick, *Akhbar al-Marifat*, p. 12.

70 Suniti Kumar Chatterji, *The Origin and Development of the Bengali Language*, Part I, Calcutta 1926, p. 210; also J.C.Ghosh, *Bengali Literature*, London 1948, p. 82.

71 S.K.Chatterji, op,cit., p. 211; also Enamul Huq, op.cit., p. 192.

72 S.K.Chatterji, op.cit., p. 211; also A.Majed Khan 'Bangali Musalmaner Matribhasa ki?', *Proceedings of the Bangiya Sahitya Sanmilan* (Rajshahi), Calcutta 1910, p. 74.

73 Abdul Ghafur *Khair Barkat*, Dacca 1870, pp. 3-4.

74 Maleh Muhammad, *Ketab Shahi Ahkam-i-Jumah*, p. 71.

75 Muhammad Naimuddin, *Zubdat al-Masail*, Calcutta 1873, pp. 1-2;

76 Ibid.

77 Kazi Abdul Mannan, *Adhunik Bangla Sahitye Muslim Sadhana*, Rajshahi 1961, pp. 169-72.

78 Incidentally, the first Bengali translation of the *Koran* was done by a Hindu, Bhai Giris Chandra Sen, who also published several other valuable works on Islam.

79 Enamul Huq, op.cit., 276-7; also *Bangiya Musalman Sahitya Patrika*, vol.I, No.I, 1918, 8-9.

80 *The Moslem Chronicle*, 13 December 1902, 697; also Kazi Abdul Mannan, op.cit., pp. 147-8.

81 For an account of the life and works of Sir Sayyid Ahmad Khan, see G.F.I. Graham, *The Life and Works of Sir Syed Ahmed Khan*, second edition, London 1909; J.M.S.Baljon, *The Reforms and Religious Ideas of Sir Sayyid. Ahmad Khan*, third edition, Lahore 1964.

82 For Syed Ameer Ali, see K.KAziz, (ed.), *Ameer Ali:His Life and Work*, Lahore 1968; P.Hardy, *The Muslims of British India*, Cambridge 1972, pp. 105-7; Aziz Ahmad, *Islamic Modernism in India and Pakistan 1857-1964*, London 1967, pp. 86-97;

For Nawab Abdul Laṭif, see Enamul Haque, *Nawab Bahadur Abdul Latif: His writings and related Documents*, Dacca 1968; Bradley Birt, *Twelve Men of Bengal in the nineteenth century*, Calcutta 1910.

83 See P.Hardy, op.cit., pp. 94-107; Aziz Ahmad, *Islamic Modernism*, pp. 30-56, 86-97.

84 In a letter addressed to Reazuddin Ahmed, Syed Ameer Ali himself admitted of his poor knowledge of Bengali; see Reazuddin Ahmad, *Arab Jatir Itihas*, Rangpur 1912-13, Introduction.

85 Aziz Ahmad, *Islamic Modernism*, pp. 77-86; P.Hardy, op.cit., pp. 112-15.

86 Aziz Ahmad, op.cit., p.104; also Z.H.Faruqi, *The Deoband School and the Demand for Pakistan*, Calcutta 1962, *passim*.

87 Anisuzzaman, op.cit., p. 74; also *The Moslem Chronicle*, 5 September 1903, 505-7.

88 See *Census of India 1901*, vol. VI:I, Appendix II, pp. i-x; also Nowsher Ali Khan Eosufzai, *Note on Muhammadan Education* (1903), Printed as an Appendix to *East Bengal and Assam General Proceedings*, April 1906, p. 2.

89 T.W.Arnold, op.cit., p. 286.

90 N.A.K.Yusufzai, *Bangiya Musalman*, first published 1891 and reprinted Calcutta 1914, pp. 2-3; Kaikobad, *Maha Smasan Kavya* (1904), Reprinted Dacca 1940, Introduction to second edition; also Anisuzzaman, *Muslim Manos*, p. 402.

91 T.W.Arnold, op.cit., pp. 33,286; also S.M.Zamiruddin, op.cit., pp. 17,47-8.

92 *The Sudhakar*, 5 December 1890, *Bengal Native Newspaper Reports* (*BNNR*) 1890, p. 1137; *The Mihir O Sudhakar*, 30 June 1899; 29 September 1899; 17 November 1899.

93 *The Sudhakar*, 5 December 1890, *BNNR* 1890, p. 1137.

94 Anisuzzaman, *Muslim Manos* p. 325.

95 S.M.Zamiruddin, op.cit., pp. 7,12,42; Muhammad Asiruddin Pradhan, *Meherullahr Jivani* Jalpaiguri 1909, p. 9.

96 Quoted in *The Mihir O Sudhakar*, 30 June 1899; see also Rev. J.Long, *Muhammader Jivan Charita* Calcutta 1855, *passim*.

97 See Rev. W.Goldsack, *A Musalmani Bengali-English Dictionary* Calcutta 1923, p. 1; and *The Calcutta Christian Observer*, January-December 1852, pp. 279-80, 334-6.

98 Quoted in Sufia Ahmed, 'Some Aspects of the History of the Muslim Community in Bengal 1884-1912' (Ph.D., London 1960; since published), p. 466.

99 *The Mihir O Sudhakar*, 30 June 1899.

100 Muhammad Asiruddin Pradhan, op.cit., pp. 13,15,25,27; also S.M.Zamiruddin, op.cit., pp. 68,69,73,91.

101 For details, see Anisuzzaman, 'Munshi Meherullah O Zamiruddin', *Sahitya Patrika*, 4th year, vol.2, Winter 1367 B.S./1960, 92-7.

102 For an account of the life and work of Pir Shah Abu Bakr of Furfura, see Mozammel Huq, *Moulana Parichaya*, Calcutta 1914; Benoy Gopal Roy, *Religious Movements in Modern Bengal*, Visva Bharati 1965, pp. 192-3.

103 Sufia Ahmed, op.cit., p. 435; also Anisuzzaman in *Sahitya Patrika*, Winter 1367 B.S./1960, 88.

104 S.M.Zamiruddin, op.cit., p. 10; Anisuzzaman, *Muslim Manos*, p. 325.

105 Among his published works were: *Kshristiya Dharmer Asarata* (1886), *Meher al-Islam* (1890), *Bidhaba Ganjana* (1898?); *Pandnamah* (trs. of SK.Sadi's *Pandnamah*, second edition 1908; *Radde Kshristan O Dalilol Islam*, (n.d.).

106 See for example, *Meher al-Islam*; he discusses details of the basic tenets of Islam in this work for the edification of the ordinary people.

107 S.M.Zamiruddin, op.cit., pp. 73-8.

108 He took a leading role in the establishment of an All-India Propagation Society in Calcutta about this time. The details are not known.

109 S.M.Zamiruddin, op.cit., p. 56.

110 Muhammad Asiruddin Pradhan, op.cit., p. 14.

111 Mirza Yusuf Ali, *Dughdo Sarobar*, Calcutta 1895, Introduction; see also *The Mussalman*, vol.III, April 16, 1909, 8; *Islam Pracharak*, vol.VII, 1312 B.S./1906, 477.

112 *The Mussalman*, 16 April 1909, 8.

113 *The Moslem Chronicle*, 29 November, 1902; 13 December 1902; also *Census of India 1901*, vol.VI:I, Appendix II, p. x.

114 *The Dhaka Prakash*, vol.19 No.6 (1879), p. 71; *Islam Pracharak*, vol.5 No.2, February 1903, pp. 75-6; vol.7, 1312 B.S./1906, p. 485; also Mozammel Huq, *Moulana Parichaya*, p. 28.

115 Muhammad Asiruddin Pradhan, op.cit., p. 13.

116 *The Moslem Chronicle*, 11 April 1895, 15; *The Mussalman*, vol.III, 1 December 1908, 7.

117 Ibn-e-Maaz (pseud.), 'Amar Samsar Jivana O Islamer Jwalanta Pravaba' *Islam Pracharak*, vol.VII, 1312 B.S./1906, 482-3

118 Ibid., 483.

119 *Islam Pracharak*, vol.5, No.2, February 1903, 75-6.

The Social Organization of the Sinhalese Sangha in an Historical Perspective

MICHAEL CARRITHERS
Wolfson College, Oxford

In this paper I will describe the social organization of the Sinhalese Buddhist Sangha. I do so however not so much as a response to the demand for such studies in social anthropology — though I hope it may fulfil that purpose as well — but in response to nexus of problems which arose in my research on the recent history of forest-dwelling monks in Ceylon. First, I found that in the last two hundred years a number of reform or forest-dwelling groups of monks had arisen and then declined or disappeared. These seem to be examples of the central theme of Sangha history: the repeated reforms of the Sangha throughout its two millenia in Ceylon (and in Burma and Thailand as well). Second, I found that each of the modern reform movements had overcome, or succumbed to, more or less substantial resistance among the rest of the Sangha. At one level, of course, this dynamic of reform and decay, which is so conspicuous among Western Christian monastic orders as well, is the fruit of natural human propensities. The reforms of ascetic idealists, in the course of time, naturally exhaust themselves and the Sangha returns to a dead level of indifferent morality and worldly involvement: this process is suggested in the phrase 'routinization of charisma'. Similarly, worldly monks with vested interests naturally resent reformers whose moral stand threatens their legitimacy. However true these explanations are to human nature, they do not explain what is characteristically Buddhist about the process, or why it should be the chief issue of Sangha history. I aim to produce an account which finds an explanation in the enduring conditions and ideals of Sangha life.

In its most general form the tension between reform and decay stems from two missions laid down for the Sangha by the Buddha: the mission of preaching, and the mission of contemplative self-cultivation. The mission of preaching is enjoined in the following words, which are often and eagerly quoted by Buddhist preachers and missionaries: 'Fare forth, monks, for the blessing of the many, out of compassion for the world, for the welfare, the blessing and the happiness of gods and men. Let not two of you go the same way. Monks, teach the Dhamma which is lovely at the beginning, lovely in the middle, and lovely at the end.'* This call to pastoral life in the world stands in contrast to equally firm calls to the contemplative life, such as this: 'If there is anything to do which has been taught by a teacher to his disciples out of compassion, wishing their welfare, that has been taught by me. Here, monks, are the roots of trees and empty places (in which to meditate). Do not be negligent, do not be remorseful later. This is my command to you.' (Majjhima Nikaya, I, 118.) The inherent tension between the active and contemplative lives is familiar from Christian monasticism as well, of course; but since all Buddhist clergy are first and foremost meant to be monks, it reaches to the very heart of Sangha life. The unintended complications arise when the contemplative order envisaged in canonical texts tries to fulfill its clerical duties toward a Buddhist populace; or, seen the other way round, it arises when a peasant sangha confronts its own monastic ideal.

I will argue from present-day Sangha organization in Ceylon, because of the richness of material available to me. I assume, however, that the argument can be applied, with suitable adjustments, to the rest of the Theravāda world, and throughout Theravāda history. I think, for example, that the origin of many of the rules of the canonical monastic code (*Vinaya*) could profitably be seen in the light of these unintended complications. The chief obstacle to accepting the universality of my explanation lies in the argument that most of the reforms in Buddhist history have been carried out by Buddhist kings, and have therefore sprung from the demands of religious polity rather than from the internal

**Mahāvagga*, I, 11. It is significant, however, that this passage goes on to say that what is to be preached is the life of a monk. Thus: '. . . sātthaṃ savyañjanaṃ kevalaparipuṇṇaṃ parisuddhaṃ brahmacariyaṃ pakāsetha.' 'Announce, in the letter and in the spirit, the celibate life which is wholly pure and completely fulfilled.'

necessity of the Sangha itself. In this view, my explanation from present-day Ceylon (and by extension, from present-day Burma) would apply only to the colonial and post-colonial periods, when government either was not interested in the Sangha, or did not have the power to influence it. I will deal with this at the end of the paper.

My thesis is as follows. There is, on the one hand, a Sangha of peasant clergy, which I call the village Sangha, whose duties are chiefly pastoral, and whose values and social organization stem from their involvement with the laity. On the other hand, some monks comprise a reform Sangha, whose values and organization are oriented toward communal life and meditation. This distinction is recognized in later Pali literature — the commentaries and the Sinhalese chronicles —, which reflects a Buddhism already well-entrenched as the national religion of Ceylon. These sources distinguish between village dwelling (*gāmavāsin*) and forest-dwelling (*arraññavāsin*) monks. A similar distinction is made between the duty of scholarship (*ganthadhura*) and the duty of meditation (*vipassanādhura*). This latter distinction, though in intention it cuts across the distinction between village and forest monks, is very often taken to mean roughly the same thing: in this context the duty of scholarship means the duty of teaching and preaching. These are ideal types, of course: a village monk may live a relatively pure and meditative life, while a forest monk may participate intimately in the affairs of his lay supporters.

The basic fact of the Sangha's social organization — this applies to both village and reform monks — is its perpetual division into small units: individual monks, single monasteries, or at most small groups of monks connected by pupillary succession. Three factors provide the logic for this situation. The first is the egalitarian principle enshrined in Buddhist doctrine and particularly in the Vinaya. The Sangha is foremost a brotherhood of equals, so that the principles of hierarchy and obedience which play such a conspicuous part in, for example, Roman Catholic church organization, are limited — and that with reservations — to the personal teacher-pupil relationship. Furthermore, the principle of deference to age which orders life within the Sangha reinforces egalitarianism insofar as it ensures that every monk, as he attains a venerable age, will command respect and obedience. Though monks do form small groups organized through pupillary succession, direct control within this group does not survive the death of the eldest monk.

The second perduring condition of Sangha social organization is the relationship between monks and laymen, which is that of recipient to donor. Monks receive all their material support as gifts from laymen, and indeed they are constrained, by Vinaya rule, to eat only food received directly from the hands of a layman. Where monks are given land to provide their living, it is ideally administered by laymen. (Though here, of course, lies one of the greatest potential abuses of the relationship: that monks will become landlords in their own right.) Laymen in return receive merit. For all that it is impalpable, merit is a spiritual value which is axiomatically prized — one may as well ask why gold is prized.

The third condition, then, arises from the fact that Theravāda flourishes in peasant societies, so that the Sangha is spread evenly across the landscape with its donors. Though monks may ideally be supported by anyone, convenience dictates that they be supported chiefly by those in their local area. This further promotes the monks' mutual independence while it inhibits the growth of hierarchically ordered groups in the Sangha. Consequently the Sangha tends to resemble a professional class — like, say, medical doctors in the United States — rather than a unified monastic order.

These conditions hold, as I say, for both the village and reform Sangha; but it should be clear that, insofar as they create a natural equilibrium toward which the Sangha has tended throughout its history, that equilibrium state is the village Sangha and not the reform Sangha. The monks of the village Sangha, while they seldom act in concert, share values through which they act uniformly in similar situations.

These values stem from their role in the village. There are three features of their role which are important here: they are necessary participants in much of the village ceremonial life; they are, if even on a very small scale, property holders; and they are teachers. As participants in ceremony, much of their time is given to village-wide *pinkama* (Pali *puññakamma*), or merit-making. These include not only calendrical celebrations, such as Vesak and the *Kaṭhina pinkama* at the end of the rainy season retreat (*vas*), but also *ad hoc* celebrations such as ordinations, *salpila* (fairs to raise money for the temple), and *suvisi vivaraṇa* (an all-night dancing ceremony which likewise raises money for the temple). Monks are also called upon to make merit for private individuals. They participate in funerals, chant *pirit* (Pali *paritta* — or protective verses to avert disease or bad fortune), or preach. Indeed, any meal offered to the monks can be an occasion for some more or less lengthy preaching or chanting.

As property holders monks are responsible for the various buildings of the temple, which are commonly the largest and best-kept buildings in the village. This involves them in fund-raising activities — such as the fairs I have already mentioned — as well as planning and organizing for repairs and improvements. Furthermore, there may be lands attached to the temple for its maintenance, and the monks sometimes administer these.

Finally, monks are the repositories of culture and therefore traditionally the village schoolmasters.

These are the demands, then, which inform the village Sangha proper. First, their Buddhist learning, rather than being turned to the purpose of self-cultivation, is put to use for ceremony and teaching. Their close contact with the villagers — and indeed they are usually sons of the village — means that their values are in and of the village. Furthermore, insofar as they are property holders, they share the proprietary interests and values of fellow-villagers. In the perspective of Buddhist asceticism these are the values of the householder's estate, rather than those of homelessness — or, as we might put it in a more familiar idiom, these are the values of the marketplace. Though the monks' special status is founded on their moral purity — especially celibacy — and though they might remain morally pure relative to their fellow villagers, relative to the very detailed monastic code they fail on many counts. What is important here is not the actual behaviour of the village monks — which is anyway quite varied — but its contrast with monastic ideals, or with the actual behaviour of reform monks.

Here I will turn to the life of a modern Sinhalese monk who began as the incumbent of a village temple, but who later left the village and became a leading figure in a nascent reform movement. Through his life I will illustrate the values I have already described, show the social structure which accompanies those values, and then show how his values and role changed when he became a forest-dwelling monk. This material is drawn from the diaries and autobiographical writings of Asmaṇḍala Ratanapāla, and from interviews with his associates. I shall of course emphasize the typical, rather than the idiosyncratic, in his life.

Ratanapāla was born in 1900, and grew up in Asmaṇḍala, a small Kandyan village. He was exceptionally intelligent and pious — a perfect candidate to take the robes — and so was ordained at the age of twelve by the village monk. By his own admission he was himself enthusiastic to be ordained, and his ordination was accompanied by pious satisfaction in both his parents and the village monk. Religious sentiment aside, however, his ordination was desirable for a number of less spiritual reasons. In gaining an able and devoted pupil, the monk was ensuring his own succession to the village temple, and the villagers were likewise assured of continued spiritual care. The village monk was also assured of having someone to look after him in his old age.

Most important, however, is this: in taking Ratanapāla at a tender age, the village monk could impress on him paternal authority, and train him in the duties and, equally vital, the deportment expected of a monk. (As monks and soldiers know, the younger the recruit, the better.) The monastic code, of course, stresses obedience of pupil to teacher, but there the relationship is meant to be transferable to any elder monk, and the pupil is meant to retain his autonomy, which provision is consistent with the notion of training for self-reliance. It is true that Sinhalese monks, in keeping with this canonical assumption, do not usually differentiate in speech between their original teacher — in this case Ratanapāla's village monk — and the others who may have authority over them in their education. Nevertheless the original teacher — Sinh. *mulguruvarayā* — stands *in loco parentis* toward the novice, and retains this authority — as is characteristic of parents in the rest of Sinhalese society — until death. Hence, whenever the novicc goes somewhere else for training, he is entrusted (*bāra dīla*) by his own teacher to the other, temporary, teacher.

While Ratanpāla was still a novice, in his teens, his teacher died. Ratanpāla became the responsibility of a brother-monk (Sinh. *sahōdara hāmuduruvō*), of his first teacher, that is, a monk who shared the same teacher. He went to live at that monk's nearby temple, and it is clear that his new teacher fully replaced his old in the parental relationship. The fate of Ratanapāla's village temple is instructive: it passed into the trusteeship of the new teacher, but was essentially held for Ratanapāla. The traditional principle of inheritance here mirrors that of Sinhalese lay society: property passes from father to son, but may be held in trusteeship by the father's brothers until the son reaches majority.

At the age of twenty, Ratanapāla received his higher ordination in Kandy. He then spent most of the next ten years at seminary (Sinh. *pirivena*) in Colombo. Whatever other reasons there might have been for this, the most salient is that a certain venerable age is required in monks. In fact the ten years at education that Ratanapāla spent after his higher ordination correspond to the period of dependence on a teacher (Pali *nissaya*) required by the monastic code.

When he reached thirty, in 1930, Ratanapāla returned to take over his village temple. In what followed he showed particular energy and initiative. He had his work cut out for him: the temple buildings were decaying, the villagers had no strong connections with the temple, and there was no school. He set to work, preaching, organizing committees, and rebuilding his temple. Within a few months he had preached twenty five public sermons. Early in 1931 he organized a *suvisi vivaraṇa* ceremony to raise money for the temple. In September 1931 he founded a Sunday school for the children of the village, and a society to run it. In March 1932 he founded another Sunday school in a nearby village. Meanwhile the monk's dwelling (Sinh. *āvāsa*) was repaired, and in November 1933 work on a new image house (Sinh. *vihāragē*) was begun. He also started another temple in the adjoining village, Wattegedara. Throughout this period, too, he took such an active interest in the ongoing repair of the great pilgrimage centres of Ceylon that he gathered money for them and led his villagers on pilgrimages.

This is uncharacteristically active for the upcountry Sangha, and would have counted as remarkably resourceful even among conscientious Low Country Sangha. At the same time it does not take note of the daily activities (such as attending funerals and chanting *pirit*) which formed the more typical substance of Ratanapāla's duties. Most significant for my argument, however, is the autonomous responsibility the monk takes in initiating action to further the religious and educational life of the village. By virtue of his education and his position of moral authority, the monk is a leader in village affairs. In this respect we can group village monks together with ayurvedic doctors and local headmen as an indigenous élite: an élite to which S.W.R.D. Bandaranaike turned so successfully for political support in 1956.

The circumstances which create the equilibrium of the village Sangha should now be clear. However, for all that the village Sangha is, so to speak, a natural and inevitable growth in a Buddhist country, so too is the reform Sangha. The fundamental claim of the monk to his position is based on his moral purity, his renunciation of the world. Though the actual practice of moral purity is very often effaced by the demands or privileges of village life, the ideal of asceticism is nevertheless perennially alive: in the ceremonies of ordination; in the sermons of the monks; and in the folklore — Jātaka tales, poetry, and temple art — of the countryside. Every Buddhist has a firm (though perhaps unclear) image of the proper behaviour of a monk, and is more than willing to discuss the shortcomings of any particular monk of his acquaintance. Furthermore the notion of moral purity for monks is founded on a more extensive idea of morality (propagated by the monks themselves) which identifies sensual indulgence as being evil. Here the adjective 'evil', which may seem to smack too much of Christian ethnocentrism, has a very good Sinhalese translation: *pāpa*, and similarly Sinhalese has a very accurate translation of the English noun 'sin': *pau*. We need not assume, of course, that Sinhalese Buddhists are any better than English Christians. Nevertheless, the idea of moral purity is imbibed with one's mother's milk in Ceylon, and can be enlisted to justify reform as a natural and necessary step.

Here I will return to Ratanapāla. From 1930 to 1938, Ratanapāla poured his energies into the village. In 1938 he renounced the village and his temple completely, and went to the forest to meditate. The reasons for this step are as characteristic of his personality as his activity in the village, but they exemplify at the same time the basic nature of Theravāda reform. In his diaries Ratanapāla reveals that, from adolescence, he had been involved in some sort of sexual activity. Reading between the lines — which we must do because of the rigorous propriety of his clerical style — we are forced to conclude that this was nothing worse than masturbation and mild homosexuality (by our jaded standards). There is nothing to indicate that homosexuality was very widespread in the Sangha of his youth, but Ratanapāla does emphasize that, when he received his higher ordination, he was taught only to avoid the most grievous transgressions, such as sexual intercourse proper. This reveals the tendency among the village Sangha to educate monks for their ceremonial role, rather than for a thorough observance of the monastic life.

Ratanapāla was not, of course, oblivious to the significance of his habits, but the discrepancy between this supposed monastic purity and his actual behaviour might have done little more than make him uncomfortable for the rest of his life, had he not developed a chronic infection which plagued him for years, and finally left him deaf. Ratanapāla attributed this illness directly to his moral turpitude, an attribution which expresses a very strong strand in Sinhalese medical thinking. Underlying his dilemma was his very real vocation to monastic life — he had, after all, been trained as a monk since his childhood, and could not very well conceive an alternative.

The infection, and with it Ratanapāla's spiritual crisis, flourished during his days at seminary in Colombo. Here he learned the rules of discipline (*Vinaya*), and in particular he learned that he could attain purity (Pali *parisuddhi*) from his faults by confessing them before an assembly of twenty monks, after which he would be rusticated, and then reaccepted into full communion by a similar assembly (*the sanghādisesa* ceremony). At the time, however, this remained merely a piece of scholastic knowledge, for the ceremony was not then in use. Nevertheless, at seminary he imbibed the ascetic principles of the Sangha, and when he took over his village temple he began to put many of them into practice — he began eating out of his monk's bowl, for example, and he gave up using money. It was not until his ear infection began, though, that he was driven to his final crisis. In the midst of his busy life as a village monk, he turned more and more to reading the scriptures and, as he went deaf, he began meditating. He did not, however, attain purity from his transgressions until a former teacher came to him and offered to resurrect the requisite ceremony. (This must have presented considerable problems, since it had to be resurrected almost totally from texts.)

The purification was duly undertaken, and was completed by

the end of 1935. During the next two years Ratanapāla's relations with his fellow monks of the area gradually worsened. Unfortunately I do not have a very detailed account of this process, but, insofar as it seems to have resembled similar events elswhere, the argument must have arisen when Ratanapāla's newly founded claims to the legitimacy of moral purity became an implicit — or explicit — criticism of the other monks' legitimacy. Neither Ratanapāla nor any of the other reform monks in latter Sinhalese Sangha history seem to have kept their opinions to themselves. On the other side, the village monks seem to have been sufficiently threatened by the example of preaching or asceticism to have reacted with some vehemence. In December 1937, Ratanapāla went to hospital in Colombo, and when he returned home a month later, he discovered that malicious gossip by his erstwhile colleagues had ruined his support in the village. He therefore decided to go to the forest in the company of a like-minded monk. In July 1938, Ratanapāla renounced his temple and the two of them went — with elaborate support from a rich layman — to the jungle fastnesses of the Dry Zone.

The basic requirements of Ratanapāla's new life, as a monk of the reform Sangha, were relative isolation for meditation, and moral purity. In fact isolation (Pali *viveka*) is a prerequisite of both, since the peace of forest life, withdrawn from the marketplace (or the world, Pali *loka*; or the householder's life, Sinh *gṛhastha jīvitaya*) implies both physical isolation in the jungle and moral isolation from temptation. Implicit in this isolation is a social organization among reform monks, and a relationship with laymen, which are rather different from those that characterize the village Sangha. These forms are already well laid down in the canon and commentaries.

After Ratanapāla went to the forest, he left off all intercourse with his former colleagues, and established relations with a small group of fellow monks who were interested in re-establishing the forest life in Ceylon — though their interest tended to be rather more in reviving a glorious historical past than in escaping the suffering of the world. These monks identified themselves, quite properly by canonical precedent, as a community of moral purity. They revived the ceremony by which Ratanapāla purified himself, and it became a sort of initiation into the forest life. Similarly they revived and practised assiduously the fortnightly gathering (*Pali uposatha*) to recite the monastic code (Pali *Pāṭimokkha*). In the case of such meetings, moral purity is a prerequisite for participation, so their new life presupposed that purity, and set them off from the village Sangha from which they had all come. Furthermore their spirit of common enterprise in the forest life — a spirit copiously recommended in the canon — at first drew them together in fact as well as in ideal, though their necessary dispersal throughout the island was a serious obstacle to fellowship. This dispersal, of course, is conditioned by the circumstances of their support, as I have already indicated for the village Sangha.

Furthermore, since the forest monks renounced all property, the management of their hermitages had to devolve into the hands of lay managers while ownership was invested in that legal fiction, the Sangha (of the four quarters: Pali *Catuddisa Sangha*). Within the reform Sangha this tends to break down the network of father-son relationships which prevail in the village Sangha due to its concern with succession and property. Relationships between monks approximate more closely to the ideal of the Vinaya texts, wherein monks without attachment to property may choose to live anywhere, and young monks may live with whichever teacher is appropriate. In practice, among the reform Sangha this means that paternal authority is dispersed, that monks transfer easily between hermitages, and that the elder in charge of a hermitage may change at will.

The readjustment of relationships between monks and laymen is manifest in Ratanapāla's later career. After he had spent three months in the deep jungle, and another three months at a new hermitage in the south of Ceylon, a group of laymen from his home area wrote to him to tell him that they had found some unoccupied caves on a hill a few miles from the village, and they invited him to stay there. He and his companion duly moved in, and for the rest of his life Ratanapāla made that his headquarters. In 1939 the two monks, and their lay helpers, had to live in one small cave; at present there are ät least twelve individual houses for monks, as well as two Bo tree shrines, two preaching halls, a library, and sundry other installations crowded on top of the hill. In this development, however, it was not Ratanapāla who took the initiative, any more than it was he who took the initiative in moving there. Though he continued to preach

— I suppose that much of his success depended on his persuasive presentation of the values of asceticism — he left management to laymen. This, too, is provided for in scripture or at least in the commentaries, which apply to the Sangha in Ceylon. Groups of laymen came from miles around to offer support to the monks. and build buildings for them. The monks, on the other hand, were able to devote themselves to scholarship and meditation. This altered relationship between monks and laymen is expressed by the gate which appears at many hermitages, and the visiting hours conspicuously posted thereon, which contrast significantly with the more informal access available to villagers in their village temple. This very separation creates the aura of holiness which makes villagers so eager to support hermitage monks.

As holy as he was felt to be by his lay supporters, however, Ratanapāla was never reconciled to the monks of the surrounding area. In 1948 he outraged them by ordaining as novices two members of a low caste group; the same year he published a pamphlet inveighing against caste divisions in the Sangha. Consequently they refused to allow him to ordain his pupils — this control over ordination is a vestige of the feudal Sinhalese Sangha — and when the registration of monks began to be discussed in government, they further let it be known that they would not allow him to be registered with the Siyam Nikāya.

This forced Ratanapāla to re-align his allegiances once more. He had grown dissatisfied with his original association of forest-dwellers. In the first place, they had not been able to free themselves from the control of the feudal monks of the Siyam Nikāya in the crucial matter of ordinations (and in fact they were not to do so until 1968). More importantly he felt that they were not sufficiently strict. The lack of rigour among them stemmed not so much from their lack of personal self-discipline, however, as from their tendency to slide back to the state of village monk. The criticisms levelled at them, which have been borne out by later events, were, first, that they were too concerned for their buildings; and second, that they spent too much time out among laymen, chanting *pirit*, attending funerals, and generally acting not as forest-dwellers, but as village monks.

In 1952 Ratanapāla therefore joined fores with Kaḍavädduvē Jinavaṃsa, a monk of the Rāmañña Nikaya who could ordain Ratanapāla's pupils in that Nikāya. Jinavaṃsa had begun a reform movement in 1948 and had shown himself then, and subsequently, to be very sensitive to the tendency of reform groups to return to the state of the village Sangha. Ratanapāla's association with Jinavaṃsa proved very successful, and after Ratanapāla died in 1955 his pupils continued to flourish among Jinavaṃsa's group.

Jinavaṃsa's genius for guiding his movement along the narrow path between self-destructive asceticism and worldly involvement is evinced by his first major act after deciding to undertake a reform: he began preaching up and down the country in order to re-educate laymen to the less active role they must expect of reform monks. Indeed, to this day he continues to inform his lay supporters of the mass of monastic rules which are designed to free monks from material concerns. He is adamant that, for many of their ceremonial concerns, laymen should go to their village monks. By the same token he forbids his own disciples to chant all-night *piṛit*, or to get involved in village affairs. Furthermore, he refuses to allow his pupils to attend seminaries frequented by village monks, on the clear and sound principle that they would be distracted by the (relative) worldliness of such an environment. Nevertheless, neither Jinavaṃsa nor his colleagues are very sanguine about the fate of their movement: though they have expressed the hope that their pupils will be able to proceed a little further along the path to Nibbāna, they realize that many of their hermitages will eventually disappear, or become village temples. As they well know, the same fate befell an earlier forest-dwelling group in the Rāmañña Nikāya in the late nineteenth century.

I have assumed so far that this movement of reform and decay is solely the concern of the Sangha, rather than of civil government. Michael Mendelson and S.J. Tambiah (Mendelson 1975, Tambiah 1976) have argued, mostly implicitly, that the Sangha reforms of ancient Ceylon, as well as of later Burma and Thailand, were affairs of religious polity, emanating from the kings in their capacity as protectors of the religion. In this view the conditions of colonial and post-colonial Ceylon (and Burma as well) were idiosyncratically favourable to the development of pluralistic reform movements, since government did not interest itself in reform, or was unable to take an effective part. I do not disagree with this, and I think it is even clear that some of the reforms were purely political window-dressing, a form of self-legitimization by insecure kings. Nevertheless I would argue that the conditions underlying Sangha life, which produce the dynamic of decay and reform, are both logically and temporally prior to the role of the king as reformer. The need and inspiration for reform springs from within the Sangha itself, and the king merely exerts his power to weigh, more or less decisively, on the side of one party or the other. Hence what I visualize as a natural and organic movement within the Sangha is distorted and amplified by the intervention of civil power. Only the most powerful kings — such as Parakkramabāhu I of Ceylon, or Dhammaceti of Burma — were able to carry out thorough reforms. On the other hand, many kings have either quashed reform movements on the advice of entrenched monastic interests or have created conditions, such as large gifts of land to the Sangha, which encouraged its decay.

I shall briefly illustrate the role of the king in reform through the career of Väliviṭa Saraṇaṃkara. I shall take his life as read, though I know of no complete biography in English.* Saraṇaṃkara was responsible for reviving Buddhism in Ceylon when it has reached perhaps its lowest point in history: he restored Pali learning and brought the higher ordination from Thailand, and was thus the founder of the largest group of pupillary succession in Ceylon today, the Siyam Nikāya.

Born in 1698, Saraṇaṃkara early showed a predilection for asceticism and monastic life, and at the age of sixteen became a novice. In fact, since there were no fully ordained monks among the land-owning clergy of the time, he had no prospect but to remain a novice all his life. He pursued the study of Pali, sitting at the feet of perhaps the only Pali teacher in Ceylon at that time. He also undertook a thoroughly ascetic life, living in a cave and subsisting on alms. A small group of fellow-ascetics gathered around him, and they came to be called the *silvat samāgama* — the 'disciplined fraternity'. Though they were not fully ordained

*The most complete account I know of is in Kitsiri Malagoda's excellent book, *Buddhism in Sinhalese Society*, 1750-1900, University of California Press, 1976. I depend on Kotagama Vācissara, *Saraṇaṃkara Sangharāja Samaya*, Y. Don Edwin Samāgama, Colombo, 1960. This is also available in substantially the same form as Vācissara's doctoral thesis at the University of London: K. Wāchissara, 'Välivita Saraṇamkara and the Revival of Buddhism in Ceylon', London, 1961.

monks, they instituted among themselves the practice of the fortnightly confession and recital of the Vinaya. They enjoyed very enthusiastic support among the people — who are said to have vied with one another to pluck a piece of palm leaf from the roof of the palanquin in which Saraṇaṃkara was carried. Significantly, Saraṇaṃkara withdrew his respect from the feudal land-owning monks of his day. He once went to worship at a *stupa* attached to a temple, but refused to visit the incumbent on the grounds that that dignitary was no proper monk at all.

This did not sit well with the religious establishment. Saraṇaṃkara's first encounter with the royal power was the fruit of this antagonism. On the advice of the chief monks — who were also high officers of government — King Narendrasiṃha (1707-39), banished Saraṇaṃkara and his fellows to the wilds of Laggala, and forced them to wear a white cloth around their heads, which indicated that they were not true monks at all. This would have been the end of Saraṇaṃkara had the king not relented later — he was a peculiarly capricious monarch — and restored Saraṇaṃkara's freedom. Here I should note that, under the equally capricious but stronger King Bodawpaya of nineteenth century Burma, Saraṇaṃkara might well have been executed.

Saraṇaṃkara prospered thereafter: he was tutor to the next king, Śrī Vijaya Rājasiṃha (1739-47), and Rājasiṃha for his part sent two missions to Siam to bring back fully ordained monks to re-establish the higher ordination. These failed (the first because of shipwreck, the second because of the death of the Sinhalese king), but under the next king, Kīrti Śrī Rājasiṃha (1747-82), monks were finally brought from Siam. In 1753 Saraṇaṃkara and a large number of other monks, from both the landed religious establishment and from the *silvat samāgama*, received their higher ordination, and therewith the Sangha proper was re-established in Ceylon. This was the high point of Saraṇaṃkara's career. It was not, however, the decisive moment of Sangha reform it could have been. The fifteenth century Burmese monarch Dhammaceti, for example, had brought a new ordination tradition from Ceylon, and had therewith set under way massive reforms of the Sangha. In eighteenth century Ceylon, nothing of the sort happened. Though Saraṇaṃkara was appointed *Sangharāja*, or chief of the Sangha, he had very little real power. Thereafter the traditional two parties among the landed religious establishment, Malwatte and Asgiri, fell to squabbling among themselves, but managed to pin the blame for the affray onto the *silvat samāgama*. The king's final act in the struggle between reform and reaction was to outlaw the *silvat samāgama*, the monks of which had to adhere to one or the other of the traditional parties. In the end reform was quashed by the very king who had fostered it.

That the king's actions were not more decisive is attributable to two factors. First, though they had to act as Buddhist monarchs, the Kandyan kings of the time were a Hindu dynasty from India, and therefore had little personal conviction in the matter. Second, they were weak, and therefore had to play off one faction against the other — in this case, the supporters of Saraṇaṃkara against the old religious establishment — without letting either gain too much power. Hence, for example, Kīrti Śrī Rājasiṃha was forced to deal carefully with a conspiracy (presumably against the outrage of a non-Buddhist ruler) in which Saraṇaṃkara seems to have taken a part. He executed the lay ring-leaders, but soon restored Saraṇaṃkara to his position. Nevertheless, however much religious reform became the concern of the crown, or politics the concern of the Sangha, the dynamic of reform and decay itself sprang from within the Sangha as a natural consequence of its own mission and its place in a Buddhist society.

BIBLIOGRAPHY

1. *Majjhima Nikāya*, vol.1, ed. V. Trenckner, Pali Text Society, London, 1888.
2 Malalgoda, Kitsiri, *Buddhism in Sinhalese Society, 1750-1900*, University of California Press, Berkeley, 1976.
3 Mendelson, E. Michael, *Sangha and State in Burma*, Cornell University Press, Ithaca and London, 1975.
4 Tambiah, S. J., *World Conqueror and World Renouncer*, Cambridge University Press, Cambridge, 1976.
5 *Vinaya Pitakam*, vol.1, ed. H. Oldenberg, Williams and Norgate, Edinburgh, 1879.
6 Wachissara, Koṭagama, 'Välivița Saraṇaṃkara and the Revival of Buddhism in Ceylon', Doctoral Dissertation, University of London, 1961.

Language and Cultural Identity in Pakistan Panjab

C. SHACKLE
School of Oriental and African Studies, University of London.

The political implications of the extraordinary linguistic diversity of the subcontinent have been so obvious, especially in the decades immediately before and after independence, that it is hardly surprising that their analysis should have come to occupy the attention of a considerable number of social scientists. Nor, since most of the latter have been political scientists, is it remarkable that the chief focus of their attention should have been the language movements of India in the narrower sense. For it is in India, with its relative openness to political changes, that language movements have had the most striking political effects, the most notable of these being the formation of the linguistic states.

As in other fields also, however, this concentration has its dangers, for it can be too readily assumed that statements properly applicable to India are equally valid for all parts of South Asia. In fact, with the ever-lengthening separate evolution of the different countries since 1947, the *a priori* likelihood of such assumptions becomes progressively less. One purpose of the present article[1] is, therefore, simply to present a description of some aspects of language movements in Pakistan, since these have attracted so much less attention than those in India, or even than language conflict in Sri Lanka. The particular background against which these movements have come into being, and whose description forms the first part of the article, may help to show by contrast that some aspects of comparable phenomena in India have been of local, rather than pan-South Asian significance. Such contrasts will, however, for the most part be left implicit here.

The reader's attention should, on the other hand, be drawn at the outset to an explicit contrast of approach with that which has generally been adopted by analysts of the political implications and effects of language movements in South Asia. As a specialist in language and literature,[2] the present writer has sought to compensate for his palpable lack of a social scientist's theoretical rigorousness by concentrating upon the cultural implications of the language movements in Pakistan Panjab to be described in the latter part of the article. For one feature of language movements which really does seem to be universal, in Eastern Europe as much as in South Asia, is that the overtly political stage in their evolution is preceded by what may be called the cultural stage, when they are in the hands of the intellectuals — writers, teachers, journalists, secretaries of literary societies, folklore collectors, and so forth — rather than in those of the professional politicians. The striking political successes of many Indian language movements has caused this earlier stage in their evolution to be for the most part consigned to vernacular literary histories, from which, unsurprisingly, those concerned with the later phases have usually failed to disinter them. Hopefully, therefore, the later description here of language movements observed at first hand in this cultural phase may suggest the need to correct the misleading bias involved by this general disregard of comparable earlier stages in the development of more evolved language movements.

Finally, if indeed further justification for this approach is called for, it may be observed that it is the cultural rather than the political aspects of language movements which are ultimately of the greater significance. For the latter present only the intellectual fascination of analysing their patterns of evolution, while the former, by their opening fresh possiblities for literary creativity, offer — at least potentially — works of art. Even in the narrower context of the community within which language movements operate, it is perhaps in the last analysis the possibilities of fresh cultural identification which the intellectuals open that are to be seen as more significant than the jobs which, if the movements attain political success, the politicians will be able to apportion on a linguistic basis. Within the present context, certainly, it will be suggested that while the language movements in Pakistan Panjab certainly possess political implications, their main present interest, and perhaps ultimate significance, lies rather in their attempts to develop the sorts of local cultural identity that were so overshadowed in the peculiar circumstances of Pakistan's creation as the political expression of a subcontinental religious identity.

* * *

It is, however, impossible to understand the reasons for the emergence of the language movements in Pakistan Panjab without a general grasp of the rather complex linguistic history of the Panjab from the beginnings of Panjabi literature (in the sixteenth century) until 1947. The historical pattern has been fundamentally similar to that found in most other parts of the Indo-Gangetic plains, being marked by a more or less sharp distinction between the spoken languages, 'on the ground' as it were, and the written languages in use for different purposes, which may be only remotely, or not at all related to the spoken varieties.[3]

The most important category among the spoken languages is that of the 'regional standards'. Based on the speech of urban centres, whether they be centres of administration, commerce, or pilgrimage, these transcend the limitations of the endlessly graduated local dialects, and thus facilitate the needs of wider social intercourse. The spoken regional standards can be regarded on the one hand as clusters of local dialectal features, on the other as themselves 'dialects' of a single language — although at this point speakers and philologists may differ as to which language they should be assigned to. Thus in Grierson's *Linguistic Survey of India*, which remains the classic catalogue,[4] the regional standards of most of the eastern and central areas of the undivided Panjab of British India are assigned to the 'Panjabi' language, while those of the western areas are separately classed as varieties of 'Lahndā', a coinage of Grierson's from the Panjabi word for 'west'. This distinction has not, however, been universally accepted, and even Grierson was forced to invent an intermediate group labelled 'Panjabi merging into Lahndā'.

Nor is this the only complication, for the distribution of spoken linguistic varieties in the Panjab has undergone two massive displacements in the last hundred years. The first resulted from the opening of much previously barren land to cultivation when the vast extension of irrigation by canal-building was initiated towards the end of the last century, and the consequent emigration from the relatively densely populated eastern and central Panjab to the new Canal Colonies in the west: and the second from the almost total transfer of population between India and Pakistan on a communal basis in 1947. So far as Pakistan Panjab is concerned, the net effect has been that a large proportion of the population in the west of the province (historically, the so-called 'Lahndā' area) are speakers of eastern or central dialects; this proportion may be as high as fifty per cent over quite large areas. As will later be shown, this fact has led to a rivalry of language movements in the area to-day.

Historically, however, the differences between different sets of regional standards were obscured by their traditionally restricted use in writing, either for the keeping of simple commercial records, or for a quite limited number of types of literature. For most other kinds of writing, it has not been the regional standards which have been employed in the Indo-Gangetic area, but full-fledged 'standard languages', based on written norms of correctness rather than local speech. Until the mid-nineteenth century it was Persian which functioned as the main standard language of the Panjab, where it was used not only as the medium of administration, but also for courtly literature, most Islamic subjects, and so on. Only after the final conquest of the Sikh kingdom by the British in 1849 was Persian replaced as the dominant standard by Urdu, another non-localized language, based on written norms of correctness. The same description can also, of course, be applied to English, which has historically shared many standard-language functions with Urdu.

Before the British period, the written use of the regional standards was confined to certain types of Muslim and Sikh literature. This Muslim Panjabi literature was designed for a popular audience, and is all in verse, whether this be used for prosaic manuals of Islamic instruction, or at the higher literary level of Sufi mystical hymns (*kāfī*) and extended treatments of the local romantic legends (*kisse*). It is mostly written in a language much closer to Panjabi regional standards than, say, the Sikh scriptures, where 'Hindi' elements are much more prominent; and it is further distinguished by being written in the Persian, not the Gurmukhi script, and by its preference for Persian loans, rather than words of Sanskritic origin. Later Sikh writing (from about 1700 till 1870) in fact diverges even further by being largely composed in Braj, originally the 'regional standard' of Mathura in U.P., not in Panjabi at all.

From about 1870, however, this traditional pattern of different kinds of literature being produced in different kinds of language was radically altered by the increasingly sharp self-identifications on the part of the three religious communities in the Panjab, which ultimately paved the way to partition. There is an excellent account, by Paul Brass,[5] of how the Sikhs came to construct a new standard written Panjabi, based on the central Majhi regional standard of Lahore and Amritsar, and written in the Gurmukhi script, and to look upon this as a major marker of their cultural and religious identity, in conscious distinction from the identification of the Muslims with Urdu, written in Persian script, and of the Hindus with Hindi, written in the Nagari script. Here it is necessary to remark only on the qualitative change involved in this transformation of a restricted regional standard into a fully fledged standard language used for all purposes. It could be added that Brass tends to underplay the extent to which this new Sikh Panjabi was an artefact of the earlier, cultural, stage of the Sikh-Panjabi religio-linguistic movement, which achieved its final political success with the enthronement of Panjabi in the Gurmukhi script as a fully standard language of administration and higher education in Indian Panjab in 1966, after its severance from Haryana.[6]

This subsequent success of Panjabi in India should not be allowed to call into question the dominance of Urdu as the principal standard language of undivided Panjab in the period 1870-1947. Urdu was, on the one hand, the standard language of administration and education, although subordinate to English at the higher levels; and in this role it remained without serious challenge, as it did not in its 'home' province of U.P., where Hindi was an increasingly equal contender. Secondly, for the Muslims of the Panjab, the important place of Urdu in education was powerfully reinforced by its new function as the standard language of Indian Islam, a function which in the later nineteenth century came largely to replace its earlier role as the vehicle of a belated courtly literature derivative from Persian when the social basis of this classical Urdu literature was virtually destroyed by the British annexation of its centres of patronage in the Muslim courts of northern India. Just as it was in the Panjab that Urdu was most securely established as an administrative language, so too did the Muslims of the province come to make an increasingly important contribution to the new type of Urdu literature which played so significant a part in helping to develop an Indian Muslim identity suited to the new circumstances of the community in British India. In this connexion, one need only think of Hālī (1837-1914), born in present-day Haryana and later employed at the Government Book Depot in Lahore, or, later and more especially, of Iqbāl (1876?-1938), born at Sialkot, and the greatest Urdu (and Indo-Persian) poet of this century. A very high proportion of the important Urdu writers of the later generations also are Panjabi Muslims, including those associated with the Progressive Writers' Association who have made such a major contribution to Urdu literature since the 1930's. It was during the period before 1947, then, that Urdu came to be very firmly established in the hearts, as well as the minds of educated Panjabi Muslims.

* * *

In the period since 1947, too, the identifications of the preceding century have continued to support Urdu in its role as the dominant standard in Pakistan Panjab. A number of immediate effects on and subsequent implications for this role were, however, entailed by the sudden establishment of Pakistan. The most obvious immediate effect stemmed from the expulsion of virtually all the Sikhs and Hindus from the new province during partition, The Panjabi Muslim identification with Urdu was thereby transformed from being a marker of a distinct religious identity within a political system that also embraced other communities, to become a major symbol of the new national identity. While this change enhanced the status of Urdu by giving it a patriotic significance, it was clearly important for the stable maintenance of this enhanced status that all other groups in the newly formed country should equally consider Urdu to be an essential marker of the South Asian Muslim identity around which the new Pakistani identity was being created; or, in other words, that the almost perfect congruence between religious and political identity in Pakistan should be reinforced by a linguistic identity which would involve the common acceptance by all of a national standard language.

In fact, of course, this precondition for stability did not apply. Panjabi Muslims were now part of a political system that included, in place of other Panjabis, other Muslims, with their own provinces and their own languages. To some of these the Panjabi identification with Urdu as the new national standard was unacceptable. The principal reason for this unacceptability, which was of course especially pronounced in the then East Bengal, was a sociolinguistic tradition quite different from the Indo-Gangetic type described for the historic Panjab, but similar to that in many other parts of the subcontinent, where standards based on the local languages had come to be both more highly cultivated and more closely identified with than Panjabi had been by its Muslim speakers. The strength of this tradition, allied to the obvious differences of script, as well as the far greater linguistic divergence from Urdu of Bengali, as compared with Panjabi (especially in its eastern and central varieties), ensured the speedy rejection of attempts to impose Urdu as the single national language, and in 1954 enforced the recognition of Bengali as a national language of equal status with Urdu. All this preceded the later catastrophic history of East Pakistan, where local resentments against the Panjabi leadership which so quickly came to exert control over the whole country, and against the unfortunate Biharis, equally identified with Urdu, of course led to the ultimate formation, with Indian encouragement, of Bangladesh. Seen from a distance, at least, Bangladesh, now the one sovereign state in South Asia seemingly free of the problems entailed by linguistic diversity, would appear to illustrate in text-book fashion the emergence of an independent political identity, first on the basis of religious identity in 1947, and then on the basis of cultural and linguistic identity in 1971.

Developments in West Pakistan after 1947 were, on the other hand, more complex and less clear-cut. This was to be expected from the much more variegated political structure of the western wing, which rather resembled that of India in having the numerically dominant central core of West Panjab, Panjabi-speaking but identified with Urdu, (corresponding to the central bloc of 'Hindi' states) surrounded by other provinces and princely states. While effectively free of the problems of religious diversity that seemed to loom so large in newly independent India, there was, however, an additional complication in Pakistan introduced by the substantial immigration of Muslim refugees from U.P. and the surrounding regions, constituting for the first time a sizeable body of mother-tongue Urdu-speakers, who mostly settled in the cities of Panjab and Sind, especially Karachi. This immigration was certainly initially favourable for the further extension of Urdu in the country, especially as these refugees provided much of the early leadership of the country, although they were quickly joined by the increasingly dominant Panjabis, who of course controlled the army from the outset.

Now the pressures against allowing the development of a 'unity through diversity' on the contemporary Indian model were much stronger in West Pakistan, where the political leadership was not only faced with the difficult task of balancing their half of the country with the numerically dominant east, but was also constrained by the chronic Pakistani fear that any encouragement of diversity might lead ultimately, not to the strengthened unity of Pakistan, but to absorption into the ever-waiting unity of Hindu-dominated India. The opposite policy of total amalgamation was accordingly adopted with the enactment of the One Unit scheme in 1955, by which all former provincial boundaries were abolished in West Pakistan.

An essential part of this scheme was the increased encouragement of the use of Urdu over the whole of the western wing, as the chief marker of a single cultural identity which was ideally to emerge in support of the country's single religious identity. The increased powers of the central government after the military *coup d'état* in 1958 permitted a temporarily effective implementation of this linguistic policy; and the strident official emphasis upon Urdu as the ideal medium for national integration, which was so constant a feature of the cultural policy of the Ayub régime until its final collapse, naturally found a ready welcome among nearly all Panjabis and Urdu-speakers. Quite apart from the fact that the removal of provincial frontiers was naturally to the advantage of the dominant group, the Panjabis had the satisfaction of seeing the rest of West Pakistan brought into line with their own ideals of linguistic and cultural identity. To the Urdu-speaking refugees (*muhājirīn*), too, lacking a secure provincial base in their country of adoption, this policy was naturally congenial, since it maintained the superior status of a language which they alone spoke as a mother-tongue, saving them from the need to place themselves at a disadvantage by having to operate in a despised provincial language: equally importantly, the policy maintained the supremacy of that universalist tradition in South Asian Islam of which the *muhājirīn* saw themselves as the chief standard-bearers, and for whose safeguarding they saw Pakistan as having been established.

But the advantages to these two groups were naturally evident to those in other parts of the country who did not share them, or were actively disadvantaged by the official linguistic policy. These resentments eventually helped to result in the overthrow of its administrative framework, when in 1970, after the fall of Ayub, his successor Yahya Khan announced the abolition of One Unit, and the restoration of the former provinces. While leaving aside developments in the 'tribal' provinces of Baluchistan and the N.W.F.P., it will be relevant at this point to discuss briefly those in Sind, the province second in importance after Panjab.[7]

Although geographically most definitely a province of the Indus, there had before 1947 developed in Sind, which was by historical accident separately administered from Bombay, a tradition of linguistic and cultural identity which had some elements in common with the type briefly described above for East Bengal, rather than conforming strictly to the Indo-Gangetic pattern. While there had been in earlier centuries a traditional dichotomy, similar to that described for the Panjab, between the use of Sindhi for a popular Islamic verse literature and that of Persian for most formal purposes, under British rule much greater official and literary use had come to be made of Sindhi than of Panjabi in the Panjab, with a correspondingly more restricted role being available for Urdu. The relative isolation of Sind had encouraged the preservation of a quite cohesive popular culture, and the differences, both of language and script,[8] had encouraged the awareness of a separate linguistic and cultural identity. The changes brought about by the incorporation of Sind into Pakistan were such as to heighten this awareness considerably. In the first place, the replacement of the expelled Sindhi Hindu community by large numbers of obstinately non-assimilating Urdu-speaking *muhājirīn* could not but serve to make the Sindhis more aware of their separate identity, a consciousness which was further exacerbated by the Panjabi-supported encouragement of Urdu during the One Unit period. Even when this official encouragement of Urdu was most forcefully implemented, in the early years before the Ayub régime's progressive loss of morale, it cannot be said that it produced any very positive results, either in strengthening the political identity of Pakistan, or in developing a corresponding cultural identity; in fact, it would seem in retrospect that precisely the contrary purpose was achieved, that is, the development of consciously formulated provincial identities. This was especially true in Sind, where the immediate tensions with the *muhājirīn*, which received violent expression in the Sindhi-Urdu language riots of 1972, and the newly favoured position of the Sindhis in a country ruled by a Sindhi premier have combined to develop a strongly defined local identity. This has as its base the quite well-preserved popular culture,[9] the Sindhi language in its distinctive script as its primary marker, and as its major symbol the mystical poetry of the 'national' Sindhi saint, Shāh Abdul Latīf of Bhit (1689-1752). In many respects, therefore, the situation in Sind has come to resemble that found in many Indian states, where the provincial framework fosters a sub-national cultural identity through the local language. The presence of the Urdu-speaking minority suggests that the closest parallel is perhaps with Indian Panjab between 1947 and 1966, although it remains to be seen if the fate of the Urdu-speakers will follow that of the urban Panjabi Hindus, the chief losers in the division between Panjab and Haryana.

* * *

For the historical reasons which have been discussed in the earlier part of this paper, it will certainly take much longer to see if the patterns of language identity which have evolved in Indian Panjab will in any way be followed across the frontier in Pakistan Panjab. It is, however, to recent challenges to the long-established patterns in this, the core province of Pakistan, that I now turn, for developments in India do at least show that the traditional situation of the subordination of regional languages to a supra-local standard is not necessarily a stable one in the changed circumstances of the post-imperial era. From this point on I shall be drawing largely on personal observations made while living in the cities of the Panjab; for, just as it is the intellectual class who can be expected to provide the initial challenge to any established pattern of cultural identity, so it is their home, the cities, with their concentration of powerful institutions, where language patterns for the country as a whole are determined.

This is above all true of Lahore, always the provincial capital, and formerly that of West Pakistan during the One Unit period. When I first lived in Lahore in 1967-8, I was greatly struck by the complex patterns of language and identity which prevailed in the city.[10] English, Urdu, and Panjabi were, and are, all widely used, but in different contexts, forming a rough hierarchy. Thus, while Panjabi is virtually the only language of the masses, the middle class adds to this an active command of Urdu and at least a passive command of English, and the élite an active command of English. While both Urdu and English are prestige languages, their prestige derives from different identifications; for English is not only the language of higher education, administration and business, but also that of world culture, while Urdu, as has been shown, is not only the official language at all levels subordinate to English, but is particularly identified as *the* language of South Asian Islam, and hence of all that is implied by the Pakistani identity. There is, therefore, to some extent a polarity of attraction between English and Urdu; and the continuing identification with English, especially on the part of the élite, has hardly encouraged the vigorous development of an identifiable Urdu-based Pakistani cultural identity.

In contrast to both these prestige languages, Panjabi was generally held in affectionate contempt, and regarded as unsuitable for any formal use. Only in the eyes of a quite small minority of middle class intellectuals was Panjabi seen as deserving an enhanced role. It is true that, even before 1947, there had been a very small amount of writing by Muslims in Panjabi in non-traditional genres, i.e., in forms deriving from Urdu or English verse models; but, generally speaking, with the passing of the vitality of the traditional literary forms, Panjabi was effectively reduced to an oral medium, albeit still the vehicle of a lively popular oral literature. In the field of education, Panjabi was abolished as a university subject after the departure of the Sikhs. While a very small degree of official recognition was given to a few Panjabi activities in the early years of Pakistan,[11] in the succeeding period, the first and most authoritarian phase of Ayub's rule, even the modest amount of cultural activity that was being pursued in Panjabi seems to have been severely frowned upon as inimical to 'national unity': hence literary societies were dissolved, and journals closed down.

From about 1963 onwards, however, this strictness was relaxed, and a revival of activity became possible. By the time that I became involved in the Panjabi literary life of Lahore, some half-dozen literary societies were holding regular meetings in the city, and three literary journals of the familiar 'little magazine' type were appearing. Of course, these figures were extremely modest in comparison with the amount of literary activity being pursued in Urdu; for Lahore could by then claim to be, in many ways, the most important centre in South Asia of Urdu literary activity. It was, and still is, certainly the largest centre of publishing in Urdu. By contrast, only a very few Panjabi books, mostly collections of poetry, were available in publishers' general lists, although there were many crudely produced bazaar editions of Panjabi Muslim classics aimed at the popular market. Nor was there any Panjabi newspaper, and the only regular Panjabi radio programmes were a daily round-up of news and farming tips for the peasant audience, and a propaganda programme, aimed across the frontier, which was compiled in the distinctive Panjabi of the Sikhs. Whether in universities or schools, Panjabi had no officially recognized place, although a private college did run courses leading to the unprestigious qualification of 'Fāzil-e Panjābī'. Only in the film world was a respectable amount of money to be made out of Panjabi, for the Lahore film studios cater for a mass rural audience; indeed, the easy money to be made by churning out film songs has been the ruin of many a promising young Panjabi poet.

This exception apart, the cultural emphasis upon Urdu was so strong as to prompt one to ask why even a minority of intellectuals should voluntarily involve themselves in such an apparently unpromising field as that then constitued by their attempts to develop Panjabi as a literary medium to be taken seriously in Pakistan. In a society where people get so much pleasure out of their Assistant Joint Secretary-ships, or from finding an audience for their poems, the cynical explanation that this was such an easy world to get into, with every new recruit guaranteed a ready welcome, should certainly not be entirely overlooked. Similarly, it was evident that, if Panjabi were ever to be granted a more privileged official status, as everyone involved in these activities believed in some measure it deserved, then many of the activists would stand directly to gain in terms of personal status. This would apply particularly to, say, teachers, if changes in education policy were adopted. Even those not themselves directly involved in creative writing would of course welcome an extension, through official recognition or, better, official financial support, in the activities of the various small literary and cultural organizations which they helped run.

But less superficial issues than these were also raised by the Panjabi activists' questioning of the official equation between Islam, Pakistan and Urdu. For one thing, this identity seemed to an outsider to be so very unsatisfactorily based, with a profoundly negative streak directed against India, and all that India was supposed to stand for. This negativity emerged at one level in the frequent headlines of the pattern 'Nation Must Beware Of Foreign Aggressors!', which are still so constant a feature of the Pakistani press. At a more significant level it could be seen in the profound mistrust of Hindu intentions towards Muslims, and consequent need to keep the ideal Islam of Pakistan uncontaminated by any Hindu associations. One convenient way of preserving this ideal was by the identification with Urdu, which so far as possible turns its back on India in favour of the Islamic world, not only in its Perso-Arabic literary vocabulary, but also in its adherence to Persian-derived literary traditions.[12] Panjabis, however, are not Persians; and the split in cultural identity involved in most Muslim Panjabi-speakers' exclusive identification with Urdu had not been resolved by the emergence of major writers who could perhaps have done as much to heal this split as Iqbāl — posthumously declared to be the spiritual father of Pakistan — had done to widen it with the heady message of his pan-Islamic poetry. For it is literature, especially poetry, which continues to enjoy a mass audience, that dominates the other arts in Pakistan, and it is only through significant literature that any substantial reformulations of cultural identity are to be anticipated.

In fact, as was clearly seen by the more acute Panjabi activists, the removal of non-Muslims from Pakistan Panjab had undermined the previously compelling need to construct a rigidly non-Indian Muslim identity, and there was thus no absolute necessity for the Pakistani Muslim identity to exclude all recognition of local elements within itself. It was no accident that caused the activists to base their attempts to include such a recognition on the submerged and undervalued Muslim Panjabi literature of the past, since the chief characteristic of this literature, especially that important part of it which was of Sufi inspiration, was its mediation of the universal message of Islam through the symbolism of the local folk-culture. There was inevitably, it is true, a certain artificiality about some of the activists' attempts to organize 'cultural events' around the still lively popular celebrations of the festivals of the old saint-poets, or develop a valid modern literary idiom from the folk-based models of older Muslim Panjabi writing; but such attempts did, even so, seem to point hopefully to a possible way out of the apparent impasse of the split cultural identity that could be symbolized on the one hand by pretentious officially-sponsored Urdu 'talk-fests' on the occasion of Iqbal Day, on the other by the cynical commercial exploitation of the mass audience with an unending stream of dreadful Panjabi films.

In 1968 there did not, however, seem much chance of the quick realization of the Panjabi activists' aims, whether these were moderate or extreme, since they accorded so ill not only with official policy, but also with the sentiments of the majority of educated Panjabi opinion, which viewed the traditional language-identity with Urdu as an important part of the maintenance of Pakistani Muslim religious and political identity, particularly when the loyalty of other parts of the country (especially the then East Pakistan) seemed to be called into question by their assertions of local cultural identity.

But when I returned to Lahore in 1974, a major transformation had been effected in the standing of Panjabi, thanks to the unforeseen political changes that had overtaken the country in the interval. This transformation was particularly noticeable in the broadcast media, where radio programmes in Panjabi far surpassed those of six years before in quantity and range of subject, and where the much expanded television service also gave a considerable amount of its time to Panjabi programmes. Most of those working for such programmes were naturally committed activists. The ranks of the activists were also being swelled by the successful establishment in 1971 of Panjabi as an M.A. university subject, for the first time since 1947; and the achievement of this long-cherished ambition of the Panjabi movement had in turn caused a great expansion in the numbers of books being written in and about Panjabi. While there was still no Panjabi newspaper, the language had obviously passed the initial point of being employed in published form only for small collections of poems, and the broadcast programmes seemed to command large audiences.

Some of these changes were the direct products of political decisions, sometimes undertaken for rather unexpected reasons; for instance, the amount of television time allotted to Panjabi was sharply increased when it suddenly became posible to receive Panjabi programmes in Lahore from the new, strategically-sited transmitter over the border in Amritsar. The partial success of the activists' aims which these changes collectively represent is, however, partly to be explained in terms of the much more wide-spread sympathy with which many of these aims have come to be regarded by educated Panjabi opinion at large. Several reasons can be advanced for this more general questioning of the previously accepted pattern of linguistic and cultural identity. These include the disastrous war of 1971, for which the rest of the country largely blamed the ineptitude of the Panjabi general staff; the enforced withdrawal of many Panjabi officials and settlers from other provinces of Pakistan after the abolition of One Unit; and the example of the more developed evolution towards linguistic and cultural autonomy in Sind. All these factors may be assumed to have induced a readiness, hitherto lacking, to entertain the idea that previous patterns could, and perhaps should, be modified.

Such a readiness is, of course, very unevenly distributed among individuals and groups. Divisions of a different kind are naturally also to be found amongst the activists. As is to be expected in a 'movement' which consists not of a highly structured organization — even in the field of political parties such groupings are very much the exception in Pakistan — so much as a loose grouping of different coteries of intellectuals and their patrons and supporters, there is a wide range both of literary allegiance and practice and of long-term objectives of policy among them. It is, however, possible to draw a broad distinction between 'moderates' and 'extremists'. The former, who constitute the larger group, favour rather gentle adaptations of traditional Panjabi verse-genres, alongside the extension of Urdu forms into Panjabi, most notably in their Panjabi *ghazals*, which occupy so large a space in anthologies of Pakistani Panjabi poetry;[13] and in terms of language policy would be for the most part relatively content with the way in which Panjabi has come to be better recognized alongside Urdu, even if still markedly subordinate to it in many fields.

The more extreme group, on the other hand, who are particularly associated with that very dynamic cultural organization, the Majlis Shāh Husain, founded in 1965, were already prepared at the time of my first visit to see Urdu more or less totally replaced by Panjabi; and subsequent developments have only served to strengthen their conviction of the desirability of this change. To this more extreme group, sometimes dubbed 'Panjabi nationalists', the successful Sikh espousal of Panjabi is an inspiration, and they look to closer cultural links with Indian Panjab.[14] While their broad political outlook naturally tends, on the whole, to be 'on the left', in so far as this has any very specific meaning in the context of Pakistani politics, it is in the field of literature that their activities are of greater immediate interest, and perhaps ultimate significance. The work of Najm Husain Sayyid (now in charge of the Panjabi department in the University of the Panjab) and the younger writers associated with him deserves particular mention. This is characterized on the one hand by an exciting power of formal experiment, which extends to the creation of what is virtually a new literary language, based on the central dialects of Pakistan Panjab, as opposed to the hitherto dominant Majhi of Lahore, closer to and more influenced by Urdu, which is still the usual medium of most other Panjabi writing;[15] while on the other hand it attempts a basic reformulation of cultural identity through the creation of fresh historical symbols. For example, in place of the official historical pantheon of Pakistan in which Jinnah and Iqbal are seen as natural successors of the Mughal Emperors, they would place the folk-heroes of the Panjab, such as Dullā Bhaṭṭī, a local chief of the Sandal Bar who opposed the Emperor Akbar.[16] A whole gallery of historical and semi-legendary figures of this type are paraded in the popular poem *Desh Panjāb* ('Land of the Panjab') by the young poet Ahmad Salīm, which begins:

This land of the Panjab's earth
Is Dulla the Bhatti's Bar,
Where Mirza's troth was plighted:
The land of Bhagat Singh,
And the country of the Kharals . . .[17]

It would, nevertheless, be very misleading to suggest that these kinds of reappraisal have yet achieved a large place in educated Panjabi thinking at large. For the present, at least, it would be more realistic to see the changes which have been effected in the status of Panjabi as a cultural medium in Lahore and the surrounding region as representing an emerging consciousness of local cultural identity. But majority Panjabi opinion is still the chief bastion of an outspoken all-Pakistan nationalism, and the total abandonment of its identification with Urdu is not speedily to be expected.

* * *

It is, besides, not as if there were just Panjabi and Urdu in contention with one another in Pakistan Panjab. For there has recently arisen in the south-west of the province another candidate to make its claims to represent a valid local cultural identity, and hence to deserve official recognition. This is Siraiki, whose claims are advanced by an activist movement, principally based in the cities of Multan and Bahawalpur, where I was able to observe something of its operations while carrying out linguistic fieldwork in the region in 1974-5.[18] These observations may, it is hoped, provide some insight into the problems faced by a language movement in the very early stages of trying to foster an awareness of a local cultural identity.

The linguistic status of Siraiki as a set of regional standards differing in many features from those of the central Panjab has been briefly indicated above. The most obvious differences are phonological: Siraiki has the usual Indian voiced aspirates, which are reduced to tones on adjacent vowels in the speech of central Panjab, and also possesses a distinctive set of implosive consonants, which it shares with Sindhi, not Panjabi. So far as the grammar is concerned, the free use of pronominal suffixes with verbs, and the relatively archaic richness of inflexion for both verbs and nouns also serve to align Siraiki rather with Sindhi. But many shared morphological details, as well as overall agreement in much of the vocabulary and syntax, link it quite closely to Panjabi, with which it has a higher degree of mutual intelligibility — in all but the most extreme varieties — than with Sindhi. In broad terms, therefore, Siraiki is to be regarded as occupying an intermediate position between Sindhi and Panjabi, but is in most respects closer to the latter.[19] The ties with Panjabi have been further reinforced, as has already been mentioned, by the major change in the composition of the population which has resulted from substantial immigration from central and eastern Panjab into the Siraiki-speaking area, especially that of the Muslim refugees from India in 1947.

In former times Siraiki was used for the same types of Muslim verse literature as have been described for Panjabi and Sindhi. As in the case of Panjabi proper, this literature was overlaid by the dominant standards, first of Persian, then of Urdu, which became the official language not only in the areas under direct British control, but also in the princely state of Bahawalpur, which formerly constituted a large part of the region. In many respects, therefore, the cultural base from which a Siraiki movement could operate was at least superficially similar to that of the Panjabi movement.

At first sight, many aspects of the operations of the Siraiki activists were immediately familiar after my experience in Lahore; probably these are, indeed, features common to all language-movements at an early stage of development. There was, for instance, the same social grouping in the leadership of teachers, journalists, broadcasters, lawyers and some public officials. They too were on the one hand encouraging the literary efforts of each other, their juniors or their social inferiors, while on the other seeking support for their aims from higher authority, and trying to develop public opinion to back these aims. They too were seeking to draw attention to the not inconsiderable Siraiki literary heritage, whose particular glory is the collection of mystical hymns by the great saint-poet of Bahawalpur, Khwāja Ghulām Farīd (1845-1901),[20] and to build upon the veneration he still commands by organizing special 'cultural events' in his memory with items of wide popular appeal.

On a more routine level, much of their practical activity was, as in Lahore, built around the meetings of literary societies, or embodied in small literary journals. All this activity was, however, on a much more restricted scale even than that described above for Panjabi in Lahore in 1968. Moreover, the obstacles faced by the protagonists of Siraiki are in many ways much more formidable than those which have lain in the path of the Panjabi activists. First, although Multan is much the largest city of the region, with a population of some half-million, it is a city which almost entirely lacks the long-established cultural resources of Lahore. Until 1970 it had no radio station, and many of the programmes are still relayed from Lahore. There is only one Urdu daily newspaper, whose principal edition is anyway prepared in Lahore. There is almost no publishing industry, and most of the physical processes of production of the few Siraiki books have to be carried out in Lahore. Until 1974 there was no university, and that now established is unlikely to rival the long-established prestige of the University of the Panjab in Lahore. Given this scantiness of resources in Multan, it can be imagined that the much smaller centre of Bahawalpur is even worse off.

The difficulties imposed by these physical constraints are compounded by the complexities of the demographic situation. The Siraiki speech-area is certainly very extensive, although it includes many barren areas, but it is neither solid nor cohesive. On the one hand, many Siraiki-speakers do not live in the heartland of the south-western Panjab, but in Sind and in the adjacent parts of Baluchistan and the N-W.F.P. This makes for obvious difficulties of communication, especially where, as in case of Sind, a well-established local cultural identity is already in existence. It also makes attempts to secure official recognition four times more difficult; and, while the grandiose dreams of the extreme activists for a 'Siraiki Suba' would certainly be an ideal guarantee for the Siraiki identity the necessity of taking territory from all four provinces of Pakistan hardly makes them likely of fulfilment.

On the other hand, Panjabi-speakers have now come to form a very significant proportion of the inhabitants of the Siraiki heartland. It is true that the Siraiki movement derives much of its appeal from the resentments of the Siraiki-speakers against the extraordinary success with which these immigrants have taken over and expanded upon the position vacated by the once prosperous and powerful Hindu community of the region; but the demographic and economic balance of power is weighted much more heavily against the Siraiki-speakers than it ever was for the Sindhis vis-à-vis the *muhājirīn* in Sind. Nor, given the historic language patterns of the Panjab, is it easy to oppose an easily understood Siraiki cultural identity to the increasingly well-established Muslim Panjabi cultural identity, which has, so to speak, pre-empted many of the available geographical, historical, literary, and even linguistic symbols to its own use. As a token of this imbalance, it may be pointed out that in both Multan and Bahawalpur there are moderately active Panjabi literary societies linked to the parent orgaizations in Lahore, where the numbers and organization of educated Siraiki-speakers are, by contrast, practically negligible.

Lastly, there is to some extent a division of aim amongst the ranks of Siraiki activists. Differences of moderation and extremism, although certainly present, are less important here than the regional differences between Multan and Bahawalpur. In the latter, formerly the premier Muslim princely state of British Panjab, there exists a quite deeply held consciousness of local identity, which receives political expression in the demand for the restoration of provincial status to Bahawalpur: but such assertions of separate Bahawalpuri identity are themselves in conflict with the aims of activists from other areas, to whom this princely past has no special meaning.

Against these negative factors there can, however, be set the one basic achievement of the activists, that they have given Siraiki its name. The closely related regional standards were in the past called by a variety of such local names as 'Multānī' in Multan, or 'Riyāsatī' in the princely state of Bahawalpur. Only in Sind, where it was probably introduced by immigrants from the north some centuries ago, and where it is still widely spoken bilingually with Sindhi, was it called 'Siraiki'.[21] It was only a little more than a decade ago — just about the time when the Panjabi movement revived in Lahore — that this term came to be adopted in the heartland, where its subsequent successful propagation by the activists has indeed served to strengthen a previously weak sense of a common language-identity among its speakers.

But there has yet to emerge a term which will describe these speakers, who, unlike Panjabis and Sindhis, remain just 'Siraiki-speakers' (like 'Urdu-speakers'). The implied uncertainty of identity is also acutely expressed in the frequently heard local complaint that 'the Panjabis think of us as Sindhis, and the Sindhis regard us as Panjabis'. In the same way, there has yet to evolve a coherent symbolic ideology which will allow a viable cultural identity to develop around the new-found sense of linguistic identity. It is interesting, though, that the attempts which are made in this direction concentrate for the most part on a specifically Islamic symbolism, relying on the substantially Islamic character of the region's past and its historical monuments. Such slogans as 'Siraiki, language of the heart of Pakistan' suggest the possible future development of a local cultural identity which will seek its validation in terms quite close to those of the official ideology of Pakistan, though with a suitable stress on local elements, thus nicely turning the flank of the aggressive ideals of cultural identity put forward by the more extreme Panjabi activists on the basis of a secular historical symbolism in opposition to this official ideology. For the present, this combination of praise of the beloved mother-tongue with an emphasis on its particular associations with Islam is nicely captured in the opening line of a poem entitled *Zabān-e Sirāikī* ('The Siraiki Language'):

Sweet as honey or as sugar,
Like the language of Arabia — Siraiki![22]

Even my own limited experience of the language scene over barely a decade in Pakistan Panjab is sufficient to induce a very marked caution where future prediction is concerned: in the words of the cliche, 'only time will tell'. But I hope to have shown during the course of this article that a clear typology of language movements, even in South Asia, is still very far from being properly established. Even in Pakistan, indeed, I have instanced four types: the emergence of Bangladesh as a nation state, of Sind as a secure provincial base for a distinct local cultural identity, of the Panjabi movement as providing a serious challenge to accepted cultural and lingustic identifications, and of the Siraiki movement as providing a fresh local challenge to this in turn. In a sense, these four can be regarded as being on a continuum of success or of development; and I hope that the more detailed treatment which has been given the last two will have helped justify the stress laid at the beginning of the article upon the importance in understanding any language movement, however successful, of investigating its cultural beginnings. Finally, while I regret that it has not been possible to enter here into a more detailed discussion of literary works, which would have helped underline my opening point about the greater satisfaction to be drawn from studying literature rather than politics, I hope that this article may have served to throw some light on a further episode in the fascinating saga of problems of cultural identity caused by the tensions between the universal and the local in the history of Islam in South Asia.

NOTES

1 A modified and expanded version of a paper first given in November 1976 in the seminar on Language, Religion and Political Identity organized by the Centre for South Asian Studies, S.O.A.S.

2 As Lecturer in Urdu and Panjabi at S.O.A.S.

3 For this distinction, cf. J. Gumperz, 'Some remarks on regional and social language differences' in *Language in Social Groups*, ed. A.S. Dil (Stanford University Press, 1971), pp. 1-11.

4 The relevant volumes of the *LSI* are vol.viii, part I, *Sindhī and Lahndā* (Calcutta, 1919), and vol.ix, part I, *Western Hindī and Panjābī* (Calcutta, 1916).

5 In his *Language, Religion and Politics in North India* (Cambridge University Press, 1974), part IV. The development of the more specifically religious symbols of revivalist Sikhism is well analysed in W.H. Mcleod, *The Evolution of the Sikh Community* (Clarendon Press, 1976), pp. 37-58.

6 It could also be pointed out that many of the Sikh intelligentsia in India tend to deprecate the artificiality of this 'neo-Panjabi', in contrast to the supposedly more vital Panjabi of Pakistan, where the language has received so much less official encouragement.

7 The 1961 Pakistan Census lists the numbers of the speakers of the principal languages in West Pakistan as Panjabi 26.2m.; Sindhi, 5m.; Urdu 3.3m. The 1972 Census, which significantly, does not appear to record languages, gives the population figures for Panjab as 37m. and for Sind as 14m. (constituting 58 per cent and 19.5 per cent of the country's population respectively).

8 Sindhi is much less similar than Panjabi to Urdu. It is written in a much modified form of the Arabic script, different both in style of writing and in principles of formal organization from the Perso-Urdu script which is also used for writing Panjabi in Pakistan. The importance of script as an obvious symbol of separate local cultural identity is thus apparent in Pakistan as well as India, in spite of the common Islamic heritage.

9 The recording of this culture has been eagerly prosecuted by intellectuals and folklorists. The most impressive testimony to this eagerness is to be found

in the extensive collection of folklore materials published under the editorship of Dr. N.B. Baloch as the *Lok adab silsilo* by the officially-backed Sindhi Adabi Board: this series had reached its thirty-third volume by 1975.

10 My impressions of the general situation at the time, and of the Panjabi movement in particular, were published as 'Punjabi in Lahore', *Modern Asian Studies*, 4, 3 (1970), 239-67.

11 Notable among these was the Panjabi Adabi Academy (founded in 1956), devoted to the publication of reasonably critical editions of Panjabi Muslim classics, and works on the Muslim history of the Panjab. It was at one time slightly comparable to the Sindhi Adabi Board mentioned in n.9 above, although always far less influential in scope and support.

12 There is an interesting, if rather disconnected, discussion of this aspect of Urdu in Aziz Ahmad, *Studies in Islamic Culture in the Indian Environment* (Clarendon Press, 1964), chapters X-XI.

13 Typically enough, the best of such anthologies has been produced in India: this is *Dukh daryāon pār de* ('Sorrows from the other bank'), ed. Attar Singh, with a stimulating introduction that is duly cautious about the future of Panjabi vis-à-vis Urdu in Pakistan (Jullundur, 1975).

14 There is, of course, a serious barrier of intelligibility between the Persian and the Gurmukhi scripts, and the latter can be read only by a minority even of the more extreme 'Panjabi nationalists'. The closure of the frontier between India and Pakistan for the decade 1965-75, including a ban on postal traffic, seriously hampered the development of cultural interchange between the two Panjabs.

15 The use of this literary language, based on the 'mid-western' regional standard (i.e., half-way to Siraiki!) is advocated in the interesting pamphlet *Hamlets will hum again* (Lahore, *c.* 1971), which reflects the views and practice of Najm Husain Sayyid. At present, however, this language, whatever its long-term merits as a literary medium decidedly different from Urdu, can be difficult of comprehension even by educated Panjabis, especially in the more exaggerated form represented by the practice of such younger poets as Mushtāq-Sūfī, whose collection *Sāvī dā ḍholā* (Lahore, 1972) is liberally provided with footnotes explaining the rarer words. It is interesting that the work of the leading 'Sindhi nationalists', especially that of Shaikh Ayāz, their senior poet, should reflect a similar obsession with the use of recherché dialect words. Parallels from the work of poets in the minor European languages during their literary renaissance in the nineteenth century would of course be easy to cite.

16 A traditional folk-poem in praise of Dullā Bhaṭṭī is published in *Lok vārān* (Islamabad, 1971), edited by Ahmad Salīm, who has played an important part in collecting the folklore of the Panjab at the National Council of the Arts in Islamabad. The best-known modern re-working of the symbol of Dullā Bhaṭṭī is in Najm Husain Sayyid's poem *Dulle dī vār*, prefixed to his play *Takhat Lahaur* (Majlis Shah Husain, Lahore, n.d.). In Sindhi, too, a similar sort of reversal of the accepted scheme of historical values is to be found, as in the play by Rashīd Bhaṭṭī, '*Āshiq zahar-piyāk* (Sukkur, 1968), which exalts the martyred Sindhi Jewish mystic Sarmad over his persecutor, the Mughal Emperor Aurangzeb, still one of the major figures in the Pakistani pantheon.

17 The poem is included in *Dukh daryāon pār de* (see n.13), pp. 24-5.

18 My impressions are recorded at greater length in 'Siraiki: a language movement in Pakistan', *Modern Asian Studies*, 11, 3 (1977), 379-403.

19 A more detailed account of the linguistic background is given in the introduction to my grammar, *The Siraiki language of central Pakistan* (S.O.A.S., 1976). I have given a general account of the early development of studies of the language during the British period in *From Wuch to Southern Lahnda, A century of Siraiki studies* (to be published by the Research Institute for Siraiki Literature and Culture, Bahawalpur), and have treated some of technical linguistic issues in 'Problems of classification in Pakistan Panjab' (to appear in *Transactions of the Philological Society*).

20 A few of these hymns are considered in my article 'The Pilgrimage and the extension of sacred geography in the poetry of Khwāja Ghulām Farīd' in *Socio-cultural impact of Islam on India*, ed. Attar Singh (Panjab University, Chandigarh, 1976), pp. 159-70: see also my translation of part of a disciple's account of the saint-poet, *The Teachings of Khwaja Farid* (Bazme-Saqafat, Multan, 1978). I have dealt more generally with the Sufi literature in *Styles and themes in the Siraiki mystical poetry of Sind* (Bazme-Saqafat, Multan, 1976); and with the very different tradition of Shiite literature in 'The Multani *marsiya*', *Der Islam*, 55, 2 (1978), pp. 100-128.

21 While various etymologies — both flattering and derogatory — have been advanced, the name is probably derived from the Sindhi word *siro*, meaning 'up-river, north'.

22 The poem, by Dilshād, is included in *Rat dīān hanjūn* ('Tears of blood'), ed. Sādiq Bashīr (Siraiki Adabi Majlis, Bahawalpur, 1967), p. 11. Such eulogies, usually with the refrain (*radīf*) 'Siraiki!', are frequently recurring items in the Siraiki literary magazines.

Caste and Politics: A Survey of Literature

D.L. SHETH
Centre for the Study of Developing Societies, Delhi.

Political sociology in India has not yet acquired the status of an independent social science discipline. It is a joint protectorate of sociologists, social anthropologists, social psychologists and political scientists interested in borderline areas of inquiry in their respective disciplines. Although there is some agreement on the subject matter, broadly conceived as the study of interactions between political processes and the social order, profound differences prevail with respect to the formulation of research problems, methods of inquiry and data-gathering. Occasional cross-stepping between disciplines is not uncommon; but, by and large, studies in the field are distinctly discipline bound.

These studies, although carried out from different disciplinary perspectives, have generated a wealth of empirical data and a variety of significant insights which, if brought together in a unified body of theoretical knowledge, are likely to enrich the field of political sociology.

Literature on the Indian caste system is extensive and includes general ideological discussions as well as specific studies carried out in different social science disciplines. Attempts have earlier been made to review parts of this literature around specific problem areas of sociological research.[1] No systematic account is, however, available of the studies in the area of caste-politics interaction.[2] In the present paper, we shall review studies of

I am thankful to Shyamoli Chakravarti and Dr. Subrato Mitra for bibliographical assistance. Dr. Ghanshyam Shah made available to me his valuable notes and annotations on the subject. This paper was originally prepared for the Indian Council of Social Science Research, and has since been revised. The assistance of the Council is gratefully acknowledged.

caste-politics interaction as constituting a sub-field of political sociology.[3]

Before we take up the review of specific studies, however, it is necessary to examine the ideological and disciplinary contexts of research in this area.

I
Alternative Vantage Points of Research

Discussions and studies of interaction between political processes and the caste system are dominated by controversies about the nature of political and social changes that occur through such an interaction. Surprisingly, despite the growth of numerous empirical studies in the field, these controversies are still couched in terms of the nineteenth century universal theory of social change inspired by the impact of industrialization; it is as if social scientists in India are still fighting the battle of Marx and Weber. Marx believed that the growth of industrialization would lead to the dissolution of the caste system and its progressive replacement by a class system.[4] Weber, on the other hand, argued that the caste system was inimical to the emergence of 'capitalism' and would always stand in the way of the growth of legal-rational norms inherent in the development of a modern polity.[5]

These problem-formulations of nineteenth century western social science were reinforced by the 'reformist' views of Indian intellectual and political élites with western education. The controversies centred around the issue of whether a caste-ridden society was fit for democratic self-government, or whether modern political institutions can perform democratic functions without uprooting the traditional social structure of the caste system. This was first reflected in the late nineteenth century controversy between social reformers who believed in the prior eradication of the social evils of the caste system before political democracy was introduced and the political leaders for whom political independence was a pre-condition for social change. The latter, however, agreed with the former that ultimately, for political democracy to succeed in India, the caste system would have to disappear.[6] Pronouncements of leading intellectual and political leaders during the independence movement and in the post-independence period reflect a continuity of this attitude in the elite strata of

Indian society. Nehru voiced it for all when he declared:

It is sometimes said that the basic idea of caste might remain, but its subsquent harmful development and ramifications should go; that it should not depend on birth but on merit. This approach is irrelevant and merely confuses the issues. . . . In the soical organization of today it [caste] has no place left. If merit is the only criterion and opportunity is thrown open to everybody, then caste loses all its present day distinguishing features and in fact, ends. . . . It [the caste system] was an aristocratic approach based on traditionalism. This outlook has to change completely, for it is wholly opposed to modern conditions and the democratic ideal. . . .[7]

Ambedkar, Lohia and others have expressed even more radical views.[8]

In contradistinction to this outlook there also prevailed a tendency to preserve national self-esteem by defending and at times glorifying the traditional social order as a product of 'Indian genius', and to hold that the indignities of this order pointed out by the radicalists were only aberrations from the original social order, and hence were external to the basic system. This gave rise to nationalistic reinterpretations of traditions by which modernist changes were not considered as discontinuous with what had existed in the traditional social system but rather as continuous in one form or the other.[9]

How social and political conditions of a prior age continue to influence social investigation and theory formulation — the classic problem of the sociology of knowledge — can be pursued as an independent inquiry promising rich dividends. It is sufficient to note here that in the course of India's political development over the last hundred and fifty years, the Indian elites have from time to time experienced extreme feelings of self-denigration and self-esteem, and this has greatly influenced their present ambivalent attitude towards the traditional social order. Indian social scientists, sharing the elite culture of their society, have been subject to this attitude of ambivalence while approaching the problem of caste-politics interaction.[10] This confusion between ideological stances and scientific investigation has given rise to endless, and at times unfruitful, controversies and a plethora of speculative writings far removed from the emerging empirical theory of political and social change.[11] Srinivas showed the social scientists' awareness to this situation when he said:

Most of us — not only our politicians but our intellectuals as well — are bamboozled into agreeing with something merely because we are afraid to be mistaken for being reactionary. . . . In case of caste this disease has proceeded so far that our talk and policy will leave reality far behind.[12]

Research efforts in the area of caste-politics interaction have been greatly influenced by the intellectual environment traced above. Specific formulations, however, have been guided by the researcher's identification with a particular social science discipline. Let us examine, briefly, how formulations on this problem by a sociologist, a social anthropologist and a political scientist differ according to their different disciplinary concerns and preoccupations.

A sociologist concerned with the processes of stability and change in society is drawn to examine the influence of 'political forces' on the system of social stratification. For him political development is one of the independent variables (alongside industrialization, urbanization and modern technology) which influences the traditional social system. In his view, all elements in society are functionally integral, and hence he perceives the relationship between politics and 'social structure' in a dichotomous framework of modernity and tradition. Any change is contemplated as a replacement of traditional, ascriptive stratificatory systems by modern universalistic norms and an achievement-oriented stratificatory system. Of course, in a 'transitional' stage the 'mixes' between the two are conceded but nonetheless the traditional forms of social living are viewed as incongruous with the functioning of modern political institutions. Following the much prevalent 'convergence theory' of social change, a sociologist holds that it is in the logic of development that modern (political) institutions produce, though with different time-lags and with some alterations in the sequential order of development, similar responses in the traditional segments of a society.

A social anthropologist, who feels comfortable to work with an isolable whole of a little community, brings a different perspective to the field of political sociology. For him, political authority, alongside other elements of social structure, is an endogenous variable operating within the social whole (a well-defined and more or less autonomous structural entity). It constitutes one of the *functional elements* of the 'total social structure' which orders the arrangement of roles and determines one's social status in the stratificatory system of the community. By concentrating on endogenous variables he implies a high degree of autonomy for the social structure which absorbs exogenous political (and other) influences through expansion of its roles and functions. Changes in the social structure are indeed recorded, but as the analysis is focussed almost exclusively on the internal changes in the social structure of a microcosmic entity, the discontinuities in this structure as well as the processes of structural integration taking place at a wider level of society through interactions between macro and micro processes are by and large ignored.

A political scientist is drawn to political sociology through his pursuit of exploring different contexts (social, economic and demographic) of political behaviour and to systematize these for a theory of political power. For him 'political development' is a dependent phenomenon which is either facilitated or undermined by a pre-existent system of norms and stratification. He assumes that certain contexts and behaviours are relevant for the functioning of modern political institutions and he further assumes that the norms and structure of a traditional society like India are inconsistent with the values and institutions of political democracy. The prevailing structure of loyalties and allegiances in Indian society is held as preventing the growth of new collective identities which are secular and universalistic in nature. For democratic political institutions to strike roots in Indian society, modern secular institutions like political parties and elections must get adjusted to the demands of the traditional social order rather than the traditional order being transformed. Hence, political behaviour in India is viewed as dominated and determined by the traditional social order characterized, for instance, by the caste system.

On the basis of the same assumption of consistency where the form determines the substance, however, a political scientist may sometimes take a different position. He looks upon Indian tradition as one capable of serving modern functions. In this case the traditional social order is observed as flexible and mutable, performing new roles and functions, and adjusting to the working of modern political institutions. Like a sociologist a political scientist perceives the relationship between political processes and social order as dichotomous, but treats the political process as a dependent variable; and unlike a social anthropologist he views the traditional social structure only as an inevitable milieu *through* and *beyond* which political processes operate. He is less concerned with observing changes in the social structure that may or may not occur through 'politicization'. His primary interest is to examine how different social milieus intervene in the process of generation and distribution of political power. In his analysis of interaction between modern political institutions and traditional society, therefore, a political scientist tends to ignore the social anthropologist's notion of a social structure as a homogenous and autonomous social whole. He rather tends to take the same position as the social psychologist for whom 'social groups' are entities more or less independent of a social structure. For the political scientist these social groups are drawn into the political process as independent units and can forge horizontal and vertical links with other groups for purposes of political mobilization, undermining or disregarding their membership of a specific structure. In the process these groups acquire new characteristics which are essentially 'political'. They provide bases of support and recruitment for a new elite (in defiance of principles informing the prevailing social structure), may divide or align among themselves as necessitated by the exigencies of political parties (again cutting across traditional hierarchical divisions), and thus gradually come to function as 'interest' or 'pressure' groups undermining their social and ritual characteristics. Whether such a politicization of social groups effects discontinuities and disintegration of a traditional social structure or only modifies it in some respects is of no concern for the political scientist. His principal concern is rather with the processes of articulation and mobilization, division and aggregation, of the prevailing constellation of social groups for political ends.

II
Studies of Interaction Between Caste and Politics

It is in the above context of disciplinary perspectives that the substantive issues in the area of caste-politics interaction can be explored for a fruitful aggregation of findings. Accordingly, we can classify the literature in this field into three major categories:

A. Studies focussing on the continuity and extensiveness of the traditional social structure

B. Studies focussing on the differentiation of social structures under the impact of economic and political change

C. Studies focussing on the politicization of castes

A. *The Continuity of Traditional Social Structure*

These studies are not directly concerned with the phenomenon of caste-politics interaction. Their primary concern is to study the social structure of little communities.[13] They conceive traditional social structure as a total entity, which, while responding to exogenous influences, maintains its structural integrity. As part of this general research pursuit, they make important observations about how the caste system is responding to processes of representational politics. In the absence of any explanatory model of analysis, such studies provide a selective documentation of evidence on how caste structures persist and even expand under the impact of adult franchise and political parties.[14]

These writings, no doubt, take note of changes that have occurred in the traditional system of social stratification, but these are not perceived as causing such structural alterations which might lead to discontinuities in, or disintegration of, the traditional caste system. On the contrary, according to these studies the kinds of changes that have taken place only suggest re-affirmation of the basic principles of India's traditional social structure. The new political forms are perceived as responding to the needs of the 'total social structure' of the traditional order rather than as providing any serious challenge to its existence and continuation.[15]

These studies have accumulated a mass of data and have generated some important concepts. What follows is a brief summary of the findings and conceptual thinking reflected in the numerous descriptive essays and specific studies of caste and village social structure.

1. Status mobility is still by and large a group phenomenon, and individuals aspiring to a higher status cannot do so by contracting out of the traditional status system. They can hope to improve their status only as members of a specific caste group; and in their effort to improve their status they have to carry other members of their caste-group along with them.[16]

2. This is so because ritual status is still a predominant cri-

terion of social stratification, and the acquisition of economic and political power by a status group in itself does not assure its rise in the social ladder.[17]

3. A status group aspiring to upward mobility in the system of social stratification tends to emulate the life-style of higher castes and seeks acceptance within the 'great tradition' of Sanskritic norms and the *varna* system.[18] Thus, mobility is the property of a group and it takes place within the confines of the traditional social structure. It is governed by the principles inherent in the caste system. And there are certain limits beyond which even this kind of vertical mobility cannot take place.[19]

4. The social status of a group, however, is not always commensurate with its ritual status. This is revealed in the phenomenon of the dominant caste.[20] In a village community there usually is a dominant caste. Besides its ritual status, its dominance is derived from several factors such as numerical strength, economic and political power, etc.[21] The importance of these factors has lately increased with the introduction of modern political institutions. Adult franchise, for example, has made the numerical strength of a group an important criterion of dominance. Similarly, the expansion of economic frontiers of a village society and the democratic decentralization of political power have undermined the hereditary prerogatives of some status groups to political and administrative offices. Hence, caste-groups with relatively low ritual status have been successful in acquiring a dominant position from previously dominant castes with high ritual status.[22] Despite the exogenous causes of these shifts and variations in the dominant status of a caste, the phenomenon of dominance is essentially a characteristic of the caste system. While a caste group may avail of new opportunities to maintain or increase its dominance, the functions it performs are in respect of the traditional social structure.[23] Besides, in so far as ritual status is a factor determining dominance, the economic and power structures of a village community are not dissociated from its caste structure. It is a well known fact that when a group relatively low in ritual status acquires economic and political dominance, it is likely to try to establish its claim to a higher ritual status also. A few groups at the higher and intermediate levels of the caste hierarchy may succeed in some measure in establishing such a claim. But a group located at the bottom of the hierarchical

system, even if it fulfils all other criteria of dominance, cannot hope to become a dominant caste.[24] Even if it temporarily succeeds in establishing its economic and political power, its dominance cannot be sustained by the system. It is further argued that shifts in the dominant status of caste-groups at higher and intermediate levels of the system, including changes in their ritual status, have occurred throughout the history of the caste system in India, and these have not disrupted the traditional structure of social stratification.[25]

5. In their pursuit of social mobility castes also take on new functions such as the provision of educational and welfare facilities for their members. They participate in political decision making as well, — at least with respect to decisions about electoral support for political parties or candidates. This generates new leadership processes within the caste groups as well as within village communities in which the political role of a leader is emphasized over his traditional role of a patriarch. But he still remains a mediator between his caste or village and the political broker who operates at higher levels of politics, with whom he exchanges votes of his caste or village for whatever political and administrative benefits he can secure for them. Besides this, the proliferation of caste functions has not resulted in structural changes in the caste system. It has only provided castes with new fields of activity and a new lease of life.[26]

6. The expansion of caste functions has another important consequence for the structure of the caste system. For purposes of social mobility, self help and political power, castes seek more viable social organizations. An all-inclusive social structure in a village where caste-groups are bound together in a system of vertical interdependence marked by a patron-client relationship no longer provides an adequate basis for castes to perform these new functions. This has forced caste-groups to forge horizontal ties beyond the territorial and hierarchical boundaries known to them in the localized social structure of a village.[27] Several intermediate categories between *varna* and *jati* have emerged, and they provide new referents of status allocation in the traditional system of social stratification. These intermediate categories, however, have not brought about vertical mobility of status groups to any significant extent. They only provide referents for members of small *jatis* bearing similar status in the

traditional hierarchy to unite into wider caste-categories.[28]

The formation of horizontal alliances between caste, therefore, does not destroy *jati*, the basic component of the caste system. In important matters like diet, inter-dining and marriage, they still follow by and large the rules prescribed for them in the traditional order of social hierarchy.[29] In fact, such changes as brought about by the functioning of modern political institutions have evoked caste identities and sentiments, making horizontal caste structures more viable and solidary social entities.[30] The role of caste, which was confined to local politics, has now acquired significance at higher levels of politics.

Thus, according to the 'total social structure approach', whatever changes have occurred in the traditional social structure consequent upon the introduction of modern political institutions, are far from being disruptive or disintegrative for the caste system. This, in fact, demonstrates its propensity to survive and expand, rather than suggest any transformation of the basic principles, norms and ethos of the system. Representative politics, in particular, has strengthened rather than weakened castes, and the politics itself is being overcome and absorbed by the traditional structure of social stratification. Some adjustments in the hierarchical ordering of staus groups and flexibility of functions are not unknown to the historical caste system; and therefore, the adoption of new functions by castes and changes in status locations of a few caste-groups, are not indicative of basic discontinuities in the ongoing traditional social structure.

B. *Differentiation of Social Structures*

These studies are also concerned with the examination of social structures. Their notion of social structure, however, is not of an involute and undifferentiated system of roles. Instead, they conceive the institutions of 'macro society' as *generative spheres of social change* which bring about structural differentiation and discontinuities in the traditional social order. Though caste is viewed as a category of social structure, it is not considered as a singular principle of social organization. Not only have other elements of status (like power and class) entered the system of social stratification, but caste itself is undergoing a process of transformation.[31]

These changes in the traditional system of social stratification are attributed to the processes of economic and political change operating at the macro level of society. While no systematic effort is made to operationalize these macro-level changes as explanatory variables in study designs, frequent reference is made to these changes as independent influences impinging on the traditional social order. Substantively, these influences pertain to universal education, wide-ranging social legislation affecting age-old institutions and inequities, incipient changes like land reforms, urbanization and industrialization, the consequent diversification of occupational structures giving rise to a number of new 'caste-free' occupations, the penetration of impersonal bureaucratic norms in all sectors of life, the new institutions of planning, *panchayati raj* and community development, and above all to elections based on adult franchise, a highly competitive party system and increasing decentralization of political power at state, district and lower levels.

'The implication of these changes on caste structures', it is observed, 'has been of accretion and differentiation of roles, of fusion and fission of segments, of formation of new corporate groups or caste associations, and of the emergence of classlike structures within the framework of caste.'[32] It is as part of this general concern that these studies examine the influence of modern secular and political institutions on caste structures.

Thus while they do recognize the power of resilience of such a long established and complex system of social stratification as caste, these studies emphasize certain structural changes that have come about in the system. While it is often conceded that the microcosms of *jatis* may still persist as primary social groups based on kinship and endogamy (though significant changes are noticeable even in this respect), it is at the same time recognized that with progressive differentiation of economic and power structures new structural categories have been formed which are independent of, and discontinuous with, the traditional social structure and which cannot be located in the *varna* and *jati* schemes of caste stratification. These new structural entities are variously characterized as social circles, social networks, political factions or factional alignments, pressure groups, and sometimes even as socio-economic classes.

Although the studies in this category share in common the above theoretical concerns, they differ significantly among themselves with respect to their methods of inquiry and analysis. Accordingly, we can consider these studies in two sub-categories: descriptive theoretical essays and case studies on the theme of structural changes and differentiation; and systematic studies of the changing economic and power structures of village communities.

Descriptive Essays and Case Studies

Quantitatively, such studies dominate the literature on change in social stratification.[33] While they take as their point of departure the examination of structural changes and differentiation in the traditional system of social stratification, they fail to operationalize their theoretical concerns into systematic research. Instead, their attempt is to argue out a case with the help of descriptive material. Having chosen an *ad hoc* theoretical position, they go about descriptively recording such facts and events as are illustrative of their theoretical point. Sometimes illustrations are drawn from other similar descriptive writings, newspaper reports, the researcher's own field notes and general observations which he would make as a participant of the society he lives in. At other times an edifice of theoretical argument is built upon the description of a single event. Thus, on the one hand we have a few theoretical essays full of empty generalizations, and on the other, numerous case studies replete with theoretical assertions.

Although concerned with explaining the differentiation of social structures with reference to changes in 'macro-society' in their data base and methods of inquiry, these studies do not significantly differ from those that emphasize continuity and extensiveness of the traditional social structure. Instead of devising appropriate methods of inquiry and analysis for the problem they have posed for themselves, they only introduce formalistic and definitional variations in their discussions.[34] By redefining the phenomena (especially of caste) they offer different interpretations of the same facts presented by the studies in the previous category. In these writings, inference is often substituted by argumentation and generalizations rest on the kinds of facts they prefer to highlight. In the process, they sacrifice the good exploratory style by which descriptive anthropological studies have held their own in social science literature. One marvels at their superbly clever use of the English language by which contradictory assertions are made to appear as interrelated statements explaining a phenomenon. Often a proposition is followed by a series of qualifying statements which negate the proposition.[35] Instead of a proposition which can be tested and verified, one is left with a collection of independent assertions. More often than not, what we get is a piece of journalistic writing reported in social science jargon.

While emphasizing changes in the traditional system of social stratification, these studies simultaneously perform two rather contradictory operations. On the one hand, they purport to establish that the caste system has never been the kind of closed system it has generally been made out to be. Basing their argument on the same evidence cited by those who argue in favour of the resilience of caste-structures, these studies emphasize the differentiated nature of the traditional system of social stratification. It is argued that the instances of vertical mobility of status groups incongruence between ritual status and economic and political power of a caste, difference in ritual status of similar occupational groups in various regions, and dissociation between religious and secular functions of caste have all been present throughout the history of the caste-system, and they indicate the relatively open and differential character of the ongoing system of social stratification in India. On the other hand, it is held that the traditional system of social stratification is antithetical to the processes of structural differentiation brought about through the modernization of Indian society. With their universalistic value system, modern economic and political institutions introduce new principles and criteria of social stratification alien to the caste system. The interaction between these two divergent systems brings about the dissociation of the traditional order of caste on the one hand and class, power and other elements of status on the other.[36]

In arguing their case on the phenomenon of structural differentiation, however, these studies point to some important, even if sweeping, findings which should be taken note of.

1. The new economic order has produced basic changes in the traditional social structure. Mobilization of the economy and the growth of new occupational opportunities have induced large-scale transfers of land ownership in villages. The one-caste monopoly of land is now broken, and a more hetrogenous class

of land owners has come into existence. The ownership of land being an important source of local power, transfers of land ownership have also influenced the power structure of the rural society.[37] The traditional class of land owners, composed of priestly, managerial and merchant castes is being increasingly replaced by a new group of land owners composed mainly of peasant castes. This has increased the dominance of peasant castes in the political and social life of different regions of the country. Instances are cited of Jats in Haryana and Western U.P., Marathas in Maharashtra, and Kammas and Reddis in Andhra Pradesh.[38] Case studies of shifts in dominant status from one caste to another at village level are also described.

2. The new system of education has also brought about important changes in the traditional social structure. Modern education has spread common universal values among individuals of different castes. In the initial stage this was restricted to a few higher castes who first availed of new educational opportunities. This gave rise to a new group of intellectual and political elites, different from the traditional group of Brahminic elites.[39] The gradual expansion of modern education diversified the social base of intellectual and professional elites. This has resulted in bridging cultural gaps, and at times in reducing structural differences between castes, especially through the expansion of the effective unit of endogamy.[40] Instances of inter-marriage between previously endogenous groups of a larger caste category are cited in support of this observation.

3. Besides changes in the caste structure, new categories of social belonging have emerged in the urban-industrial sectors of society. This is reflected in the phenomenon of urban middle classes, which cannot be explained in the 'caste frame of reference'.[41] Several caste-free occupations and professions are now being followed by members of different castes. Since recruitment to these new occupations is open (in fact more open for the 'lower' castes), mobility has greatly increased. Around these occupational groups have evolved distinct life-styles and interest perceptions characteristic of a social class. The cultural and structural differences between caste-groups are being increasingly minimized through the acquisition of a new occupational status and similar economic interests.

4. Similarly, western education and urbanization have initiated

several reformist movements, giving rise to new social entities which cannot strictly be described as status groups or as socio-economic classes. The emergence of Brahmos in Bengal is cited as an example of such a new social entity. Though a socially cohesive group, the Brahmos are neither a caste nor a class, they can best be described as a 'social circle' or a 'social set'.[42]

5. Another important process of structural differentiation is initiated by modern political institutions. Being universalistic in their organization, they introduce new principles of organization and open up new avenues of status mobility for caste-groups as well as for individuals. Instances are cited of specific individuals from lower social strata who could improve their status through political activities. Further, the differentiation of political structures has introduced several loci of power in rural society. This has led to a shift of dominant status from one caste to another. What is more important, the locus of power has begun to shift from the caste-system itself to a structure of power whose mode of differentiation is based on new principles.[43]

6. The processes of distribution of power in the new political order have inducted into politics social strata hitherto far removed from political life. Since modern politics have to accomodate a variety of interests beside caste, new components of social status have entered the traditional system of social stratification. The numerical strength of a social group and its ability to organize itself politically have become more important than ritual status or ownership of land. Although the involvement of castes in politics has strengthened particularistic loyalties, in the long run caste solidarities have to dissolve into social groups based on economic and political interests, or at least compete with other, non-caste, loyalties.[44] Political parties, in their bid to secure the support of different castes, promote dissensions and splits in caste associations, and also enter into alliances across castes. Meanwhile, political alliances among castes and between castes and political parties tend to be untenable. To the extent that these processes of generation and distribution of power lead to new forms of association, they tend to loosen the traditional structure.[45]

Studies of Changing Economic and Power Structures of Village Communities

A few studies investigate the problem of structural differentiation in a more systematic manner.[46] These are the studies of changing economic and power structures of village communities. Focussing on situations of inter-group tensions and conflicts in village society, they examine structural changes in the caste system. Basing their analysis on comparative data obtained from a number of carefully selected village communities they draw attention to new patterns of conflict and integration that have emerged in the village social structure, patterns which are characteristically different from those in a caste society. Instead of making vague references to 'forces of modernization' in the macro society, some of these studies select a specific change-variable like the abolition of *zamindari*, the introduction of community development or *panchayati raj*, the functioning of political parties and the holding of elections, as an explanatory variable and examine its influence on village social structure or specifically on caste structure. There are a few other studies which do no more than identify and locate changes in the village social structure in an exploratory manner and question established categories of social structure analyses. There are, however, also some extreme cases which, while repudiating the caste frame of reference in the analysis of Indian rural society, substitute it by an equally problematic 'class frame of reference'.[47]

What follows is a brief summary of some important findings of these studies.

1. The traditional system of economic and social interdependence between castes, (known as the *jajmani* system) is disintegrating. In the place of cooperation, competition between castes and between groups of castes, has become an active principle of village social structure.[48] The authority of a dominant caste which regulated the *jajmani* system and functioned as an agency enforcing the norms of the traditional social structure is now being challenged by hitherto dependent caste groups occupying lower and dependent status in the traditional social hierarchy.[49]

2. Often, such competition assumes the form of acute tensions and violent conflicts between caste groups. It is, however, misleading to view these conflicts in terms of an intercaste relationship.

For, the issues on which the different castes come into conflict have no bearing on caste beliefs and values. The conflict between castes does not stem from the fact that they are caste. The people belonging to different castes may be treated as groups of people and these, like groups in any society, come in conflict with one another for such reasons as control over economic resources, social dominance, self assertion, or the desire for autonomy.[50] In brief, the relationship of conflict and cooperation between these social groups is determined by the place they occupy in the changed economic and power structure of the village community rather than by their status in the traditional hierarchy.

3. The built-in mechanism of traditional social structure which helped reduction of tensions within a caste and resolutions of inter-caste disputes (which indeed existed even in a traditional village system characterized by functional interdependence and caste groups) have also become ineffective. The caste *panchayat*, the village council of castes, and even the dominant caste have lost their sanction to enforce any settlement between contending parties. This has led to fragmentation of the caste-based power structure of a village community, and the emergence of new integrative principles of allocation and distribution of power.[51]

4. In order to cope with the insecurities generated by these changes in the traditional social structure, castes take recourse to political organization. Political organization provides caste with a new source of security which helps to reduce tensions.[52] Inter-group conflicts are also contained by political parties and leaders seeking the support of various social groups. In the process, political factions rather than castes become important units of village power structure. These factions are not concomitant with castes. Their membership consists of individuals and families belonging to several castes. They are more like personalized groupings or multi-caste power alliances.[53]

5. The concept of 'dominant caste' is, therefore, not adequate in explaining the changes that have occurred in the village power structure. With large-scale economic and political changes, several castes have been brought nearer to the nucleus of local power. Attributes of dominance are possessed by more than one caste in a village, and no one caste can be said to enjoy exclusive dominance. Thus dominance is no longer the property of a single caste but is diffused among individuals and families

of different castes, high and low. Instances may be found in which politically and economically powerful individuals exercise dominance on the members of their own caste, as well as on others.[54]

6. The social categories involved in conflict situations are, therefore, essentially class categories based on economic interest and political affiliation. The inter-class relationship of conflict, however, is superimposed on the traditional social hierarchy, so that castes with high social status may also be found in control of economic resources, and those with low social status in a state of economic deprivation.[55]

C. *Politicization of Castes*

The primary concern of these studies is to examine political processes rather than social structures. These studies view the interaction between caste and politics in terms of a *process* which has implications for the generation and distribution of political power in society.

Deriving their frame of reference from the comparative analyses of political development, these studies conceive involvement of castes in politics as a process of 'politicization'. Two divergent views of politicization, however, are discernible from these studies. Following the convergence theory of modernization, one view of politicization is that of a process moving inevitably towards the growth of a modern political community which transcends primordial loyalties, brings about open competition between groups as well as between individuals in pursuit of political power, and introduces associational and non-ascriptive principles of political organization. The implications of this process for the caste system are, first, to transform castes into an infra-structure of a modern democratic polity, and, second, to transform castemen into a citizenry participating at different levels of politics.

Another view of politicization reflected in these studies stems from a more dynamic notion of tradition. Tradition is viewed neither as an immutable element of old society, nor as an element antithetical to the functioning of modern political institutions. Discarding the 'pre-requisites' concept of political development, these studies view castes as more flexible and adaptive structures of Indian society. India's success in managing important crises of political development, especially those of political participation and mobilization, is attributed, among other things, to the ability of the structure of traditional society in containing the disruptive effects of rapid political mobilization.

It should, however, be noted that, for a large part of writings in this category, the above views of politicization serve only as *ad hoc* value positions, rather than as theoretical rubrics under which specific hypotheses are formulated and examined. Consequently, we have only a few systematic studies of the politicization of castes in the midst of a huge quantity of polemical discussions and subjective writings on the role of castes in politics. For example, the discussions and writings based on evolutionary and linear views of political development lament the evils of casteism in modern politics, whereas those based on a functionalistic view of tradition go as far as reifying the caste system as a bastion of democracy in India.

If we eliminate such polemical writings from our review, we are left with only a few specific studies which systematically examine how caste influences politics and is in turn influenced by the functioning of political institutions.[56] These studies are based on intensive field investigations (carried out in different regions of India) of the political movements of castes,[57] the relationship between caste associations or federations and political parties,[58] and intra-party and inter-party processes in which caste loyalties play a part.[59] There are also some analyses based on aggregate electoral and socio-demographic data and on documentary evidence with a view to highlighting the support structure of political organizations.[60] Finally there is now coming to the fore a systematic analysis of this interaction based on survey interviews of political leaders and cross-sections of the population.[61]

It should be noted that these studies are primarily concerned with the study of political behaviour, but in so far as caste constitutes an important element of political behaviour in India, they also deal with the problem of caste-politics interaction. For our purpose, these studies can be considered in the following sub-categories: (i) Studies of political mobilization, (ii) Studies of voting behaviour, and (iii) Studies of local and state level politics.

Studies of Political Mobilization

These studies view the involvement of castes in politics as a process of mobilization of different sections of society into organized politics.[62] Being in the form of case studies, they describe various processes through which castes are being politicized. Important among these are case studies of the formation of caste associations and caste federations,[63] the role of caste associations and federations in mobilizing mass support for political movements,[64] and the participation of wider caste-groups in politics for purposes of social mobility, economic well-being and political articulation.[65]

As case studies of political movements of wider caste categories, these studies emphasize the regional context of caste-politics interaction.[66] Being exploratory in nature, they help in the clarification of issues and the formulation of research problems. The main import of these studies can be summarized here.

1. The process of political mobilization inevitably involves indigenous social structures in politics. In a society where caste groups are basic social entities, it follows that they will constitute an important segment of the infra-structure of its political order.[67]

2. Having come closer to each other, modern political institutions and caste structures enter into a process of interaction in the course of which both change. By drawing castes into its competitive structures politics finds its bases in society, and by subjecting itself to the rules of competitive politics, caste acquires political characteristics.[68]

3. The controversy whether caste serves functions of politics or politics serves functions of caste is, therefore, entirely misplaced. Instead, the interaction between caste and politics should be conceived as a two-way process of the politicization of castes and the institutionalization of politics.[69]

Studies of Voting Behaviour

Studies of voting behaviour deal mainly with the role of caste in elections.[70] On the one hand, there are studies showing how caste sentiments and loyalties are activated through elections and how electoral support for a candidate or a party is mobilized on caste lines. These studies point to the incidence of group-voting based on caste. Several instances are cited to show how, during elections, informal leaders of various castes or formal organizations of castes commit the support of their entire membership to particular candidates or political parties. It is argued that inter-party competition, in fact, reflects caste-based cleavages rather than differences in the political identification and party loyalties of the electorate.[71]

On the other hand, a large number of voting behaviour studies emphasize the increasing role of non-caste factors in determining voting behaviour. These studies show how caste loyalties and caste identities are often undermined by political factors such as party loyalties of the electorate, ideological appeals of political parties and issue orientation of voters.[72] Instances of split-voting in the same castes and of factional alignment between and across castes are cited in support of this argument.[73] Thus, according to these studies, elections have given rise to new interests and new identifications and these have resulted in weakening hierarchical as well as solidarity features of the caste system.[74]

From the above two kinds of studies, it is difficult to establish the relative strength of caste and non-caste variables in determining voting behaviour. Since most studies of voting behaviour are in the form of case studies of a constituency, a town or a village, their generalizations apply to a specific place at a given point in time. All that one can conclude from these studies is that at some places and in some elections caste is an important factor influencing voting behaviour; whereas at some other places and at other times it is not that important an element in voting behaviour.[75] This state of affairs, however, cannot be entirely attributed to the case-study method of inquiry. From well-conceived case studies it should be possible to identify and locate conditions which either activate or undermine the influence of caste in voting behaviour. Hypotheses generated from such case studies could then be tested through an explanantory design of a large-scale survey. Barring a few systematic case studies,[76] however, most studies of voting behaviour at best view the influence of caste as a function of the place and time of investigation and at worst only assert the typicality or universality of the place. For example, a multi-caste village or town in which major political parties are fighting an election is claimed to be a representative situation from which generalizations can be made about political behaviour in India.[77] Sometimes a mere assertion that what is true of the place under investigation may also be true of many other places in the country is considered enough justification for making country-wide generalizations. To the best of my knowledge, no systematic secondary analysis for comparative or aggregative purposes has yet been carried out.

Besides being non-representative, voting behaviour studies suffer from a serious theoretical misconception. By and large, characteristics of individual voters are derived from observations of group behaviour.[78] The unit of observation in these studies is a group and not an individual voter. As an onlooker of an election event in a community, a researcher usually has his eye on caste leaders negotiating among themselves and with political activists about the electoral support of their caste members. The queries he makes of individuals also refer to their membership of caste groups. From such observations of group situations, inferences are made about the presence or absence of the caste element in the voting behaviour of individuals. For example, if individuals who were so far deprived of political rights due to their low social status now unite to assert their political independence, their behaviour will be perceived as a caste-group behaviour. Similarly, if members of a caste sharing common economic interests, vote for a political party which guarantees protection of their interests, they will be attributed with caste considerations in their voting behaviour.

Another way of deriving individual characteristics of voters from the observation of groups is found in the use of electoral statistics in the studies of voting behaviour. Often, statements are made about the presence or absence of caste considerations in voting behaviour on the basis of polling-booth analyses of election returns. By matching estimates of the caste composition of a constituency or a polling-booth area with the division of votes between candidates or parties in that area, these studies infer the role of the caste factor in voting behaviour.[79]

A few studies of voting behaviour, however, directly examine individual characteristics of voters as determinants of their voting behaviour. Their information is based on systematic interviews of a cross-section of voters in which they are asked about their voting preferences as well as about their personal dispositions and attitudes on various matters including caste.[80] These studies show that besides casteism several other constellations of individual attributes of voters influence voting behaviour.

Studies of Local and State Level Politics

These studies deal with the role of caste at different levels of politics. Studies of local level politics describe how the functioning of modern political institutions, especially elections and political parties, influences the leadership and power structures of a village or a constituency. Like voting behaviour studies, these are also in the form of case studies based on field investigation and analyses of electoral data. Their investigation, however, is usually confined to a longer period of time and covers changes over two or more elections.

Different case studies of changing leadership and power structures emphasize different aspects of the interaction between caste and politics at the level of local politics. On the one hand, there are a few studies which show that while elections and political parties bring about some adjustments in the traditional leadership and power structure, local politics still continue to be caste-oriented.[81] These studies point to cases of increased control by dominant caste groups on local power structures like *panchayats* and cooperatives,[82] continuing hold of traditional leadership on these power structures and the caste basis of political factions. On the other hand, a large number of studies describe how competition for political power as introduced by elections and political parties has brought about basic changes in the leadership processes and power structures of local communities.[83] Some important observations made by these studies relate to the increasing political autonomy of local leaders,[84] the growth of political factions which operate as interest groups rather than as caste groups,[85] attempts by traditional leaders to perform new political roles[86] and the emergence of a new leadership which represents economic and political interests rather than merely caste interests.[87] They report changes in the social composition of local leaders from election to election and emphasize the growing importance of political skills rather than a leader's membership of a caste or his ascriptive position.

Studies of state politics describe interaction between political parties and social groups at the state level. These studies are based mainly on analyses of electoral data and documentary information on political parties.[88] A large number of these studies describe state politics in terms of a competition between major caste groups for political power within a state;[89] as chief contenders of power, these caste groups work through political parties.[90] Others, however, directly focus on the recruitment process and support bases of political parties.[91] They show how the requirement of numbers and hence hetrogenous support bases for a political party undermines the importance of caste as a factor in state politics.

III
Caste-Politics Interaction: Developments and Gaps in Research

Our review suggests some developments as well as gaps in research in the area of caste-politics interaction.

In the past two decades important developments have taken place, especially with respect to identification of issues, specification of units and levels of inquiry, development of concepts and expansion of fields of inquiry covering various aspects and levels of the relationship between caste institutions and the political process.

While these developments are heartening, several theoretical and methodological problems remain unsolved. Important among these are: interlinking of various conceptual categories and aggregation of findings into a common all-India theoretical framework of political and social change; differentiation of political and social structural variables; generation of testable hypotheses from the findings of numerous case studies through secondary and aggregative analysis; and growth of individual-based survey research for a better understanding of the true dynamics of caste-politics interaction. Following considerations should, therefore, inform the strategy of new research in this area.

1. In general the caste-politics interaction aspect of political sociology in India has been extensively investigated. Since these investigations are carried out from different disciplinary perspectives, often prompted by a sense of professional autonomy instead of being required by the nature of the problem under investigation, their conceptual categories and findings do not provide a satisfactory basis for an empirical theory of political and social change. The need is for evolving a theoretical framework which undermines constraints born of individual disciplinary

traditions and makes interlinking of concepts and generalizations at various levels of analysis possible.

2. Literature in this field is dominated by case studies, aggregative analyses and polemical discussions. Very few systematic studies with an explanatory model of analysis are available. The need is rather to systematize findings of these studies in the form of testable hypotheses than to proliferate the literature still further by more case studies and descriptive writings which hardly throw any new light on the nature and direction of political and social change in India. In other words, a re-analysis of existing data and formulation of new research problems in a theoretical context of political and social change should receive greater priority than a continuation of the present trend of research in this area. For example, from several descriptions of movements of specific castes for the acquisition of political power, it should be possible to identify the conditions and processes through which different social groups gain solidarity or get fragmented in the course of their involvement in politics, and then to hypothesize about the 'stages of politicization'.

Similarly, from the findings of numerous case studies on the role of caste in elections, it should be possible to classify different conditions and contexts under which primordial sentiments and identifications are either activated or attentuated. This would inevitably involve a multi-variant examination of the relationship between the caste variable (which itself needs to be broken up into several variables) and other variables of political and social change. This would also permit the formation of several hypotheses on the differential role of caste at different levels of politics and in different sectors of social life.

In brief, re-analyses of available findings on the relationship between caste and politics should be canalized in two directions: (i) development analyses focussing on the changing role of caste and community with increasing politicization of citizens and institutions, and (ii) cross-sectional analyses in a comparative perspective which evaluate the role of primordial affiliations like caste in different socio-cultural and political milieus.

3. Finally the question what is happening to caste — is it strengthening or weakening or disappearing — cannot be wished away either by resorting to smart definitional exercises or through

micro-research that is carried out without reference to an adequate theoretical framework. The fact is that even the allegedly 'micro' studies often presuppose an *ad-hoc* all-India framework of the caste *system* based on unstated ideological propositions. It will be theoretically more profitable to recognize explicitly how *ideas* and *ideals* operate independently of the empirical reality and influence not only categories of social analysis and research, but also the processes of social change. It will, therefore, be a wrong start for an empirical theory of social change in India not to address itself first to the issues of how the prevalent tools of analysis are embedded in an ideological framework, in this case an all-India caste system. The question is whether an all-India framework is such that it continuously generates new data and hypotheses which then makes a re-statement of the possible, or does it only deductively generate lower order propositions which are sought to be corroborated by 'micro' studies.

It is probably the *structural* concept of caste that underlies the present all-India framework, which has inhibited the development of an empirical theory of social and political change based on substantive concerns. The first step towards an empirical theory in this area can be of generating new sets of data and hypotheses stemming from an alternative theoretical orientation which conceives caste not as a structural entity but as an aggregate of attributes (of casteness) possessed by concrete individuals. To be more precise, the need is to demonstrate empirically whether caste, as it enters politics, continues to be an ongoing structural whole in the strict sense of the term or remains as mere sentiment, a category of interest identification, operative at the individual level only. It can well be hypothesized, for example, that with growing individuation and differentiation in society, the social structure of a specific caste, or of the caste system, will break down. What may still persist are psycho-cultural attributes of casteness possessed by specific individuals and aggregable at the collective level. The loss of structural characteristics of caste becomes more pronounced when observed in the sector of political behaviour. Hence an appropriate researchable question to ask is not whether the phenomenon of caste is disappearing but whether caste is losing its *structural* characteristics when penetrated by electoral politics and other 'modernizing' processes in society.[92]

In the absence of an alternative theoretical orientation such as the one illustrated above, the concept of caste in most studies tends to be all-inclusive and totalistic, with the result that aggregative behaviour of individuals is often confused with the structural behaviour of a group. This has given rise to several misconceptions about the role of caste in politics. For example, any attempt on the part of certain individuals to organize politically or assert their political right is viewed as caste behaviour, for the trivial reason that, due to an historical accident of being born with a caste label, these individuals share that label with several others. Whether their motivations and aspirations are for pursuing interests of the collectivity of a caste or of themselves as individuals, and whether their behaviour in politics is regulated by norms and values governing caste membership or by rules of competitive politics, is nowhere ascertained in these studies. What is important, therefore, is to know how far casteness as an attribute of an individual constitutes an element of his political behaviour and how far it influences his perceptions and choices in politics; and what implications this has for both the political system and the social structure.

NOTES

1 Two comprehensive reviews of literature, covering social structural and cultural aspects of the Indian caste system, are already in existence. André Béteille, Y.B. Damle, S. Shahani and M.N. Srinivas, *Caste: A Trend Report and Bibliography*, *Current Sociology*, 8(3), UNESCO, 1958; and Y.B. Damle, *Caste: A Review of the Literature on Caste*, M.I.T., Centre for International Studies, 1961.

2 A.P. Barnabas and S.C. Mehta, in their *Caste in Changing India*, New Delhi: Indian Institute of Public Administration, 1965, examine the literature concerning effects of modern developments (industrial, political educational, etc.) on caste. The essay reviews numerous writings on the subject with a view to finding out whether caste is getting stronger or weaker under the impact of modern developments. While not satisfactory as a systematic assessment of evidence and findings on changes in caste, the essay provides an inventory of viewpoints, speculations and value-judgements of politicians, journalists and social scientists on the subject of the resilience and adaptability of caste.

3 Unfortunately, the excessive preoccupation of Indian social scientists with the phenomenon of caste has caused severe neglect of other important areas

of study in the field of political sociology. The present review is confined to an examination of studies relating to caste-politics interaction and leaves out whatever little has been done in other areas of political sociology. It also excludes studies of political involvement of Scheduled Castes and Scheduled Tribes and of the politics of 'communalism'. Besides, the present review focusses almost exclusively on the contributions of Indian scholars in the field.

4 Karl Marx, 'The British Rule in India', *Selected Works*, 2, pp. 652-61.

5 Max Weber, *The Religion of India: The Sociology of Hinduism and Buddhism*, translated and edited by H.H. Gerth and D. Martindale, Glencoe, Ill., 1958. Also see Milton Singer's explication of Weber's theory in 'Religion and Social Change in India: The Max Weber Thesis, Phase Three', *Economic Development and Cultural Change*, July 1966; and A.K. Singh's persuasive criticism of Weber's thesis as applied to India, in 'Hindu Culture and Economic Development in India', *Conspectus*, 3(1), 1967.

6 These controversies have been made well-known through the biographies of leading social reformers and political leaders of the nineteenth century. For two comprehensive works on the history of nineteenth century social reform movement in India which highlight the intellectual and political context of this debate, see S. Natarajan, *A Century of Social Reform in India*, Bombay, Asia Publishing House, 1962; and, Charles H. Heimsath, *Indian Nationalism and Hindu Social Reform*, Princeton, Princeton University Press, 1964.

7 Jawaharlal Nehru, *Discovery of India*, Calcutta, Signet Press, 1948, p. 440.

8 B.R. Ambedkar, *Annihilation of Caste*, Bombay, The Bharat Bhushan P. Press, 1945; and, Ram Manohar Lohia, *The Caste System*, Hyderabad, Navahind, 1964.

9 Heimsath, op. cit.

10 The debate was once again revived in the post-independence period soon after the First General Elections of 1952 which drew attention to the 'evils of casteism' in Indian political life. A new wave of indignation and self-disregard became noticeable in the speeches and writings of intellectuals and political leaders alke. See, *Report on Casteism and Removal of Untouchability*, Delhi, September 26 — October 2, 1955 (Bombay, Indian Conference of Social Work, 1955). The feeling was heightened on the eve of the next general elections of 1957. Political leaders, party functionaries and intellectuals feared subversion of democracy in India due to the rise of 'casteism' in national and local elections. The General Secretary of the Indian National Congress, Mr. Sriman Narayan, wrote in the editorial of the official party organ, 'the present system of elections has undoubtedly given strength and encouragement to casteism.' (see *A.I.C.C. Economic Review*, April 15, 1956, p. 4). M.N. Srinivas, in his presidential address to the Anthropology and Archaeology Section of the Fifty-Fourth Session of the Indian Science Congress in January 1957, took upon himself to demonstrate that '. . . the power and activity of caste has increased in proportion as political power passed increasingly to the people from the rulers.' See M.N. Srinivas, *Caste in Modern India and Other Essays*, Bombay, Asia Publishing House, 1962, p. 23. The climax of despondency and frustration was attained when an American journalist echoed these anxieties of Indian élites in his book and declared that India

had already entered the most dangerous decades of her existence as a nation and as a democracy. See, Selig S. Harrison, *India: The Most Dangerous Decades*, Princeton, Princeton University Press, 1960.

11 The study of caste once again acquired a practical focus in the perspective of its role and future in modern politics. What by and large took place, however, were torrents of ideological and speculative writings. Basic inquiries directed towards an empirical theory of social and political change were conspicuous by their absence. This continued throughout the fifties and upto the early sixties. Even the social anthropologists and sociologists addressed themselves to ill formulated problems of inquiry. The questions raised were: Was caste disappearing? Was caste serving functions of modern politics, or was modern politics serving functions of caste? By using different definitions of what constituted caste, and with selective use of relevant instances supporting the case one way or the other, the contenders of opposite viewpoints on the issue sought to maintain their respective positions. See, for instance, the Srinivas-Leach controversy on the issue in *Caste in Modern India*, op. cit., and in E.R. Leach, ed., *Aspects of Caste in South India, Ceylon and North-West Pakistan*, Cambridge, 1960.

It was in the sixties that the assessment of political sociologists about the role of caste began to change. One cannot say that this shift was due to any significant change in the empirical phenomenon itself. Srinivas, five years after his presidential address to the Anthropological and Archaeological Section of the Science Congress, wrote in 1962, 'I must confess that I was somewhat distrubed by what I felt was an increased activity of caste in certain areas of public life.' (Srinivas, *Caste in Modern India and Other Essays*, op. cit., p. 1). Since the mid-sixties the pendulum seems to have taken a full swing. Now caste began to be viewed as a medium of mobilization of the masses in organized politics and even as an instrument of political education of the masses. See Lloyd I. Rudolph and Susanne H. Rudolph, 'The Political Role of India's Caste Associations', *Pacific Affairs*, 32(1), March 1960; and later Rudolph and Rudolph, *The Modernity of Tradition*, Chicago, University of Chicago Press, 1967.

12 M.N. Srinivas, 'Castes: Can they exist in the India of tomorrow?', in *Caste in Modern India*, op. cit., p. 71.

13 Important among these are a number of carefully done studies of village social structure and descriptive writings on the role of caste in modern times. For studies of village social structure, see M.N. Srinivas, 'The Social Structure of a Mysore Village'; and S.C. Dube, 'Deccan Village', in M.N. Srinivas, ed., *India's Villages*, Bombay, Asia Publishing House, 1960. See also M.N. Srinivas, 'The Social System of a Mysore Village', in McKim Marriot, ed., *Village India*, Bombay, Asia Publishing House, 1961; S.C. Dube, *Indian Village*, Ithaca, N.Y., Cornell University Press, 1955; and R.D. Singh, 'The Unity of Indian Village', *Journal of Asian Studies*, 16(1), 1956. Of numerous descriptive writings on caste based on researchers' field notes and newspaper reports, see especially, M.N. Srinivas, *Caste in Modern India and Other Essays*, op. cit.

14 M.N. Srinivas, 'Caste in Modern India', and 'Castes: Can they exist in the India of tomorrow?', in *Caste in Modern India and Other Essays*, op. cit.

15 André Béteille has characterized this approach as 'total social structure approach.' According to him, this approach fails to take into account differentiation and discontinuation of social structures effected through changes at the macro level of the society. See André Béteille, *Caste: Old and New*, Bombay, Asia Publishing House, 1969, pp. 85-6.

16 G.S. Ghurye, *Caste and Class in India*, Bombay, 1952.

17 M.N. Srinivas, 'A Note on Sanskritsation and Westernisation', in *Caste in Modern India*, op. cit., pp. 57-8.

18 This phenomenon is conceptualized as 'Sanskritization'. The concept was first used by M.N. Srinivas in his book, *Religion and Society Among the Coorgs of South India*, London, Oxford University Press, 1952, and later developed by him in various papers dealing with internal processes of cultural and social structural changes in India. For a detailed explication of the concept, see 'A Note on Sanskritisation and Westernisation', in *Caste in Modern India*, op. cit. Some others, however, who examined the phenomenon empirically in their specific studies, have pointed to the inadequacy and untidyness of the concept. For the latest among these comments, see for example, S.L. Srivastava, 'The Concept of Sanskritisation: A Re-Evaluation', *Economic and Political Weekly*, 4(16), April 19, 1969. Also see, S.K. Chauhan, 'Social Mobility in Upper Assam: A Note on Sanskritisation', *Social Action*, New Delhi, 22(3), January-September 1972, 231-6.

19 M.N. Srinivas, 'A Note on Sanskritisation and Westernisation', op. cit., pp. 58-9. Since Sanskritization has been viewed as the general mode of upward mobility, the studies of downward mobility have not received much attention. Downward mobility, according to a recent article, can be characterized as a failed attempt at Sanskritization wherein the group gives up lucrative occupations that are low in status and takes to norms associated with groups higher in status. However, they do not always succeed in this, resulting in the process, in actual downward mobility in terms of status. The article contains an illustrated typology of downward mobility. K.L. Sharma, 'Downward Social Mobility: Some Observations', *Sociological Bulletin*, 22(1), March 1973, 58-77. Also see, Shyam Lal, 'Sanskritisation and Social Change Among the Bhangis in Jodhpur City: A Case Study', *Indian Journal of Social Work*, 34(1), April 1973, 37-41.

20 'Dominant caste' is another important concept that has been developed in the studies of village social structure. The concept was first used systematically by M.N. Srinivas in his various studies, especially in 'The Dominant Caste in Rampura', *American Anthropologist*, 61(1), February 1959. The concept of dominant caste has also been critically examined by other researchers in their studies. See S.C. Dube, 'Caste Dominance and Factionalism', *Contributions to Indian Sociology*, 2, December 1968; Yogesh Atal, *The Changing Frontiers of Caste*, Delhi, National Publishing House, 1965; André Béteille, *Caste, Class and Power: Changing Patterns of Stratification in a Tanjore Village*, Berkeley and Los Angeles, University of California Press, 1965; P.N. Rastogi, 'Dominant Caste and Faction Situation in Brahminpura', *Man in India*, 43, October 1963; G. Chattopadhyay, *Ranjana: A Village in West Bengal*, Calcutta, Bookland Private Limited, 1964; K. Iswaran, *Tradition and Economy in Village India*, London, Routledge and Kegan Paul, 1965;

Mathur, K.S., 'Leadership in Rural India', in L.P. Vidyarthi (ed.), *Leadership in India*, Bombay, Asia Publishing House, 1967; K. Ranga Rao and Radhakrishna Murthy, 'A Note on Public Office, Legitimacy and Flow of Political Power in Village India', in *Sociological Bulletin*, 24(2), September 1975, 204-9; K.L. Sharma, 'Power Elite in Rural India: Some Questions and Clarifications', *Sociological Bulletin*, 25(1), March 1976.

21 M.N. Srinivas defines dominant caste as follows: A caste may be said to be 'dominant' when it preponderates numerically over other castes, and when it also wields preponderant economic and political power. A large and powerful caste group can be more easily dominant if its position in the local caste hierarchy is not too low. See M.N. Srinivas, 'The Social System of a Mysore Village', in McKim Marriot, ed., *Village India*, op. cit., p. 18.

22 André Béteille describes how Kallas and few other castes acquired control over village politics from Brahmins in Sripuram. See his *Caste, Class and Power*, op. cit. The concept of dominant caste, however, has created a great deal of confusion on the question of whether it suggests continuity or change in the traditional social structure. Much of this confusion is due to the fact that the relative importance of elements involved in the phenomenon of a dominant caste has not been empirically established. For a theoretical critique of the concept, in this respect, see T.K. Oomen, 'The Concept of Dominant Caste: Some Queries', *Contributions to Indian Sociology*, New Series, No. IV, December 1970.

23 M.N. Srinivas makes this point in his Introduction to *India's Villages*, '. . . the dominant caste supports and maintains the total system. The dominant caste respects the code of every caste, even when some features of it are different from the code of dominant caste.' M.N. Srinivas, *India's Villages*, Bombay, Asia Publishing House, 1960, p. 7.

24 M.N. Srinivas, 'A Note on Sanskritisation and Westernisation', in *Caste in Modern India*, op. cit. See also M.N. Srinivas, 'The Dominant Caste in Rampura', op. cit.

25 M.N. Srinivas makes this point very effectively in his book, *Religion and Society Among the Coorgs of South India*, op. cit. He emphasizes the continuity of the caste system in the face of various movements of caste mobility. According to him the change took place within the structure — in hierarchy, but not in the system. 'Even revolutionary movements which had aimed at the over-throw of the caste system ended by becoming castes themselves. . . . Thus the caste system effectively neutralised all attempts to change it.'

26 See M.N. Srinivas, 'Castes: Can they exist in the India of tomorrow?', and 'Indian Road to Equality', in *Caste in Modern India and Other Essays*, op. cit. In a recent study Uma Ramaswamy shows how the policy of preferential treatment to scheduled castes has not succeeded in bringing about any structural changes in their socio-economic status. 'Scheduled Castes in Andhra: Some Aspects of Social Change'. *Economic and Political Weekly*, 9(29), July 20, 1974, 1153-58. Also see Lalit K. Sen, 'The Concepts of Tradition and Modernity: A Re-evaluation', *Behavioural Sciences and Community Development*, 7(2), September 1973, 83-105.

27 See V.V. Nath, 'Village, Caste and Community', *The Economic Weekly*, 14(49), December 1962.

28 See Irawati Karve, *Hindu Society: An Interpretation*, Poona, Deccan College, 1961. For a discussion of the historical process by which the scheduled castes in Andhra Pradesh have gained a sense of shared identity through a process of horizontal mobilization, see Uma Ramaswamy, 'Self-Identity Among Scheduled Castes: A Study of Andhra', *Economic and Political Weekly*, 9(47), November 23, 1974, 1959-64. Also see, Ghanshyam Shah, 'Growth of Group Identity among the Adivasis of Dang', *Gujarat Research Society Journal*, 34(2). April 1972, 164-84.

29 M.N. Srinivas, 'Castes: Can they exist in the India of tomorrow?', op. cit., p. 7.

30 Of the few studies emphasizing the continued hold of caste on its members through formation of caste associations and expansion of caste activities mention may be made of V.A. Sangve, 'Changing Patterns of Caste Organisation in Kolhapur City', *Sociological Bulletin*, 11(1, 2), 1962; S.G. Morab, 'Caste Council of the Bhandari of Depoli', *Man in India*, 46(2), April-June 1966; M.S.A. Rao, 'Caste and the Indian Army', *The Economic Weekly*, 16(35), August 29, 1964.

31 As against the 'total social structure approach', this approach emphasizes independent influences of macro-level changes in society on micro structures of caste and village. Consequences of these changes are observed in terms of vertical differentiations of social structures, giving rise to new criteria and principles of social stratification. The development of differentiated political structures like political parties, legislatures and organs of local governments is considered as introducing such new elements in the prevailing system of caste stratification. For a formulation of this approach, see André Béteille, 'Closed and Open Social Stratification in India', in *Castes: Old and New*, op. cit., and in *Caste, Class and Power*, op. cit. Yogendra Singh, 'Caste and Class: Some Aspects of Continuity and Change', *Sociological Bulletin*, 17(2), 1968; Satish Saberwal, 'Towards a Model of Indian Society: Urgent Research in Social Anthropology', *Transactions of the Indian Institute of Advanced Study*, 10, Silma, 1969. A significant departure from 'total social structure' approach is especially noticed in works of those few social anthropologists who have extended their area of inquiry to urban-industrial communities. For example, see Satish Saberwal, 'Status, Mobility and Networks in a Punjabi Industrial Town', in S. Saberwal (ed.), *Beyond the Village: Sociological Explorations,* Simla, Indian Institute of Advanced Study, pp.111-84. See especially his recent book, *Mobile Men,* New Delhi, Vikas Publishing House Pvt. Ltd., 1976.

32 Yogendra Singh, op. cit., p. 175.

33 Numerous articles can be recorded under this category. Most of these are general descriptive writings focussing on change in the caste system as brought about by modern political and economic developments. Representative of writings of this kind are some essays of André Béteille, especially, 'Closed and Open Social Stratification in India', 'Caste and Politics in Tamilnadu', 'Changing Pattern of Status Groups', 'Elites, Status Groups and Castes in Modern India', all of which are reproduced in *Castes: Old and New*, op. cit.; M.N. Srinivas, 'Changing Institutions and Values in Modern India', *The Economic Weekly*, 14(28-30), February 1962; V.K.N. Menon 'Caste, Politics

and Leadership in India', *Political Sciences Review*, 3(2), October 1964; Pradeep J. Shah, 'Caste and Political Process', *Asian Survey*, 6(9) September 1966. While the present section reviews such writings in general, it deliberately concentrates on the essays of André Béteille, as he is perhaps the best exponent of this style of writing, and thus illustrates its main characteristics.

34 André Béteille, for example, views caste as a status group and equates its behaviour with that of a status group in any other society. Whatever difference that is noticeable between castes in India and status groups in other societies is, according to him, essentially a difference of degree and not of kind. Accordingly, with the changes in the criteria of status in Indian society, there also occurs a 'transformation from closed status groups based on caste to more open ones which accomodate other components as well.' ('Closed and Open Social Stratification', op. cit., p. 70.) He elaborates this point at great length. But when confronted with E.R. Leach's pertinent question, 'If a caste group turns itself into a political faction does it then cease to be a caste?', which Leach himself answers, in clear affirmative, (Leach, op. cit., p. 6.), Béteille finds it difficult to agree with him. He finds Leach's affirmative answer 'based on a peculiarly personal view of caste'. ('Caste and Politics in Tamilnadu', op. cit., p. 192). Also see the Srinivas-Leach controversy on the same definitional issues in *Caste in Modern India,* op. cit., and the Béteille-Bailey controversy on referents of caste in *The European Journal of Sociology*, 4, 1963, 107-24, and 5, 1964, 130-4.

35 For example, 'The new economic order and the new educational and political system are almost all based on universalistic principles of organisation. *Of course*, the mere adoption of universalistic principles of recruitment does not lead to the dissolution of particularistic modes of grouping. It is well known how, for instance, actual recruitment to universities, professions or political parties has in the past been highly selective in terms of religion, caste and region. *Nonetheless*, it is important to investigate the changes brought about in the individual's life chances by the extension of principles of recruitment which either did not exist or were of little or no significance in the past'. Béteille, *Caste*: *Old and New*, op. cit., p. 60 (emphasis added).

36 Béteille, 'Closed and Open Social Stratification', op. cit. Also see, V. Gomathinayagam, 'Rural Social Change: Its Correlation to Caste Ranking, Economic Position and Literacy Level', *Indian Journal of Social Research* (Meerut), 13(3), December, 1972, pp. 224-30; and, M.S.A. Rao, *Tradition*, *Rationality and Change*: *Essays in Sociology of Economic Development and Social Change*, Bombay, Popular Prakashan, 1972.

37 Ibid., p. 61.

38 Ibid., p. 62.

39 Béteille, 'Elites, Status Groups and Caste in Modern India', op. cit.

40 Béteille, 'Changing Pattern of Status Groups', op. cit., pp. 200-1.

41 Béteille, 'Closed and Open Social Stratification', op. cit., pp. 65-78. See also, Y.B. Damle, 'Reference Group Theory With Regard to Mobility in Caste', in James Silverberg, (ed.), *Social Mobility in Caste System*, Comparative Studies in Society and History, Supplement III, Mouton, The Hague. Basing his discussion on 'some cases from urban areas' with which he is 'personally

familiar', Damle examines the phenomenon of mobility in the caste system in the light of the reference group theory.

42 Ibid., pp. 74-8.

43 Béteille, 'Caste and Politics in Tamilnadu', op. cit., p. 155. Also see, S.K. Chauhan, 'Caste, Class and Power: An Analysis of the Stratification System in Upper Assam', *Eastern Anthropologist*, 25(2), May-August 1972, 149-60.

44 Ibid., p. 191. For a carefully done study showing how the traditional power structure of a village community is undermined by urbanization, especially through the expansion of economic opportunities outside the agricultural system, see M.S.A. Rao, *Urbanization and Social Change: A Study of a Rural Community on a Metropolitan Fringe*, Orient Longman Ltd., New Delhi 1970.

45 Ibid., p. 192.

46 Important among these are André Béteille, *Caste, Class and Power*, op. cit.; K.K. Singh, *Patterns of Caste Tension*, New Delhi, Asia Publishing House, 1967; Yogesh Atal, *The Changing Frontiers of Caste*, Delhi, National Publishing House, 1968; Yogendra Singh, 'The Changing Power Structure of Village Community — A Case Study of Six Villages in Eastern U.P.', in A.R. Desai, (ed.), *Rural Sociology in India*, Bombay, Popular Prakashan, 1969; S.C. Dube, 'Caste Dominance and Factionalism', *Contributions to Indian Sociology*, II, New Series, December 1968; Brij Raj Chauhan, 'Phases in Village Power Structure and Leadership in Rajasthan', in L.P. Vidyarthi, (ed.), *Leadership in India*, Bombay, Asia Publishing House, 1967; Ramkrishna Mukherjee, 'Caste and Economic Structure in West Bengal in Present Times', in R.N. Saksena, (ed.), *Social Research and Social Problems in India*, Bombay, Asia Publishing House, 1961; *The Dynamics of Rural Society*, Berlin, Akademic Verald, 1957; 'Six Villages of Bengal', *Journal of Asiatic Society of Bengal*, 24(1, 2), Calcutta, 1958.

47 See A.R. Desai, *Rural India in Transition*, Bombay, Popular Prakashan, 1969; S.M. Shah, 'Rural Class Structure in Gujarat', in A.R. Desai, (ed.), *Rural Sociology in India*, op. cit. For an illuminating empirical investigation of the emergence of class structure over time in an urban area, see, Y.P. Chibbar. *From Caste to Class*, Delhi, Associated Publishing House, 1968.

48 Yogendra Singh, op. cit.

49 Béteille, op. cit.

50 K.K. Singh, op. cit. For a criticism of the 'overemphasis' on caste as a category of social conflict that results in the 'lumping together of landlords and labourers' of heterogeneous economic status leading to the loss of the differentiation among various economic categories, see Krishna Bharadwaj, 'Understanding Rural Social Change.' *Economic and Political Weekly*, 10(8), February 21, 1976, 321-4.

51 Yogendra Singh, op. cit.

52 K.K. Singh, op. cit. Also see, Santosh Singh Anand, *The Changing Concept of Caste in India*, Delhi, Vikas Publishing House Pvt. Ltd., 1972.

53 S.C. Dube, op. cit.

54 Ibid.

55 Ramkrishna Mukherjee, *The Dynamics of Rural Society*, op. cit.

56 For a clear formulation of the issue of how modern politics undermines basic

elements of caste, especially its hierarchies and solidarity features, see, I.P. Desai, 'Caste and Politics', *Economic and Political Weekly*, 2(17), April 1967. Also see, R.K. Hebsur, 'Caste and Politics,' *Economic and Political Weekly*, 11(19), May 8, 1976, 691-2.

57 A series of such studies appeared in Rajni Kothari (ed.), *Caste in Indian Politics*, New Delhi, Orient Longman Ltd., 1970.

58 See, for example, Rajni Kothari and Rashikesh Maru, 'Federating for Political Interests: The Kshatriyas of Gujarat'; and, Anil Bhatt, 'Caste and Political Mobilization in a Gujarat District', in *Caste in Indian Politics*, Rajni Kothari (ed.), op cit. For a detailed account of interaction between caste associations and political parties, see Ghanshyam Shah, 'Caste Association and Political Process in Gujarat: A Study of Gujarat Kshatriya Sabha', Ph.D. Thesis submitted to Gujarat University, Ahmedabad, 1970. Also see, J.C. Johari, 'Caste Politicisation in India', *Indian Political Science Review*, 7(2), April-September 1973, 184-216.

59 See, for example, Ramashray Roy, 'Inter-Party Conflict in Bihar Congress', in Centre for the Study of Developing Societies' Occasional Papers-I, *Party System and Election Studies*, New Delhi, Allied Publishers, 1966; 'Dynamics of One Party Dominance in an Indian State', *Asian Survey*, 7(7), 1968; 'Selection of Congress Candidates' (a series of five articles), *Economic and Political Weekly*, 1(20), 1966, and 2(1, 2, 6, 7), 1967; and Rajni Kothari, 'Party Politics and Political Development', *Economic and Political Weekly*, 2(3, 4, 5), 1967.

60 See, for example, Gopal Krishna, 'Electoral Participation and Political Integration', *Economic and Political Weekly*, 2(3, 4, 5), February 1967.

61 See, for example, Bashiruddin Ahmed, 'Caste and Electoral Politics', *Asian Survey*, 10(11), November 1970; and D.L. Sheth, 'Political Development of Indian Electorate', *Economic and Political Weekly*, 5(3, 4, 5), 1970. See, also, D.L. Sheth (ed.), *Citizens and Parties: Aspects of Competitive Politics in India*, New Delhi, Allied Publishers, 1975. For an account of political consciousness and the process of electoral mobilization among scheduled tribes and Harijans based on survey data, see Ghanshyam Shah, 'Voting Behaviour of Adivasi and Harijan Leaders: A Study of the 1971 Elections', *The Indian Journal of Political Science*, 33(4), October-December 1972. Also see, Anil Bhatt, *Caste, Class and Politics: An Empirical Profile of Social Stratification in Modern India*, Delhi: Manohar, 1975.

62 Kothari (ed.), *Caste in Indian Politics*, op. cit.

63 Kothari and Maru, op. cit.

64 Anil Bhatt, op. cit.

65 Ghanshyam Shah, op. cit.

66 For a leading formulation of the issues related to caste-politics interaction, see 'Introduction' by Rajni Kothari, in Kothari (ed.), *Caste in Indian Politics*, op. cit.

67 'Introduction', in *Caste in Indian Politics*, op. cit. Also see, Chapter VI, 'Social Infra-Structure', in Rajni Kothari, *Politics in India*, New Delhi, Orient Longman Ltd., 1970.

68 'Introduction', in *Caste in indian Politics*, op. cit.

69 'Introduction', in *Caste in Indian Politics*, op. cit.

70 See Myron Weiner and Rajni Kothari (eds.), *Indian Voting Behaviour*, Calcutta, Firma K.L. Mukhopadhyay, 1965.

71 See, for example, Rajni Kothari and Ghanshyam Shah, 'Caste Orientation of Political Factions', in *Indian Voting Behaviour*, op. cit.

72 See, for example, V.M. Sirsikar, 'Party Loyalties vs. Caste and Communal Pulls', Baldev Raj Nayar, 'Religion and Caste in the Punjab', Rajni Kothari and Tarun Sheth, 'Extent and Limits of Community Voting', all in *Indian Voting Behaviour*, op. cit. Also see, O.P. Goyal, 'Caste and Politics — A Conceptual Framework', *Asian Survey*, 5(10), 1965; V.K. Gokte, 'The Role of Caste in Outer Delhi Parliamentary Elections', *The Indian Political Science Review*, April-September 1967.

73 See, for example, O.P. Goyal, 'Caste Split in Voting Behaviour', *Political Scientist*, 2(2), January-June 1966. For the role of multicaste factions in electoral politics, see also M.S.A. Rao, 'The Mid-Term Poll in a Village in Outer Delhi Constituency', *Sociological Bulletin*, 21(1), March 1972, 17-35.

74 I.P. Desai, op. cit. For the role of caste in mobilizing voters from the lower social strata, see Satish Saberwal, 'The Reserved Constituency: Candidates and Consequences', *Economic and Political Weekly*, 7(2), January 8, 1972, 71-80; and, Ghanshyam Shah, 'Voting Behaviour of Adivasi and Harijan Leaders: A Study of the 1971 Elections', *Indian Journal of Political Science*, 33(4), October-December 1972, 431-42.

75 See, for example, Sirsikar, op. cit.

76 Among few such exceptions are Rajni Kothari and Tarun Sheth, 'Extent and Limits of Community Voting', and, Baldev Raj Nayar, 'Religion and Caste in the Punjab: Sidhvan Bet Constituency', in *Indian Voting Behaviour*, op. cit.

77 See, for example, V.M. Sirsikar, *Political Behaviour in India*, Bombay: Manaktalas, 1968, p. 8, where the author argues that due to religious, linguistic, occupational and caste diversities of voters and due to many political parties contesting the election, 'the four constituencies (under study) together could be regarded as a microcosm of Indian political life'.

78 See, for example, Rajni Kothari and Ghanshyam Shah, op. cit.

79 See, for example, H.R. Chaturvedi and Ghanshyam Shah, 'Fusion and Fission of Castes in Elections: A Case of Chhata, U.P.', *Economic and Political Weekly*, 5(40), October 1970.

80 See Bashiruddin Ahmed, 'Caste and Electoral Politics,' op. cit. Ahmed's study is the first systematic attempt at testing hypotheses generated in case studies and analytical essays through national cross-sectional survey data.

81 See, for example, C. Parvathamma, 'Election and Traditional Leadership in a Mysore Village', *Economic Weekly*, 17(10, 11), March 1964.

82 See, for example, B.S. Baviskar, 'Cooperatives and Politics'., *Economic and Political Weekly*, 3(12), March 1968.

83 See, for example, K.L. Sharma, 'Social Structure and Political Change'., *Political Science Review*, 8(1), January-March 1969; R.S. Khare, 'Groups and Processes of Political Change in North India: Gopalpur'., *Man in India*, 49(2), April-June 1969. Also see, P.N. Sheth, 'Politics of Participation'., Department of Political Science, University of Gujarat, 1970, mimeo.

84 See, for example, A.H. Somjee, 'Groups and Individuals in the Politics of an Indian Village'., *Asian Survey*, 2(4), June 1962.

85 See, for example, P.N. Rastogi, 'Dominant Caste and Faction Situation in Brahminpura', op. cit.; N. Patnayak and H.D. Lakshminarayana, 'Factional Politics in Village India'., *Man in India*, 49(2), April-June 1969.

86 See K.L. Sharma, 'Social Structure and Political Change'., op. cit. K.C. Panchnadikar, *Social Structure and Social Change in India*, Bombay, Popular Prakashan, 1970. Also see A.H. Somjee, *Democracy and Political Change in Village India: A Case Study,* New Delhi, Orient Longman, 1971.

87 See, for example, Iqbal Narain, 'Politics and Panchayati Raj'., *Indian Journal of Political Science*, 23(4), October-December 1962; R.Chaudhari, 'Panchayats and Interest Groups: Study of a Bengal Village', *Economic Weekly,* 16(38), September 1964.

88 See, Iqbal Narain (ed.), *State Politics in India*, Meerut, Meenakshi Prakashan, 1967.

89 See, for example, K.D. Desai, 'Socio-Economic Infra-Structure of Gujarat Politics'; G.N. Sharma, 'Aspects of Andhra Politics'; N.G.S. Kini, 'Caste as a Factor in State Politics'; Chetkar Jha, 'Caste in Bihar Congress Politics'; K.S. Mune Gowda, 'The Influence of Caste in Mysore Politics', all in Iqbal Narain (ed.), op. cit.

90 See, for example, K.D. Desai, 'The Swatantra Party in Gujarat Politics'; and Ramashray Roy, 'Politics of Fragmentation', in Iqbal Narain, op. cit.; Babu Naik, 'Who should rule the Samyukta Maharashtra or its Caste Patterns?', *Mankind*, 4(12), 1960; K.L. Kamal, *Party Politics in an Indian State*, New Delhi, S. Chand and Co., n.d.

91 See, for example, Ramashray Roy, 'Caste and Political Recruitment in Bihar', in Rajni Kothari (ed.), *Caste in Indian Politics*, op. cit.

92 A few studies of caste done by social psychologists focus on the individual, as against the collectivity. However they are not free from the 'caste frame of reference' in so far as they examine how caste membership influences and shapes the attitudes, beliefs and behaviour of individuals, rather than study how 'castensess' as a property of an individual enters as a *variable* in the motivational and behavioural structures of people. For a very competent social-psychological study of caste on these lines see A.C. Parnajape, *Caste Prejudice and the Individual*, Bombay, Lalvani Publishing House, 1970. Also see, *The Changing Concept of Caste in India*, New Delhi, Vikas Publishing House Pvt. Ltd., 1972.